OLE Automation
Programmer's Reference

Creating Programmable 32-Bit Applications

PUBLISHED BY
Microsoft Press
A Division of Microsoft Corporation
One Microsoft Way
Redmond, Washington 98052-6399

Library of Congress Cataloging-in-Publication Data
OLE automation programmer's reference
      p.   cm.
   Includes index.
   ISBN 1-55615-851-3
    1. Object-oriented programming (Computer science)   2. OLE
(Computer file)
QA76.64.O45   1996
005.7--dc20   95-47175
                                             CIP

Printed and bound in the United States of America.

1 2 3 4 5 6 7 8 9 QMQM 1 0 9 8 7 6

Distributed to the book trade in Canada by Macmillan of Canada, a division of Canada Publishing Corporation.

A CIP catalogue record for this book is available from the British Library.

Microsoft Press books are available through booksellers and distributors worldwide. For further information about international editions, contact your local Microsoft Corporation office. Or contact Microsoft Press International directly at fax (206) 936-7329.

Acquisitions Editor: David J. Clark
Project Editor: Brenda L. Matteson

Contents

Introduction

This book provides procedural and reference information for OLE Automation. While OLE Automation runs on other platforms, such as the Apple® Macintosh® system, the focus of this document is applications that use the Microsoft® Windows® 32-bit operating system.

To get the most out of this book, you should be familiar with:

- The C++ programming language.
- The Microsoft Windows programming environment, version 3.1 or later. The OLE protocols are implemented through dynamic-link libraries (DLLs) that are used in conjunction with other Microsoft Windows programs.
- The OLE Component Object Model (COM). This model is the foundation of OLE. It is explained in depth by the books listed in "Other Books and Technical Support."

About This Book

The book contains three parts:

Part 1 About OLE Automation

Chapter 1 "Overview of OLE Automation," introduces the basic concepts of OLE Automation and identifies the components you'll use.

Chapter 2, "Exposing OLE Automation Objects," shows how to write and expose programmable objects for use by OLE Automation controllers.

Chapter 3, "Accessing OLE Automation Objects," explains how to write applications and programming tools that access exposed objects.

Chapter 4, "Standards and Guidelines," lists the standard OLE Automation objects that are recommended for most applications, and describes naming conventions for objects.

Part 2 Reference Information

Chapter 5, "Dispatch Interfaces," describes the interfaces and functions that support access to exposed objects.

Chapter 6, "Data Manipulation Functions," describes functions that manipulate arrays, strings, and variant types of data within OLE Automation.

Chapter 7, "MkTypLib and Object Description Language," describes the MkTypLib tool and its source file language. MkTypLib creates type libraries according to the description you provide.

Chapter 8, "Type Description Interfaces," describes the interfaces and functions that allow programs to read and bind to the descriptions of objects in a type library.

Chapter 9, "Type Building Interfaces," describes the interfaces and functions that are used by tools like MkTypLib to describe objects and build type libraries.

Chapter 10, "Error Handling Interfaces," describes interfaces and functions that allow OLE Automation objects to return detailed error information.

Part 3 Appendixes

Appendix A, "National Language Support Functions," describes functions for 16-bit systems that support multiple national languages.

Appendix B, "Files You Need," lists the files you and your customers need to run OLE Automation applications.

Appendix C, "Information for Visual Basic Programmers," lists the OLE API's called by Microsoft Visual Basic® statements.

Appendix D, "How OLE Automation Compares Strings," describes the string comparison rules applied by OLE Automation.

Appendix E, "Handling GUIDs," provides supplemental information on GUIDs.

The **Glossary** defines terms useful in understanding OLE Automation.

Other Books and Technical Support

OLE Automation is part of OLE, which provides mechanisms for in-place activation, structured file storage, and many other application features. These other parts of OLE are fully described by two books:

- *OLE Programmer's Guide and Reference* describes the component object model, in-place activation, visual editing, structured file storage, and application registration in terms of the APIs and interfaces provided by OLE.
- *Inside OLE* (second edition) by Kraig Brockschmidt provides introductory and how-to information about implementing OLE objects and containers.

If you are developing C++ applications, see either the Books Online or the hardcopy documentation for Microsoft Visual C++™, version 4.0.

For technical support, see the Win32 SDK and the documentation for the product with which you received OLE. Support for OLE Automation is also provided through a forum on Compuserve. To access this forum, type **GO WINOBJ** at any Compuserve prompt. Once you are in the forum, ask your questions in Section 8.

Document Conventions

The following typographical conventions are used throughout this book:

Convention	Meaning
bold	Indicates a word that is a function name or other fixed part of a programming language, the Microsoft Windows operating system, or the OLE Application Programming Interface (API). For example, **DispInvoke** is an OLE-specific function. These words must always be typed exactly as they are printed.
italic	Indicates a word that is a placeholder or variable. For example, *ClassName* would be a placeholder for any OLE object class name. Function parameters in API reference material are italic to indicate that any variable name can be used. In addition, OLE terms are italicized at first use to highlight their definition.

Convention	Meaning
UPPERCASE	Indicates a constant or an MS-DOS® path and name. For example, E_INVALIDARG is a constant. C:\OLE2\INCLUDE\OLE2.H is an MS-DOS path and name.
InitialCaps	Indicates the name of an object, method, property, user-defined function or event. For example, the Application object has a Visible property.
monospace	Indicates source code and syntax spacing. For example:
	`*pdwRegisterCF = 0;`

Note The interface syntax in this book follows the variable-naming convention known as Hungarian notation, invented by programmer Charles Simonyi. Variables are prefixed with lowercase letters indicating their data type. For example, *lpszNewDocname* would be a long pointer to a zero-terminated string named *NewDocname*. See *Programming Windows* by Charles Petzold for more information about Hungarian notation.

P A R T   1

About OLE Automation

CHAPTER 1

Overview of OLE Automation

OLE Automation is a technology that lets software packages expose their unique features to scripting tools and other applications. OLE Automation uses the OLE Component Object Model (COM), but may be implemented independently from other OLE features, such as *in-place activation*. Using OLE Automation, you can:

- Create applications and programming tools that expose objects.
- Create and manipulate objects exposed in one application from another application.
- Create tools that access and manipulate objects. These tools can include embedded macro languages, external programming tools, object browsers, and compilers.

The objects an application or programming tool exposes are called *OLE Automation objects*. Applications and programming tools that access those objects are called *OLE Automation controllers*. OLE Automation objects and controllers interact as follows:

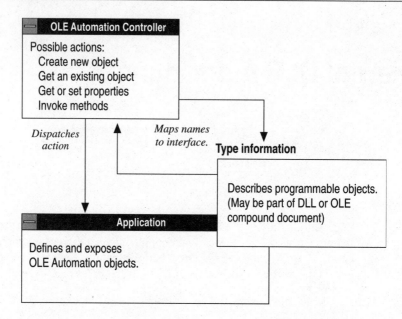

Applications and other software packages define and expose objects, which can be acted upon by OLE Automation controllers. Type information describes the exposed objects, and can be used by OLE Automation controllers at either compile time or run time.

Why Expose Objects?

Exposing objects provides a way to manipulate an application's tools programmatically. This allows your customers to use a programming tool to automate repetitive tasks that you might not anticipate.

For example, Microsoft® Excel exposes a variety of objects that you can use to build applications. One such object is the Workbook, which contains a group of related worksheets, charts, and macros—the Excel equivalent of a three-ring binder. Using OLE Automation, you could write an application that accesses Excel Workbook objects, possibly to print them, as in the following diagram:

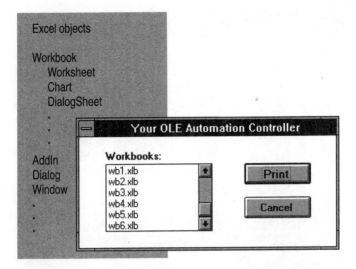

With OLE Automation, solution providers can use your general-purpose objects to build applications that target a specific task. For example, a general-purpose drawing tool could expose objects that draw boxes, lines, and arrows, or insert text, and so forth. Another programmer could build a flowcharting tool by accessing the exposed objects and adding a user interface and other application-specific features.

Exposing objects to OLE Automation or supporting OLE Automation within a macro language offers several benefits:

- Exposed objects from many applications are available in a single programming environment. Software developers can choose from these objects to create solutions that span applications.

- Exposed objects are accessible from any macro language or programming tool that implements OLE Automation. Systems integrators are not limited to the programming language in which the objects were developed; instead, they can choose the programming tool or macro language that best suits their own needs and capabilities.

- Object names can remain consistent across versions of an application.

- Object names can automatically conform to the user's national language.

What Is an OLE Automation Object?

An *OLE Automation object* is an object that is exposed to other applications or programming tools through OLE Automation interfaces. An *OLE Automation server* is an application, type library, or other source that makes OLE Automation objects available for programming by other applications, programming tools, or scripting languages. For example, Microsoft Excel exposes many objects, which you can use to create new applications and programming tools. Within Excel, objects are organized hierarchically, with an object named Application at the top of the hierarchy. The following figure shows some of Excel's objects.

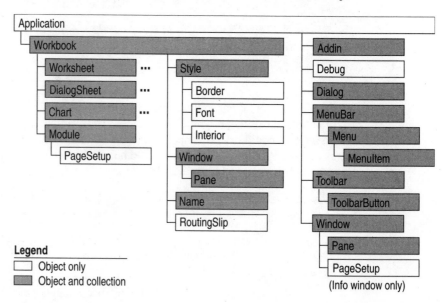

Each OLE Automation object has its own unique member functions. Exposing the member functions makes the object programmable by OLE Automation controllers. You can expose two types of members for an object:

- *Methods* are actions that an object can perform. For example, Excel's Worksheet object provides a Calculate method, which recalculates the values in the worksheet.

- *Properties* are functions that access information about the state of an object. The Worksheet object's Visible property determines whether the worksheet is visible on the display.

For example, you could expose the following objects in a document-based
application by implementing these methods and properties:

OLE Automation object	Methods	Properties
Application	Help Quit Save Repeat Undo	ActiveDocument Application Caption DefaultFilePath Documents Height Name Parent Path Printers StatusBar Top Value Visible Width
Document	Activate Close NewWindow Print PrintPreview RevertToSaved Save SaveAs	Application Author Comments FullName Keywords Name Parent Path ReadOnly Saved Subject Title Value

Often, an application needs several instances of an object. For example, an OLE
application based on Excel may have multiple workbooks. To provide an easy way
to access and program the workbooks, Excel exposes an object named Workbooks,
which refers to all the current Workbook objects. Workbooks is a *collection object*;
other collection objects in Excel are shaded in the preceding figure. Collection
objects let you iterate over the objects they manage. If you create an application
with a multiple-document interface (MDI), you might expose a collection object
named Documents with the following methods and properties:

Collection object	Methods	Properties
Documents	Add Close Item Open	Application Count Parent

What Is an OLE Automation Controller?

An *OLE Automation controller* is an application, programming tool, or scripting language that accesses one or more OLE Automation objects. The objects may exist in the same application or in another application. OLE Automation controllers can use existing objects, create new instances of objects, get and set properties, and invoke methods that the object supports.

Microsoft Visual Basic™ is an OLE Automation controller. Using Visual Basic and similar programming tools, you can create packaged scripts to access OLE Automation objects. You can also create controllers by:

- Writing code within an application that accesses another application's exposed objects through OLE Automation.

- Revising an existing programming tool, such as an embedded macro language, to add support for OLE Automation.

- Developing a new application, such as a compiler or type information browser, that supports OLE Automation.

How Do Controllers and Objects Interact?

OLE Automation controllers can access OLE Automation objects in two different ways:

- By using the **IDispatch** interface.
- By directly calling one of the member functions in the object's virtual function table (VTBL).

An *interface* is a group of related functions that provide a service. All OLE Automation objects must implement the **IUnknown** interface, which manages all the other interfaces that the object supports. The **IDispatch** interface, which derives from **IUnknown**, consists of functions that allow access to the methods and properties of OLE Automation objects. A *custom interface* is a Component Object Model interface that is not defined as part of OLE; in short, any user-defined interface is a custom interface.

The *virtual function table* (VTBL) lists the addresses of all the properties and methods that are members of the object, including the member functions of the interfaces that it supports. The first three members of the VTBL are the members of the **IUnknown** interface; and subsequent entries are the members of the other supported interfaces. The following figure shows the VTBL for an object that supports the **IUnknown** and **IDispatch** interfaces:

IUnknown::QueryInterface
IUnknown::AddRef
IUnknown::Release
IDispatch::GetIDsOfNames
IDispatch::GetTypeInfo
IDispatch::GetTypeInfoCount
IDispatch::Invoke

If the object does not support **IDispatch**, the entries for the members of the object's custom interfaces immediately follow the members of **IUnknown**. For example, the following figure shows the VTBL for an object that supports a custom interface named IMyInterface:

IUnknown::AddRef
IUnknown::Release
IMyInterface::Member1
IMyInterface::Member2

: Remaining members
. of IMyInterface

When you expose an object for OLE Automation, you must decide whether to implement an **IDispatch** interface, a VTBL interface, or both. Microsoft strongly recommends that your objects provide a *dual interface*, which supports both access methods. In a dual interface, the first three entries in the VTBL are the members of **IUnknown**, the next four entries are the members of **IDispatch**, and the subsequent entries are the addresses of the members of the dual interface. The following figure shows the VTBL for an object that supports a dual interface named IMyInterface:

IUnknown::QueryInterface
IUnknown::AddRef
IUnknown::Release
IDispatch::GetIDsOfNames
IDispatch::GetTypeInfo
IDispatch::GetTypeInfoCount
IDispatch::Invoke
IMyInterface::Member1
IMyInterface::Member2

: Remaining members
. of IMyInterface

In addition to providing access to objects, OLE Automation provides information about exposed objects. Using **IDispatch** or a type library, an OLE Automation controller or programming tool can determine the interfaces a object supports and the names of its members. Type libraries are especially useful for this purpose because they can be accessed at compile time. For more information, see "What Is a Type Library" later in this chapter, and "Type Libraries" in Chapter 2.

Accessing an Object Through the IDispatch Interface

OLE Automation controllers can use the **IDispatch** interface to access objects that implement this interface. The controller must first create the object, then query the object's **IUnknown** interface for a pointer to its **IDispatch** interface.

Although programmers know objects, methods, and properties by name, **IDispatch** keeps track of them internally by a number, the *Dispatch ID* (DISPID). Before an OLE Automation controller can access a property or method, it must have the DISPID that maps to the name of the member.

With the DISPID, it can call **IDispatch::Invoke** to access the property or invoke the method, packaging the parameters for the property or method into one of the **IDispatch::Invoke** parameters.

The object's implementation of **IDispatch::Invoke** must then unpackage the parameters, call the property or method, and be prepared to handle any errors that occur. When the property or method returns, the object passes its return value back to the controller through an **IDispatch::Invoke** parameter.

DISPIDs are available at run time and, in some circumstances, at compile time. At run time, controllers get DISPIDs by calling the **IDispatch::GetIDsOfNames** function. This is called *late binding* because the controller binds to the property or method at run time.

The DISPID of each property or method is fixed, and is part of the object's type description. If the object is described in a type library, an OLE Automation controller can read the DISPIDs from the type library at compile time, and thus avoid calling **IDispatch::GetIDsOfNames**. This is called *ID binding*. Because it requires only one call to IDispatch (that is, the call to **Invoke**) rather than the two calls required by late binding, it is generally about twice as fast. Late binding controllers can improve performance by caching DISPIDs after retrieving them, so that **IDispatch::GetIDsOfNames** is called only once for each property or method.

Accessing an Object Through the VTBL

OLE Automation allows an OLE Automation controller to call a method or property accessor function directly, either within or across processes. This approach, called *VTBL binding*, does not use the **IDispatch** interface. The controller gets type information from the type library at compile time, then calls the methods and functions directly. VTBL binding is faster than both ID binding and late binding because access is direct; no calls are made through **IDispatch**.

In-Process and Out-of-Process Server Objects

OLE Automation objects may exist in the same process as the OLE Automation controller or in a different process. *In-process server* objects are implemented in a DLL and run in the process space of the controller. Because they're contained in a DLL, they can't be run stand-alone. *Out-of-process server* objects are implemented in an .EXE file and run in a separate process space. Access to in-process objects is much faster than access to out-of-process server objects, because OLE Automation does not need to make remote procedure calls across the process boundary.

The BrowseH sample is an in-process server OLE Automation object. The Hello and Lines samples are both out-of-process server OLE Automation objects.

The access mechanism (**IDispatch** or VTBL) and the location of an object (in-process or out-of-process server) determine the fixed overhead required for access. Note that the most important factor in performance, however, is the quantity and nature of the work performed by the methods and procedures being invoked. If the method is time-consuming or requires remote procedure calls, the overhead of one additional call to **IDispatch** may be negligible.

What Is a Type Library?

A *type library* is a file or component within another file that contains OLE Automation standard descriptions of exposed objects, properties, and methods. Type libraries do not store objects; type libraries store type information. By accessing a type library, applications and browsers can determine the characteristics of an object, such as the interfaces the object supports and the names and addresses of each interface's members. You can also invoke a member through a type library. See Chapter 8, "Type Description Interfaces," for more details.

When you expose OLE Automation objects, you should create a type library to make your objects easily accessible to other developers. The simplest way is to describe your objects in an Object Description Language (ODL) file, and then compile the file with the MkTypLib tool, as described in Chapter 7.

C H A P T E R   2

Exposing OLE Automation Objects

Exposing objects makes them available for programmatic use by other applications and programming tools. To expose objects, you need to implement the objects using OLE Automation; create a type library that describes the exposed objects; and register the objects with the system.

This chapter discusses how you should design an application that exposes objects, then uses the Hello and Lines samples from the Win32 SDK to demonstrate how to implement the design. Throughout the chapter, the filename for the example precedes the example in parentheses.

Design Considerations

When you expose objects to OLE Automation, you need to decide which interfaces to implement and how to organize your objects. In addition, you should create a type library. This section provides information to guide you in designing an OLE Automation application.

Dual Interfaces

Although OLE Automation allows you to implement an **IDispatch** interface, a VTBL interface, or a **dual** interface (which encompasses both), Microsoft strongly recommends that you implement dual interfaces for all exposed OLE Automation objects. Dual interfaces have significant advantages over **IDispatch**-only or VTBL-only interfaces:

- Binding can take place at compile time through the VTBL interface, or at run time through **IDispatch**.

- OLE Automation controllers that can use the VTBL interface may benefit from improved performance.

- Existing OLE Automation controllers that use the **IDispatch** interface will continue to work.

- The VTBL interface is easier to call from C++.

- Dual interfaces are required for compatibility with Visual Basic object support features.

Converting Existing Objects to Dual Interfaces

If you have already implemented exposed objects that support only the **IDispatch** interface, you should convert them to support **dual** interfaces.

▶ **To convert an IDispatch interface to a dual interface**

1. Edit the Object Description Language (.ODL) file to declare a **dual** interface instead of an **IDispatch** interface.

2. Rearrange the parameter lists so that the methods and properties of your exposed objects return an HRESULT and pass their return values in a parameter.

3. If your object implements an exception handler, revise your code to use the OLE Automation error handling interface. This interface provides for detailed, contextual error information through both **IDispatch** and VTBL interfaces.

See "Setting Up the VTBL Interface," "Returning an Error," and "Creating a Type Library" later in this chapter for details.

Type Libraries

In addition to implementing dual interfaces, you should create a type library for each set of objects you expose. Because VTBL references are bound at compile time, exposed objects that support VTBL binding must be described in a type library.

Type libraries provide these important benefits:

- Type checking can be performed at compile time, helping developers of OLE Automation controllers to write fast, correct code to access your objects.

- You can use the **DispInvoke** function to implement **IDispatch** automatically. Using **DispInvoke** ensures that your implementation will be correct.

- Visual Basic applications can create objects with specific interface types, rather than the generic **Object** type, and take advantage of early binding.

- OLE Automation controllers that don't support VTBLs can read and cache DISPIDs at compile time, thereby improving run time performance.

- Type browsers can scan the library, allowing others to see the characteristics of your objects.

- The **RegisterTypeLib** function can be used to register your exposed objects.

- Local server access is improved, because OLE Automation uses information from the type library to package the parameters passed to an object in another process.

The Application Object

Document-based, user-interactive applications that expose OLE Automation objects should have one top-level object called the *Application object*. This object is initialized as the active object when the application starts.

The Application object identifies the application and provides a way for OLE Automation controllers to bind to and navigate the application's exposed objects. All other exposed objects are subordinate to the Application object; it is the root-level object in the object hierarchy.

The names of the Application object's members are part of the global name space, so OLE Automation controllers need not qualify them. For example, if MyApplication is the name of the Application object, a Visual Basic program can refer to a method of MyApplication as MyApplication.MyMethod or simply MyMethod. However, you should be careful not to overload the Application object;too many members can cause ambiguity and decrease performance. A large, complicated application with many members should be organized hierarchically, with a few generalized objects at the top, branching out into smaller, more specialized objects. Microsoft Excel is a good example of this kind of application.

Shutdown Behavior

OLE Automation objects must shut down in the following way:

- If the object's application is visible, the object should shut down only in response to an explicit user command (for example, the Exit command from the File menu) or from the equivalent command from an OLE Automation controller.

- If the object's application is not visible, the object should shut down only when the last external reference to it disappears.

Steps to Exposing Objects

To expose OLE Automation objects, you must write code to initialize the objects, implement the objects, and release OLE when your application terminates.

▶ **To initialize your exposed objects**

1. Initialize OLE.

2. Register the class factories of your exposed objects.

3. Register the active object.

▶ **To implement your exposed objects**

1. Implement the **IUnknown**, **IDispatch**, and VTBL interfaces for the objects.

2. Implement the properties and methods of the objects.

▶ **To release OLE when your application terminates**

1. Revoke the registration of the class factories and revoke the active object.

2. Unintialize OLE.

▶ **To make your objects available for use by others**

1. Create an object description (.ODL) file that describes the properties and methods of the exposed objects, and use MkTypLib to compile the .ODL file into a type library.

2. Create a registration (.REG) file for your application.

Initializing OLE

To initialize OLE and your exposed objects, you use the following functions:

- **OleInitialize**—Initializes OLE.
- **CoRegisterClassObject**—Registers the object's class factory with OLE so that other applications may use it to create new objects.
- **RegisterActiveObject**—Registers the active object, allowing other applications to connect to an existing object.

Implementing Exposed Objects

The following figure shows the interfaces you should implement in order to expose OLE Automation objects:

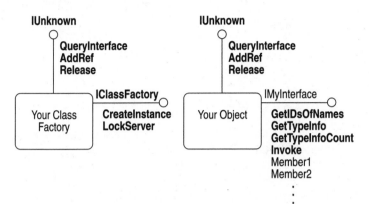

The member functions are listed under each interface name.

The *class factory* object implements the **IClassFactory** and **IUnknown** interfaces. (All objects must implement **IUnknown**, which allows OLE Automation controllers to determine what interfaces the object supports.) A class factory can create instances of a class.

The object implements two interfaces: **IUnknown** and IMyInterface. IMyInterface is a **dual** interface, which supports both late binding through **IDispatch** and early binding through the VTBL. The dual interface thus provides two ways to invoke the object's methods and properties. **IDispatch** includes the member functions **GetIDsOfNames**, **GetTypeInfo**, **GetTypeInfoCount**, and **Invoke**.

Member1 and Member2 are the members of IMyInterface. These members are available as direct entry points through the object's VTBL. They can also be accessed through **IDispatch::Invoke**.

You must also decide how to handle errors that occur in your exposed objects. If your object supports a dual interface and needs to return detailed, contextual error information, you also need to implement the OLE Automation error interface, **IErrorInfo**.

In addition to writing code to implement objects, you need to create a type library and a registration file. You describe the types of the exposed objects in the object description language (ODL), and use the MkTypLib tool to compile the ODL file into a type library (.TLB) and a header file (.H). The registration file provides information that the operating system and OLE need to locate objects.

Releasing OLE

To release OLE and your exposed objects, you use the following functions:

- **RevokeActiveObject**—Ends an object's status as the active object.
- **CoRevokeClassObject**—Informs OLE that a class factory is no longer available for use by other applications.
- **OLEUninitialize**—Releases OLE.

"Hello World" Example

The Hello example in the Win32 SDK is a simple OLE Automation application with one object. It has these characteristics:

- Supports VTBL binding
- Permits multiple instances of its exposed object to exist at the same time
- Implements **IErrorInfo** for exception handling

The sections that follow demonstrate how the Hello sample exposes a simple class. The code is abridged to illustrate the essential parts; see the source code in the Win32 SDK for a complete listing.

Initializing OLE

When the Hello application starts, it initializes OLE and the creates the object to be exposed through OLE Automation. For example (MAIN.CPP):

```
BOOL InitInstance (HINSTANCE hinst)
{
    HRESULT hr;
    char ach[STR_LEN];

    // Intialize OLE
    hr = OleInitialize(NULL);
    if (FAILED(hr))
        return FALSE;

    // Create an instance of the Hello Application object. The object is
    // created with refcount 0.
    LoadString(hinst, IDS_HelloMessage, ach, sizeof(ach));
    hr = CHello::Create(hinst, ach, &g_phello);
    if (FAILED(hr))
        return FALSE;
    return TRUE;
}
```

This function calls **OleInitialize** to initialize OLE. It loads the string ach with the initial hello message, obtained from the string table through the constant IDS_HelloMessage. Then it calls CHello::Create to create a single, global instance of the application object, passing it the initial hello message and receiving a value for g_phello, a pointer to the instance. If the function is successful, it returns True.

Registering the Active Object

After Hello creates an instance of the object, it exposes and registers the class factory (if necessary) and registers the active object (MAIN.CPP):

```
BOOL ProcessCmdLine(LPSTR pCmdLine,
                    LPDWORD pdwRegisterCF,
                    LPDWORD pdwRegisterActiveObject,
                    int nCmdShow)
{
    LPCLASSFACTORY pcf = NULL;
    HRESULT hr;

    *pdwRegisterCF = 0;
    *pdwRegisterActiveObject = 0;

    // Expose class factory for application object if command line
    // contains the /Automation switch.
    if (_fstrstr(pCmdLine, "-Automation") != NULL
        || _fstrstr(pCmdLine, "/Automation") != NULL)
    {
        pcf = new CHelloCF;
        if (!pcf)
            goto error;
        pcf->AddRef();
        hr = CoRegisterClassObject(CLSID_Hello, pcf,
                                   CLSCTX_LOCAL_SERVER,
                                   REGCLS_SINGLEUSE,
                                   pdwRegisterCF);
        if (hr != NOERROR)
            goto error;
        pcf->Release();
    }
    else g_phello->ShowWindow(nCmdShow); //Show if started stand-alone.

    RegisterActiveObject(g_phello, CLSID_Hello, ACTIVEOBJECT_WEAK,
                         pdwRegisterActiveObject);
    return TRUE;
```

```
error:
    if (!pcf)
        pcf->Release();
    return FALSE;
}
```

The sample first checks the command line for the **/Automation** switch. This switch indicates that the application should be started for programmatic access, so that OLE Automation controllers can create additional instances of the application's class. In this case, the class factory must be created and registered. If the switch is present, Hello creates a new CHelloCF object and calls its AddRef method, thereby creating the class factory.

Next, the sample calls **CoRegisterClassObject** to register the class factory. It passes the object's class ID (CLSID_Hello), a pointer to the CHelloCF object (`pcf`), and two constants (CLSCTX_LOCAL_SERVER and REGCLS_SINGLEUSE) that govern the class factory's use. CLSCTX_LOCAL_SERVER indicates that the executable code for the object runs in a separate process from the controller. REGCLS_SINGLEUSE allows only one OLE Automation controller to use each instance of the class factory. The value returned through `pdwRegisterCF` must later be used to revoke the class factory.

Finally, the sample registers the active object. Registering an active object lets OLE Automation controllers retrieve an object that is already running, rather than create a new instance of the object. The Application object must be registered.

Implementing IUnknown

Every OLE object must implement the **IUnknown** interface, which allows controllers to query the object to find out what interfaces it supports. **IUnknown** has three member functions: **QueryInterface**, **AddRef**, and **Release**. The sample implements them for the CHello object as follows (HELLO.CPP):

```
STDMETHODIMP
CHello::QueryInterface(REFIID iid, void FAR* FAR* ppv)
{
    *ppv = NULL;
    if (iid == IID_IUnknown || iid == IID_IDispatch || iid == IID_IHello
        *ppv = this;
    else if (iid == IID_ISupportErrorInfo)
        *ppv = &m_SupportErrorInfo;
    else return ResultFromScode(E_NOINTERFACE);

    AddRef();
    return NOERROR;
}
```

```
STDMETHODIMP_(ULONG)
CHello::AddRef(void)
{
    return ++m_cRef;
}


STDMETHODIMP_(ULONG)
CHello::Release(void)
{
if (--m_cRef == 0)
    {
        delete this;
        return 0;
    }
    return m_cRef;
}
```

Implementing IClassFactory

A class factory is a class that is capable of creating instances of another class. Hello implements a single class factory, called CHelloCF, as follows (HELLOCF.CPP):

```
CHelloCF::CHelloCF(void)
{
    m_cRef = 0;
}


STDMETHODIMP
CHelloCF::QueryInterface(REFIID iid, void FAR* FAR* ppv)
{
    *ppv = NULL;
    if (iid == IID_IUnknown || iid == IID_IClassFactory)
        *ppv = this;
    else
        return ResultFromScode(E_NOINTERFACE);
    AddRef();
    return NOERROR;
}


STDMETHODIMP_(ULONG)
CHelloCF::AddRef(void)
{
    return ++m_cRef;
}
```

```
STDMETHODIMP_(ULONG)
CHelloCF::Release(void)
{
    if (--m_cRef == 0)
    {
        delete this;
        return 0;
    }
    return m_cRef;
}


STDMETHODIMP
CHelloCF::CreateInstance(IUnknown FAR* punkOuter,
                         REFIID riid,
                         void FAR* FAR* ppv)
{
    HRESULT hr;

    *ppv = NULL;

    // This implementation doesn't allow aggregation.
    if (punkOuter)
        return ResultFromScode(CLASS_E_NOAGGREGATION);

    hr = g_phello->QueryInterface(riid, ppv);
    if (FAILED(hr))
    {
        g_phello->Quit();
        return hr;
    }
    return NOERROR;
}
STDMETHODIMP
CHelloCF::LockServer(BOOL fLock)
{
    CoLockObjectExternal(g_phello, fLock, TRUE);
    return NOERROR;
}
```

The class factory supports six member functions. **QueryInterface**, **AddRef**, and **Release** are the required **IUnknown** members, and **CreateInstance** and **LockServer** are the required **IClassFactory** members. The function CHelloCF::CHelloCF is a C++ constructor function. By default, the constructor function initializes the object's VTBLs; CHelloCF::CHelloCF also initializes the reference count for the class.

Implementing IDispatch

The **IDispatch** interface provides access to and information about an object. The interface requires the member functions **GetTypeInfoCount**, **GetTypeInfo**, **GetIdsOfNames**, and **Invoke**. The Hello sample implements **IDispatch** as follows (HELLO.CPP):

```
STDMETHODIMP
CHello::GetTypeInfoCount(UINT FAR* pctinfo)
{
    *pctinfo = 1;
    return NOERROR;
}


STDMETHODIMP
CHello::GetTypeInfo(
        UINT itinfo,
        LCID lcid,
        ITypeInfo FAR* FAR* pptinfo)
{
    *pptinfo = NULL;

    if(itinfo != 0)
        return ResultFromScode(DISP_E_BADINDEX);

    m_ptinfo->AddRef();
    *pptinfo = m_ptinfo;

    return NOERROR;
}


STDMETHODIMP
CHello::GetIDsOfNames(
        REFIID riid,
        OLECHAR FAR* FAR* rgszNames,
        UINT cNames,
        LCID lcid,
        DISPID FAR* rgdispid)
{
    return DispGetIDsOfNames(m_ptinfo, rgszNames, cNames, rgdispid);
}
```

```
STDMETHODIMP
CHello::Invoke(
        DISPID dispidMember,
        REFIID riid,
        LCID lcid,
        WORD wFlags,
        DISPPARAMS FAR* pdispparams,
        VARIANT FAR* pvarResult,
        EXCEPINFO FAR* pexcepinfo,
        UINT FAR* puArgErr)
{
    HRESULT hr;

    m_bRaiseException = FALSE;
    hr = DispInvoke(
        this, m_ptinfo,
        dispidMember, wFlags, pdispparams,
        pvarResult, pexcepinfo, puArgErr);
    if (m_bRaiseException)
    {
        if (NULL != pexcepinfo)
            _fmemcpy(pexcepinfo, &m_excepinfo, sizeof(EXCEPINFO));
        return ResultFromScode(DISP_E_EXCEPTION);
    }
    else return hr;
}
```

OLE Automation includes two functions, **DispGetIdsOfNames** and **DispInvoke**, which provide standard implementations for **IDispatch::GetIdsOfNames** and **IDispatch::Invoke**. The Hello sample uses these two functions to simplify the code.

Implementing VTBL Binding

In addition to the **IDispatch** interface, the Hello sample supports VTBL binding. Objects that support a VTBL interface return an HRESULT instead of a value when a member is invoked, and pass their return value as the last parameter. They may also accept a locale identifier (LCID) parameter, which allows them to parse strings correctly for the local language. The following example shows how the Visible property is implemented (HELLO.CPP):

```
STDMETHODIMP
CHello::put_Visible(BOOL bVisible)
{
    ShowWindow(bVisible ? SW_SHOW : SW_HIDE);
    return NOERROR;
}
```

```
STDMETHODIMP
CHello::get_Visible(BOOL FAR* pbool)
{
    *pbool = m_bVisible;
    return NOERROR;
}
```

Additional information must be specified in ODL to create a dual interface, as shown in "Creating the Type Information."

Handling Errors

Hello includes an exception handler, which passes exceptions through **IDispatch::Invoke** and supports rich error information through VTBLs (HELLO.CPP):

```
STDMETHODIMP
CHello::RaiseException(int nID)
{
    extern SCODE g_scodes[];
    char szError[STR_LEN];
    ICreateErrorInfo *pcerrinfo;
    IErrorInfo *perrinfo;
    HRESULT hr;

    _fmemset(&m_excepinfo, 0, sizeof(EXCEPINFO));

    m_excepinfo.wCode = nID;
    if (LoadString(m_hinst, nID, szError, sizeof(szError)))
        m_excepinfo.bstrDescription = SysAllocString(szError);
    m_excepinfo.bstrSource = SysAllocString(m_bstrName);

    m_bRaiseException = TRUE;

    // Set ErrInfo object so that VTBL binding container
    // applications can get rich error information.
    hr = CreateErrorInfo(&pcerrinfo);
    if (SUCCEEDED(hr))
    {
        pcerrinfo->SetGUID(IID_IHello);
        if (m_excepinfo.bstrSource)
            pcerrinfo->SetSource(m_excepinfo.bstrSource);
        if (m_excepinfo.bstrDescription)
            pcerrinfo->SetDescription(m_excepinfo.bstrDescription);
        hr = pcerrinfo->QueryInterface(IID_IErrorInfo,
        (LPVOID FAR*) &perrinfo);
```

```
        if (SUCCEEDED(hr))
        {
            SetErrorInfo(0, perrinfo);
            perrinfo->Release();
        }
        pcerrinfo->Release();
    }
    return ResultFromScode(g_scodes[nID-1001]);
}
```

Hello's member functions call this routine when an exception occurs. RaiseException fills in an EXCEPINFO structure that is available through **IDispatch::Invoke**. It also sets the system's error object, so that container applications that call through VTBLs can retrieve rich error information. Note that because **IDispatch::Invoke** is effectively such a container, it retrieves the rich error information and returns it through the EXCEPINFO parameter.

Hello also implements the **ISupportErrorInfo** interface, which allows OLE Automation controllers to query whether an error object will be available (HELLO.CPP):

```
CSupportErrorInfo::CSupportErrorInfo(IUnknown FAR* punkObject,
                                     REFIID riid)
{
    m_punkObject = punkObject;
    m_iid = riid;
}


STDMETHODIMP
CSupportErrorInfo::QueryInterface(REFIID iid, void FAR* FAR* ppv)
{
    return m_punkObject->QueryInterface(iid, ppv);
}


STDMETHODIMP_(ULONG)
CSupportErrorInfo::AddRef(void)
{
    return m_punkObject->AddRef();
}


STDMETHODIMP_(ULONG)
CSupportErrorInfo::Release(void)
{
    return m_punkObject->Release();
}
```

```
STDMETHODIMP
CSupportErrorInfo::InterfaceSupportsErrorInfo(REFIID riid)
{
    return (riid == m_iid) ? NOERROR : ResultFromScode(S_FALSE);
}
```

Releasing Objects and OLE

When the Hello application ends, it revokes the class factory and the active object, and uninitializes OLE. For example (MAIN.CPP):

```
void Uninitialize(DWORD dwRegisterCF, DWORD dwRegisterActiveObject)
{
    if (dwRegisterCF != 0)
        CoRevokeClassObject(dwRegisterCF);
    if (dwRegisterActiveObject != 0)
        RevokeActiveObject(dwRegisterActiveObject, NULL);
    OleUninitialize();
}
```

Creating the Type Information

Type information for the Hello sample is described in ODL. MkTypLib compiles the ODL file to create a type library (HELLOTL.TLB) and a header file (HELLOTL.H). The following example shows the description for the Hello type library, interface, and Application object (HELLO.ODL):

```
[
    uuid(F37C8060-4AD5-101B-B826-00DD01103DE1),      // LIBID_Hello
    helpstring("Hello 2.0 Type Library"),
    lcid(0x0409),
    version(2.0)
]
library Hello
{
    importlib("stdole.tlb");
    [
        uuid(F37C8062-4AD5-101B-B826-00DD01103DE1),    // IID_IHello
        helpstring("Application object for the Hello application."),
        oleautomation,
        dual
    ]
    interface IHello : IDispatch
    {
        [propget, helpstring("Returns the application of the object.")]
        HRESULT Application([out, retval] IHello** retval);
```

```
[propget,
    helpstring("Returns the full name of the application.")]
HRESULT FullName([out, retval] BSTR* retval);

[propget, id(0),
helpstring("Returns the name of the application.")]
HRESULT Name([out, retval] BSTR* retval);

[propget, helpstring("Returns the parent of the object.")]
HRESULT Parent([out, retval] IHello** retval);

[propput]
HRESULT Visible([in] boolean VisibleFlag);
[propget,
helpstring
("Sets or returns whether the main window is visible.")]
HRESULT Visible([out, retval] boolean* retval);

[helpstring("Exits the application.")]
HRESULT Quit();

[propput,
helpstring("Sets or returns the hello message to be used.")]
HRESULT HelloMessage([in] BSTR Message);
[propget]
HRESULT HelloMessage([out, retval] BSTR *retval);

[helpstring("Say Hello using HelloMessage.")]
HRESULT SayHello();
}


[
    uuid(F37C8061-4AD5-101B-B826-00DD01103DE1),      // CLSID_Hello
    helpstring("Hello Class"),
    appobject
]
coclass Hello
{
    [default]              interface IHello;
                           interface IDispatch;
}
}
```

The items enclosed by square brackets are *attributes*, which provide further
information about the objects in the file. The **oleautomation** and **dual** attributes,
for example, indicate that the IHello interface supports both **IDispatch** and VTBL
binding. The **appobject** attribute indicates that the Hello is the Application object.

Creating a Registration File

The system registration database lists all the OLE objects in the system. OLE uses this database to locate objects and to determine their capabilities. The registration file registers the application, the type library, and the exposed classes of the sample (HELLO.REG):

```
REGEDIT
; Registration information for OLE Automation Hello 2.0 Application

; Version independent registration. Points to Version 2.0
HKEY_CLASSES_ROOT\Hello.Application = Hello 2.0 Application
HKEY_CLASSES_ROOT\Hello.Application\Clsid = {F37C8061-4AD5-101B-B826-00DD01103DE1}

; Version 2.0 registration
HKEY_CLASSES_ROOT\Hello.Application.2 = Hello 2.0 Application
HKEY_CLASSES_ROOT\Hello.Application.2\Clsid = {F37C8061-4AD5-101B-B826-00DD01103DE1}
HKEY_CLASSES_ROOT\CLSID\{F37C8061-4AD5-101B-B826-00DD01103DE1} = Hello 2.0 Application
HKEY_CLASSES_ROOT\CLSID\{F37C8061-4AD5-101B-B826-00DD01103DE1}\ProgID = Hello.Application.2
HKEY_CLASSES_ROOT\CLSID\{F37C8061-4AD5-101B-B826-00DD01103DE1}\VersionIndependentProgID =
Hello.Application
HKEY_CLASSES_ROOT\CLSID\{F37C8061-4AD5-101B-B826-00DD01103DE1}\LocalServer = hello.exe
/Automation

; Type library registration information
HKEY_CLASSES_ROOT\TypeLib\{F37C8060-4AD5-101B-B826-00DD01103DE1}
HKEY_CLASSES_ROOT\TypeLib\{F37C8060-4AD5-101B-B826-00DD01103DE1}\2.0 = Hello 2.0 Type
Library
HKEY_CLASSES_ROOT\TypeLib\{F37C8060-4AD5-101B-B826-00DD01103DE1}\2.0\HELPDIR =
;US english
HKEY_CLASSES_ROOT\TypeLib\{F37C8060-4AD5-101B-B826-00DD01103DE1}\2.0\409\win16 = hello.tlb

; Interface registration. All interfaces that support vtable binding must be
; registered as follows. RegisterTypeLib & LoadTypeLib will do this automatically.

; IID_IHello = {F37C8062-4AD5-101B-B826-00DD01103DE1}
; LIBID_Hello = {F37C8060-4AD5-101B-B826-00DD01103DE1}
HKEY_CLASSES_ROOT\Interface\{F37C8062-4AD5-101B-B826-00DD01103DE1} = IHello
HKEY_CLASSES_ROOT\Interface\{F37C8060-4AD5-101B-B826-00DD01103DE1}\TypeLib = {F37C8060-
4AD5-101B-B826-00DD01103DE1}
HKEY_CLASSES_ROOT\Interface\{F37C8060-4AD5-101B-B826-00DD01103DE1}\ProxyStubClsid =
{00020424-0000-0000-C000-000000000046}
```

To merge your object's registration information with the system registry, your object should expose the **DLLRegisterServer** API, as described in the *OLE Programmer's Guide and Reference*. **DLLRegisterServer** should call **RegisterTypeLib** to register the type library and the interfaces supported by your application.

Limitations of the "Hello World" Example

The "Hello World" example was simplified for demonstration purposes. It has the following limitations:

- Has only one object.

- Uses only scalar argument types. OLE Automation also supports methods and properties that accept arguments of complex types, including arrays, references to objects, and formatted data, but not structures.

- Supports one national language. **DispInvoke** does not accommodate multiple localized member names, and therefore is useful only for single-language applications.

The remainder of this chapter explains in more detail the OLE Automation features that appear in Hello, as well as covering these more advanced features. Filenames in the rest of the chapter refer to the Lines sample.

Creating Class IDs

Each object you expose for creation must have a unique class identifier (CLSID). CLSIDs are universally unique identifiers (UUIDs, also called globally unique identifiers, or GUIDs) that identify class objects to OLE. The CLSID is included in your application and must be registered with the operating system when your application is installed.

Run the GUIDGEN.EXE utility included in the \OLE2\BIN directory to generate UUIDs. By default, GUIDGEN puts a DEFINE_GUID macro on the clipboard which you can paste into your source.

In the following example, the macro defines a class ID for Lines (TLB.H):

```
DEFINE_GUID(CLSID_Lines,0x3C591B21,0x1F13,0x101B,0xB8,0x26,0x00,0xDD,0x0
1,0x10,0x3D,0xE1);
```

When **MkTypLib** creates the optional header file (TLB.H), it inserts DEFINE_GUID macros for each library, interface, and class in your application.

Initializing OLE

OLE2.DLL provides functions to initialize OLE and to initialize exposed objects for creation using OLE Automation.

▶ **To initialize OLE**

1. Initialize the OLE DLLs by calling **OleInitialize**.

2. Create an instance of each class factory you expose. You need a class factory for the Application object and any other top-level objects.

3. Call **CoRegisterClassObject** for each class your application exposes.

The following routine initializes OLE, then creates an instance of the Lines Application object (Lines sample, MAIN.CPP):

```
BOOL InitInstance (HINSTANCE hinst)
{
    HRESULT hr;

    // Intialize OLE
    hr = OleInitialize(NULL);
    if (FAILED(hr))
        return FALSE;

    // Create an instance of the Lines Application object. The object is
    // created with refcount 0.
    hr = CApplication::Create(hinst, &g_pApplication);
    if (FAILED(hr))
        return FALSE;
    return TRUE;
}
```

Initializing the Active Object

The following function creates and registers the application's class factory, then registers the Lines Application object as the active object (MAIN.CPP):

```
BOOL ProcessCmdLine(LPSTR lpCmdLine, LPDWORD pdwRegisterCF,
                    LPDWORD pdwRegisterActiveObject, int nCmdShow)
{
    LPCLASSFACTORY pcf = NULL;
    HRESULT hr;
```

```
            *pdwRegisterCF = 0;
            *pdwRegisterActiveObject = 0;

            // Expose class factory for application object if command line
            // contains the /Automation switch.
            if (_fstrstr(lpCmdLine, "-Automation") != NULL
                || _fstrstr(lpCmdLine, "/Automation") != NULL)
            {
                pcf = new CApplicationCF;
                if (!pcf)
                    goto error;
                pcf->AddRef();
                hr = CoRegisterClassObject(CLSID_Lines, pcf,
                                      CLSCTX_LOCAL_SERVER, REGCLS_SINGLEUSE,
                                      pdwRegisterCF);
                if (hr != NOERROR)
                    goto error;
                pcf->Release();
            }
            else            // Show window if started stand-alone
            g_pApplication->ShowWindow(nCmdShow );

    // Register Lines application object in the Running Object Table (ROT)
    // Use weak registration so that the ROT releases its reference when
    // all external references are released.
            RegisterActiveObject(g_pApplication, CLSID_Lines, ACTIVEOBJECT_WEAK,
                    pdwRegisterActiveObject);
            return TRUE;

    error:
            if (!pcf)
                pcf->Release();
            return FALSE;
    }
```

OLE Automation provides several functions to identify and retrieve the running instance of an object or application:

- **RegisterActiveObject**—Sets the active object for an application. (Use when application starts.)

- **RevokeActiveObject**—Revokes the active object. (Use when application ends.)

- **GetActiveObject**—Retrieves a pointer to the object that is active. (In Visual Basic, this is implemented by the **GetObject** function.)

Applications can have more than one active object at a time. To be initialized as an active object, an object must:

- Have a class factory (that is, the object provides an interface for creating instances of itself).
- Identify its class factory by a programmatic ID (ProgID) in the system registry.
- Be registered by a call to **RegisterActiveObject** when the object is created or becomes active.

The Application object must be registered as an active object.

The example exposes the class factory for the Lines application, CApplicationCF, if the command line contains the **/Automation** switch. OLE applies this switch if it appears on the command line or in the application's registration entry. The switch indicates that the application was started for programmatic access, and therefore OLE needs to register the class factory and create an instance of the Application object. OLE also supports the **/Embedding** switch, which indicates that an application was started by a container application.

You should register the Application object's class factory only if the application is launched with the **/Automation** switch. When **/Automation** is not specified, the application was started for some reason other than programmatic access through OLE Automation. If you register the class factory under these circumstances, and the user later requests a new instance of the Application object, OLE Automation will return the existing instance instead of creating a new instance.

The sample calls **CoRegisterClassObject** to register the class factory as the active object. The CLSCTX_LOCAL_SERVER flag means that the code that creates and manages Application objects will run in a separate process space on this machine.

Because the Application object's class factory is exposed, the call specifies the REGCLS_SINGLEUSE flag. When a multiple-document interface (MDI) application starts, it typically registers the class factory for its Document object, specifying REGCLS_MULTIPLEUSE. This attribute allows the existing application instance to be used later, when instances of the document objects need to be created. Each new Application object, however, requires a new instance of the application to be launched, and therefore should specify REGCLS_SINGLEUSE. If the application registered its class factory using REGCLS_MULTIPLEUSE, the next **CreateObject** call that tried to create the application would get an existing copy.

The following chart shows how applications should expose their Application and Document objects.

Command line	MDI application	SDI application
/Embedding	Expose class factories for document classes, but not for the application.	Expose class factories for document class, but not for the application.
	Call **RegisterActiveObject** for the Application object.	Call **RegisterActiveObject** for the Application object.
/Automation	Expose class factories for document classes.	Do not expose class factory for document class.
	Expose class factory for the application using **RegisterClassObject**.	Expose class factory for the Application object using **RegisterClassObject**.
	Call **RegisterActiveObject** for the Application object.	Call **RegisterActiveObject** for the Application object.
No OLE switches	Expose class factories for document classes, but not for the application.	Call **RegisterActiveObject** for the Application object.
	Call **RegisterActiveObject** for the Application object.	

The call to **RegisterActiveObject** enters the Application object in OLE's running object table, so that OLE Automation controllers can retrieve the running object instead of creating a new instance. Thus, Visual Basic applications can use the **GetObject** statement to access an existing object.

The example specifies weak registration (ACTIVEOBJECT_WEAK), which means that OLE will release the object when all external connections to it have disappeared. OLE Automation objects should always be given weak registration. See "**RegisterActiveObject**" in Chapter 5 for more information.

The *OLE Programmer's Guide and Reference* in the Win32 SDK provides more information on the **OleInitialize** and **CoRegisterClassObject** functions. *Inside OLE* (second edition) provides more information on verifying your application's entries in the registration database.

Creating the IUnknown Interface

IUnknown defines three member functions you must implement for each object you expose. The prototypes for these functions reside in OLE2.H:

- **QueryInterface**—Identifies which OLE interfaces the object supports.

- **AddRef**—Increments a member variable that tracks the number of references to the object.

- **Release**—Decrements the member variable that tracks the instances of the object. If an object has zero references, **Release** frees the object.

These functions provide the fundmental interface through which OLE can access your objects. The *OLE Programmer's Guide and Reference* describes in detail how to implement the functions.

The **IUnknown** interface for the Line object looks like this (Lines sample, LINE.CPP):

```
STDMETHODIMP
CLine::QueryInterface(REFIID iid, void FAR* FAR* ppv)
{
    *ppv = NULL;

    if (iid == IID_IUnknown || iid == IID_IDispatch || iid == IID_ILine)
        *ppv = this;
    else if (iid == IID_ISupportErrorInfo)
        *ppv = &m_SupportErrorInfo;
    else return ResultFromScode(E_NOINTERFACE);

    AddRef();
    return NOERROR;
}


STDMETHODIMP_(ULONG)
CLine::AddRef(void)
{
    return ++m_cRef;
}
```

```
STDMETHODIMP_(ULONG)
CLine::Release(void)
{
    if(--m_cRef == 0)
    {
        delete this;
        return 0;
    }
    return m_cRef;
}
```

The Line object implements the IID_ILine dual interface for VTBL binding. It also implements the IID_ISupportErrorInfo interface, so that it can return rich, contextual error information through VTBLs.

Exposing Objects for Creation with IClassFactory

Before OLE can create an object, it needs access to the object's class factory. The class factory implements the **IClassFactory** interface. For detailed information about this interface, see *Inside OLE* and the *OLE Programmer's Guide and Reference*; this chapter only describes what you must do to expose objects for OLE Automation.

You need to implement a class factory for objects that may be created explicitly through the OLE function **CoCreateInstance** or the Visual Basic **New** operator. For example, an application exposes an Application object for creation, but may have many other programmable objects that can be created or destroyed by referencing a member of the Application object. In this case, only the Application object needs a class factory.

For each class factory, you need to implement the following two member functions, which provide services for OLE API functions. The prototypes for the member functions reside in OLE2.H:

- **CreateInstance**—Creates an instance of the object's class.

- **LockServer**—Prevents the object's server from shutting down, even if the last instance of the object is released. **LockServer** can improve the performance of applications that create and release objects frequently.

In general, the **CreateInstance** method should create a new instance of the object's class. For the Application object, however, the **CreateInstance** method should return the existing instance of the Application object, which is registered in the running object table.

The Lines sample implements a class factory for its Application object, as follows (APPCF.CPP):

```
STDMETHODIMP
CApplicationCF::CreateInstance(IUnknown FAR* punkOuter,
                               REFIID riid,
                               void FAR* FAR* ppv)
{
    HRESULT hr;

    *ppv = NULL;

    // This implementation doesn't allow aggregation.
    if (punkOuter)
        return ResultFromScode(CLASS_E_NOAGGREGATION);

    // This is REGCLS_SINGLEUSE class factory, so CreateInstance will be
    // called at most once. An application object has a REGCLS_SINGLEUSE
    // class factory. The global application object has already been
    // created when CreateInstance is called. A REGCLS_MULTIPLEUSE class
    // factory's CreateInstance would be called multiple times and would
    // create a new object each time. An MDI application would have a
    // REGCLS_MULTIPLEUSE class factory for its document objects.

    hr = g_pApplication->QueryInterface(riid, ppv);
    if (FAILED(hr))
    {
        g_pApplication->Quit();
        return hr;
    }
    return NOERROR;
}


STDMETHODIMP
CApplicationCF::LockServer(BOOL fLock)
{
    CoLockObjectExternal(g_pApplication, fLock, TRUE);
    return NOERROR;
}
```

The object's class factory must also implement an **IUnknown** interface. For example (APPCF.CPP):

```
STDMETHODIMP
CApplicationCF::QueryInterface(REFIID iid, void FAR* FAR* ppv)
{
    *ppv = NULL;

    if (iid == IID_IUnknown || iid == IID_IClassFactory)
        *ppv = this;
    else
        return ResultFromScode(E_NOINTERFACE);
    AddRef();
    return NOERROR;
}

STDMETHODIMP_(ULONG)
CApplicationCF::AddRef(void)
{
    return ++m_cRef;
}

STDMETHODIMP_(ULONG)
CApplicationCF::Release(void)
{
    if(--m_cRef == 0)
    {
        delete this;
        return 0;
    }
    return m_cRef;
}
```

Creating the IDispatch Interface

IDispatch provides a late-bound mechanism to access and retrieve information about an object's methods and properties. In addition to the member functions inherited from **IUnknown**, you need to implement the following member functions within the class definition of each object you expose through OLE Automation:

- **GetTypeInfoCount**—Returns the number of type descriptions for the object. For objects that support **IDispatch**, the type information count is always 1.

- **GetTypeInfo**—Retrieves a description of the object's programmable interface.

- **GetIDsOfNames**—Maps the name of a method or property to a Dispatch ID, which can later be used to invoke the method or property.

- **Invoke**—Calls one of the object's methods, or gets or sets one of its properties.

You may implement **IDispatch** by any of the following means:

- Calling the **CreateStdDispatch** function. This approach is the simplest, but it does not provide for rich error handling or multiple national languages.

- Delegating to the **DispInvoke** and **DispGetIDsOfNames** functions, or to **ITypeInfo::Invoke** and **ITypeInfo::GetIDsOfNames**. This is the recommended approach, because it supports multiple locales and allows you to return exceptions.

- Implementing the member functions without delegating to the dispatch functions. This approach is seldom necessary. Because **Invoke** is a complex interface with many subtle semantics that are difficult to emulate, Microsoft strongly recommends that your code delegate to **ITypeInfo::Invoke** to implement this mechanism.

The following sections explain how to use CreateStdDispatch and DispInvoke to implement IDispatch.

Implementing IDispatch by Calling CreateStdDispatch

The simplest way to implement the **IDispatch** interface is to call **CreateStdDispatch**. This approach works for OLE Automation objects that return only the standard dispatch exception codes, support a single national language, and do not support dual interfaces.

CreateStdDispatch returns a pointer to the created **IDispatch** interface. It takes three pointers as input: a pointer to the object's **IUnknown** interface; a pointer to the object to expose; and a pointer to the type information for the object. The following example implements IDispatch for an object named CCalc by calling **CreateStdDispatch** on the loaded type information:

```
CCalc FAR*
CCalc::Create()
{
    HRESULT hresult;
    CCalc FAR* pcalc;
    ITypeLib FAR* ptlib;
    ITypeInfo FAR* ptinfo;
    IUnknown FAR* punkStdDisp;

    ptlib = NULL;
    ptinfo = NULL;

    // Some error handling code omitted...
    if ((pcalc = new FAR CCalc()) == NULL)
        return NULL;
    pcalc->AddRef();
```

```
                        // Load the type library from the information in the registry.
                        if ((hresult = LoadRegTypeLib(LIBID_DspCalc2, 1, 0, 0x0409, &ptlib))
                            != NOERROR){
                            goto LError0;
                        }
                        if ((hresult = ptlib->GetTypeInfoOfGuid(IID_ICalculator, &ptinfo))
                            != NOERROR){
                            goto LError0;
                        }

                        // Create an aggregate with an instance of the default
                        // implementation of IDispatch that is initialized with our
                        // TypeInfo.
                        //
                        hresult = CreateStdDispatch(
                                pcalc,                          // controlling unknown
                                &(pcalc->m_arith),              // VTBL pointer to dispatch on
                                ptinfo,
                                &punkStdDisp);
```

Implementing IDispatch by Delegating

Another way to implement **IDispatch** is to use the dispatch functions **DispInvoke**
and **DispGetIDsOfNames**. These functions give you the option of supporting
multiple national languages and creating application-specific exceptions that are
passed back to OLE Automation controllers.

The Lines sample implements **IDispatch::GetIDsOfNames** and
IDispatch::Invoke using these functions (LINES.CPP):

```
STDMETHODIMP
CLines::GetIDsOfNames(
        REFIID riid,
        char FAR* FAR* rgszNames,
        UINT cNames,
        LCID lcid,
        DISPID FAR* rgdispid)
{
    return DispGetIDsOfNames(m_ptinfo, rgszNames, cNames, rgdispid);
}
```

```
STDMETHODIMP
CLines::Invoke(
        DISPID dispidMember,
        REFIID riid,
        LCID lcid,
        WORD wFlags,
        DISPPARAMS FAR* pdispparams,
        VARIANT FAR* pvarResult,
        EXCEPINFO FAR* pexcepinfo,
        UINT FAR* puArgErr)
{

    HRESULT hr;

    m_bRaiseException = FALSE;
    hr =  DispInvoke(
        this, m_ptinfo,
        dispidMember, wFlags, pdispparams,
        pvarResult, pexcepinfo, puArgErr);
    if (m_bRaiseException)
    {
        if (NULL != pexcepinfo)
            _fmemcpy(pexcepinfo, &m_excepinfo, sizeof(EXCEPINFO));
        return ResultFromScode(DISP_E_EXCEPTION);
    }
    else return hr;
}
```

In the preceding example, CLines::Invoke handles exceptions by initializing the variable m_bRaiseException to False before calling **DispInvoke**. If an exception occurs, the invoked member places error information in the variable m_excepinfo, and sets m_bRaiseException to True. Then CLines::Invoke copies m_excepinfo and returns DISP_E_EXCEPTION.

Setting Up the VTBL Interface

The Lines sample supports VTBL binding as well as the **IDispatch** interface. By supporting this **dual** interface, the sample allows OLE Automation controllers both the flexibility of the **IDispatch** interface and the speed of VTBLs. Controllers that know the names of the members can compile directly against the function pointers in the VTBL; controllers that don't have this information can use **IDispatch** at run time.

To have a **dual** interface, an interface must:

- Declare all its members to return an HRESULT and pass their actual return values as the last parameter.
- Have only OLE Automation-compatible parameters and return types, as described in Chapter 7.
- Specify the **dual** attribute on the interface description in the ODL file.
- Initialize the VTBLs with the appropriate member function pointers.

The IPoint, IPoints, ILine, ILines, IPane, and IApplication interfaces in the Lines sample are all **dual** interfaces. The IPoint interface defines functions that get and put the values of the X and Y properties, as follows (POINT.CPP):

```
STDMETHODIMP
CPoint::get_x(int FAR* pnX)
{
    *pnX = m_nX;
    return NOERROR;
}

STDMETHODIMP
CPoint::put_x(int nX)
{
    m_nX = nX;
    return NOERROR;
}

STDMETHODIMP
CPoint::get_y(int FAR* pnY)
{
    *pnY = m_nY;
    return NOERROR;
}

STDMETHODIMP
CPoint::put_y(int nY)
{
    m_nY = nY;
    return NOERROR;
}
```

The get_x and get_y accessor functions pass their return values in the last parameter, pnX and pnY, and return an HRESULT as the function value.

In the ODL file, the interface is described as follows (LINES.ODL):

```
[
        uuid(3C591B25-1F13-101B-B826-00DD01103DE1),    // IID_IPoint
        helpstring("Point object."),
        oleautomation,
        dual
]
interface IPoint : IDispatch
{
        [propget, helpstring("Returns and sets x coordinate.")]
        HRESULT x([out, retval] int* retval);
        [propput, helpstring("Returns and sets x coordinate.")]
        HRESULT x([in] int Value);

        [propget, helpstring("Returns and sets y coordinate.")]
        HRESULT y([out, retval] int* retval);
        [propput, helpstring("Returns and sets y coordinate.")]
        HRESULT y([in] int Value);
}
```

The **oleautomation** and **dual** attributes indicate that the interface supports both
IDispatch and VTBL binding. All the member functions are declared with
HRESULT return values. The get accessor functions, indicated by the **propget**
attribute, return their value in the last parameter. This parameter has the **out** and
retval attributes.

For more information on dual interfaces, see "The **dual** attribute" in Chapter 7.

Creating the Programmable Interface

An object's programmable interface comprises the properties and methods it
defines. Organizing the objects, properties, and methods that an application exposes
is like creating an object-oriented framework for an application. Chapter 4,
"Standards and Guidelines," discusses some of the concepts behind naming and
organizing the programmable elements your application may expose.

Creating Methods

A *method* is an action that an object can perform, such as drawing a line or clearing
the display. Methods can take any number of arguments, including optional
arguments, and they may be passed either by value or by reference. A method may
or may not return a value.

In the Lines sample, the Application object exposes the following method
(APP.CPP):

```
STDMETHODIMP
CApplication::CreatePoint(IPoint FAR* FAR* ppPoint)
{
    CPoint FAR* ppoint = NULL;
    HRESULT hr;

    // Create new item and QI for IDispatch.
    hr = CPoint::Create(&ppoint);
    if (FAILED(hr))
        {hr = RaiseException(IDS_OutOfMemory); goto error;}

    hr = ppoint->QueryInterface(IID_IDispatch, (void FAR* FAR*)ppPoint);
    if (FAILED(hr))
        {hr = RaiseException(IDS_Unexpected); goto error;}
    return NOERROR;

error:
    if (ppoint)
        delete ppoint;
    return hr;
}
```

The CreatePoint method creates a new point and returns a pointer to it in the
parameter pPoint.

Creating Properties

A *property* is a member function that sets or returns information about the state of
the object, such as color or visibility. Most properties have a pair of accessor
functions—a function to get the property value and a function to set the property
value. Properties that are read-only or write-only, however, have only one accessor
function.

In the Lines sample, the CLine object exposes the Color property. This property is
implemented by the following accessor functions (LINE.CPP):

```
STDMETHODIMP
CLine::get_Color(long FAR* plColorref)
{
    *plColorref = m_colorref;
    return NOERROR;
}
```

```
STDMETHODIMP
CLine::put_Color(long lColorref)
{
    m_colorref = (COLORREF)lColorref;
    return NOERROR;
}
```

The accessor functions for a single property have the same dispatch ID (DISPID). The purpose of each function is indicated by attributes set for the function. These attributes are set in the ODL description of the function (as in LINES.ODL) and are passed in the *wFlags* parameter to Invoke to set the context for the call. The attributes and flags are shown in the following table:

Purpose of function	ODL attribute	wFlags
Return a value	**propget**	DISPATCH_PROPERTYGET
Set a value	**propput**	DISPATCH_PROPERTYPUT
Set a reference	**propputref**	DISPATCH_PROPERTYPUTREF

The **propget** attribute designates the accessor function that gets the value of a property. When OLE Automation controller needs to get the value of the property, it passes the DISPATCH_PROPERTYGET flag to **Invoke**.

The **propput** attribute designates the accessor function that sets the value of a property. When an OLE Automation controller needs to set a property by value, it passes the DISPATCH_PROPERTYPUT flag to **Invoke**. In Visual Basic, **Let** statements set properties by value.

The **propputref** attribute indicates that the property should be set by reference, rather than by value. OLE Automation controllers that need to set a reference to a property pass DISPATCH_PROPERTYPUTREF in these cases. Visual Basic treats the **Set** statement as a by-reference property assignment.

The Value Property

The Value property defines the default behavior of an object when no property or method is specified. It is typically used for the property that users associate most closely with the object. For example, a cell in a spreadsheet might have many properties (Font, Width, Height, and so on), but its Value property is special, yielding the value of the cell. To refer to this property, a user need not specify the property name Cell(1,1).Value, but can simply use Cell(1,1).

The Value property is identified by the dispatch ID DISPID_VALUE. In an ODL file, the Value property for an object has the attribute **id(0)**.

In the Lines sample, ILines.Item, IPoints.Item, and IApplication.Name are the Value properties of the ILines, IPoints, and IApplication objects, respectively. The ILines.Item object is described as follows:

```
interface ILines : IDispatch
    {
.
.//Some descriptions omitted
.
    [propget, id(0), helpstring(
"Given an integer index, returns one of the lines in the collection")]
    HRESULT Item([in] long Index,[out, retval] ILine** retval);
.
.
.
}
```

Using this property, a user can refer to the fourth line in the collection as ILines(4).Item or simply as ILines(4).

See Chapter 4, "Standards and Guidelines," for more on recommended objects, properties, and methods.

Returning Objects

To return an object from a property or method, the application should return a pointer to the object's implementation of the **IDispatch** interface. The data type of the return value should be VT_DISPATCH or VT_UNKNOWN (if the object doesn't support **IDispatch**). The Object Description Language (ODL) for the object should specify the name of the interface, rather than **IDispatch***, as follows:

```
ICustom * MyMember(...) {...};
```

The example declares a member that returns a pointer to a custom interface called ICustom.

Passing Formatted Data

Often, an application needs to accept formatted data as an argument to a method or property. Examples include a bitmap, formatted text, or a spreadsheet range. When handling formatted data, the application should pass an object that implements the OLE **IDataObject** interface. For detailed information about the interface, see the *OLE Programmer's Guide and Reference*.

Using this interface, applications can retrieve data of any Clipboard format. Because an **IDataObject** instance can provide data of more than one format, a caller can provide data in several formats, and let the called object choose which format is most appropriate (like the Clipboard).

If the data object implements **IDispatch**, it should be passed using the VT_DISPATCH flag. If the data object does not support **IDispatch**, it should be passed with the VT_UNKNOWN flag.

Restricting Access

OLE Automation provides several ways of restricting access to objects. The simplest approach is not to document the properties and methods you don't want customers to see. Alternatively, you can prevent a property or method from appearing in type library browsers by specifying the **hidden** attribute in ODL.

The **restricted** attribute goes one step further, preventing user calls from binding to the property or method as well as hiding it from type browsers. For example, the following restricts access to the _NewEnum property of the ILines object:

```
[propget, restricted, id(DISPID_NEWENUM)] // Must be propget.
    HRESULT _NewEnum( [out, retval] IUnknown** retval );
```

Restricted properties and methods can be invoked by OLE Automation controllers, but are not visible to the customer or end user who may be using a language such as Visual Basic. In addition, they can't be bound to by user calls.

Creating Collection Objects

A collection object contains a group of exposed objects of the same type and can iterate over them. Collection objects do not need an **IClassFactory** implementation, because they are accessed from elements that have their own class factories.

For example, the Lines sample has a collection object named CLines that iterates over a group of Line objects. The following routine creates and initializes the CLines collection object (LINES.CPP):

```
STDMETHODIMP
CLines::Create(ULONG lMaxSize, long lLBound, CPane FAR* pPane,
               CLines FAR* FAR* ppLines)
{
    HRESULT hr;
    CLines FAR* pLines = NULL;
    SAFEARRAYBOUND sabound[1];

    *ppLines = NULL;

    // Create new collection.
    pLines = new CLines();
    if (pLines == NULL)
        goto error;
```

```
        pLines->m_cMax = lMaxSize;
        pLines->m_cElements = 0;
        pLines->m_lLBound = lLBound;
        pLines->m_pPane = pPane;

        // Load type information for the Lines collection from type library.
        hr = LoadTypeInfo(&pLines->m_ptinfo, IID_ILines);
        if (FAILED(hr))
            goto error;

        // Create a safe array of variants used to implement the collection.
        sabound[0].cElements = lMaxSize;
        sabound[0].lLbound = lLBound;
        pLines->m_psa = SafeArrayCreate(VT_VARIANT, 1, sabound);
        if (pLines->m_psa == NULL)
        {
            hr = ResultFromScode(E_OUTOFMEMORY);
            goto error;
        }

        *ppLines = pLines;
        return NOERROR;

error:
    if (pLines == NULL)
        return ResultFromScode(E_OUTOFMEMORY);
    if (pLines->m_ptinfo)
        pLines->m_ptinfo->Release();
    if (pLines->m_psa)
        SafeArrayDestroy(pLines->m_psa);

    pLines->m_psa = NULL;
    pLines->m_ptinfo = NULL;

    delete pLines;
    return hr;
}
```

The parameters to CLines::Create specify the maximum number of lines that the collection can contain, the lower bound of the indexes of the collection, and a pointer to a pane, which contains the lines and points in the sample.

OLE Automation defines the **IEnumVARIANT** interface to provide a standard way for OLE Automation controllers to iterate over collections. In addition, every collection object must expose a read-only property named _NewEnum to let OLE Automation controllers know that the object supports iteration. The _NewEnum property returns an enumerator object that supports **IEnumVariant**.

Implementing IEnumVARIANT

The **IEnumVARIANT** interface provides a way to iterate through the items contained by a collection object. This interface is supported by an enumerator object that is returned by the _NewEnum property of the collection object, as in the following figure:

The **IEnumVARIANT** interface defines these member functions:

- **Next**—Retrieves one or more elements in a collection, starting with the current element.
- **Skip**—Skips over one or more elements in a collection.
- **Reset**—Resets the current element to the first element in the collection.
- **Clone**—Copies the current state of the enumeration so you can return to the current element after using **Skip** or **Reset**.

In the Lines example, CEnumVariant implements the **Next, Skip, Reset,** and **Clone** member functions (ENUMVAR.CPP):

```
STDMETHODIMP
CEnumVariant::Next(ULONG cElements, VARIANT FAR* pvar,
                   ULONG FAR* pcElementFetched)
{
    HRESULT hr;
    ULONG l;
    long l1;
    ULONG l2;

    if (pcElementFetched != NULL)
        *pcElementFetched = 0;

    for (l=0; l<cElements; l++)
        VariantInit(&pvar[l]);

    // Retrieve the next cElements elements.
    for (l1=m_lCurrent, l2=0; l1<(long)(m_lLBound+m_cElements) &&
        l2<cElements; l1++, l2++)
    {
        hr = SafeArrayGetElement(m_psa, &l1, &pvar[l2]);
        if (FAILED(hr))
            goto error;
    }
```

```
        // Set count of elements retrieved
        if (pcElementFetched != NULL)
            *pcElementFetched = 12;
        m_lCurrent = 11;

        return  (12 < cElements) ? ResultFromScode(S_FALSE) : NOERROR;
error:
    for (l=0; l<cElements; l++)
        VariantClear(&pvar[l]);
    return hr;
}


STDMETHODIMP
CEnumVariant::Skip(ULONG cElements)
{
    m_lCurrent += cElements;
    if (m_lCurrent > (long)(m_lLBound+m_cElements))
    {
        m_lCurrent = m_lLBound+m_cElements;
        return ResultFromScode(S_FALSE);
    }
    else return NOERROR;
}


STDMETHODIMP
CEnumVariant::Reset()
{
    m_lCurrent = m_lLBound;
    return NOERROR;
}


STDMETHODIMP
CEnumVariant::Clone(IEnumVARIANT FAR* FAR* ppenum)
{
    CEnumVariant FAR* penum = NULL;
    HRESULT hr;

    *ppenum = NULL;

    hr = CEnumVariant::Create(m_psa, m_cElements, &penum);
    if (FAILED(hr))
        goto error;
    penum->AddRef();
    penum->m_lCurrent = m_lCurrent;

    *ppenum = penum;
    return NOERROR;
```

```
error:
    if (penum)
        penum->Release();
    return hr;
}
```

Implementing the _NewEnum Property

The _NewEnum property identifies an object as supporting iteration through the **IEnumVARIANT** interface. The _NewEnum property has the following requirements:

- Must be named _NewEnum and must not be localized.
- Must return a pointer to the enumerator object's **IUnknown** interface.
- Must have DISPID = DISPID_NEWENUM (-4)

The Lines example contains two collections, Lines and Points, and implements a _NewEnum property for each. Both are restricted properties, available to OLE Automation controllers, but invisible to users of scripting or macro languages supported by OLE Automation controllers. The property returns an enumerator (**IEnumVariant**) for the items in the collection.

The following code implements the _NewEnum property for the Lines collection (LINES.CPP):

```
STDMETHODIMP
CLines::get__NewEnum(IUnknown FAR* FAR* ppunkEnum)
{
    CEnumVariant FAR* penum = NULL;;
    HRESULT hr;

    *ppunkEnum = NULL;

    // Create a new enumerator for items currently in the collection and
    // QueryInterface for IUnknown.
    hr = CEnumVariant::Create(m_psa, m_cElements, &penum);
    if (FAILED(hr))
        {hr = RaiseException(IDS_OutOfMemory); goto error;}
    hr = penum->QueryInterface(IID_IUnknown, (VOID FAR* FAR*)ppunkEnum);
    if (FAILED(hr))
        {hr = RaiseException(IDS_Unexpected); goto error;}
    return NOERROR;

error:
    if (penum)
        delete penum;
    return hr;
}
```

Handling Events

In addition to supporting properties and methods, OLE Automation objects can be a source of events. In OLE Automation, an *event* is a method that is called by an OLE Automation object, rather than implemented by the object. For example, an object might include an event method named Button that retrieves clicks of the mouse button. Instead of being implemented by the object, the Button method returns an object that is a source of events.

In OLE Automation, you use the **source** attribute to identify a member that is a source of events. See "The Source Attribute" in Chapter 7 for more information.

Details of the OLE Automation event interfaces are provided in the *Programming with MFC* provided with Microsoft Visual C++ version 4.0.

Returning an Error

OLE Automation objects typically return rich contextual error information, including an error number, a description of the error, and the path of a Help file that supplies further documentation. Objects that do not need to return detailed error information can simply return an HRESULT that indicates the nature of the error.

Passing Exceptions through IDispatch

When an error occurs, objects invoked through **IDispatch** can return DISP_E_EXCEPTION and pass the details in the *pexcepinfo* parameter (an EXCEPINFO structure) to **IDispatch::Invoke**. The EXCEPINFO structure is defined in Chapter 5, "Dispatch Interfaces."

The Lines sample defines an exception handler that fills the EXCEPINFO structure and signals **IDispatch** to return DISP_E_EXCEPTION (APP.CPP):

```
STDMETHODIMP
CApplication::RaiseException(int nID)
{
    extern SCODE g_scodes[];
    char szError[STR_LEN];
    ICreateErrorInfo *pcerrinfo;
    IErrorInfo *perrinfo;
    HRESULT hr;

    _fmemset(&m_excepinfo, 0, sizeof(EXCEPINFO));
```

```
m_excepinfo.wCode = nID;
if (LoadString(m_hinst, nID, szError, sizeof(szError)))
    m_excepinfo.bstrDescription = SysAllocString(szError);
m_excepinfo.bstrSource = SysAllocString(m_bstrName);

m_bRaiseException = TRUE;

// Set ErrInfo object so that vtable binding containers can get
// rich error information.
hr = CreateErrorInfo(&pcerrinfo);
if (SUCCEEDED(hr))
{
    pcerrinfo->SetGUID(IID_IApplication);
    if (m_excepinfo.bstrSource)
        pcerrinfo->SetSource(m_excepinfo.bstrSource);
    if (m_excepinfo.bstrDescription)
        pcerrinfo->SetDescription(m_excepinfo.bstrDescription);
    hr = pcerrinfo->QueryInterface(IID_IErrorInfo,
                        (LPVOID FAR*) &perrinfo);
    if (SUCCEEDED(hr))
    {
        SetErrorInfo(0, perrinfo);
        perrinfo->Release();
    }
    pcerrinfo->Release();
}

return ResultFromScode(g_scodes[nID-1001]);
}
```

To raise an exception, properties and methods of the CApplication object call
RaiseException, passing an integer error ID This routine fills the global
EXCEPINFO structure, m_b_excepinfo, with information about the error. It also
sets the global flag m_b_RaiseException, which signals **IDispatch::Invoke** to
return DISP_E_EXCEPTION.

Passing Exceptions through VTBLs

The Lines example also provides rich error information for members invoked
through VTBLs. Because VTBL-bound calls bypass the IDispatch interface, they
cannot return exceptions through IDispatch. Instead, they must use OLE
Automation's error handling interfaces. The RaiseException function shown in
the example calls **CreateErrorInfo** to create an error object, then fills the object's
data fields with information about the error. When all the information has been
successfully recorded, it calls **SetErrorInfo** to associate the error object with the
current thread of execution.

OLE Automation objects similar to the CApplication object, which use the error interfaces, must implement the **ISupportErrorInfo** interface as well. This interface identifies the object as supporting the error interfaces, and ensures that error information can be propagated correctly up the call chain. The following example shows how Lines implements this interface (ERRINFO.CPP):

```
STDMETHODIMP
CSupportErrorInfo::CSupportErrorInfo(IUnknown FAR* punkObject,
        REFIID riid)
{
    m_punkObject = punkObject;
    m_iid = riid;
}


CSupportErrorInfo::QueryInterface(REFIID iid, void FAR* FAR* ppv)
{
    return m_punkObject->QueryInterface(iid, ppv);
}


STDMETHODIMP_(ULONG)
CSupportErrorInfo::AddRef(void)
{
    return m_punkObject->AddRef();
}


STDMETHODIMP_(ULONG)
CSupportErrorInfo::Release(void)
{
    return m_punkObject->Release();
}


STDMETHODIMP
CSupportErrorInfo::InterfaceSupportsErrorInfo(REFIID riid)
{
    return (riid == m_iid) ? NOERROR : ResultFromScode(S_FALSE);
}
```

ISupportErrorInfo has the **QueryInterface**, **AddRef**, and **Release** methods inherited from **IUnknown**, along with the **InterfaceSupportsErrorInfo** method. OLE Automation controllers call **InterfaceSupportsErrorInfo** to check whether the OLE Automation object supports the **IErrorInfo** interface, so that they can access the error object. For details, see Chapter 10, "Error Handling Interfaces."

Releasing OLE

> ▶ **To release OLE on exit**

1. Revoke the active object by calling **RevokeActiveObject**.
2. Revoke the classes of your exposed objects by calling **CoRevokeClassObject**.
3. Uninitialize OLE by calling **OleUninitialize**.

The following code revokes an active Lines object, revokes the Lines class, then uninitializes OLE (MAIN.CPP):

```
void Uninitialize(DWORD dwRegisterCF, DWORD dwRegisterActiveObject)
{
    if (dwRegisterCF != 0)
        CoRevokeClassObject(dwRegisterCF);
    if (dwRegisterActiveObject != 0)
        RevokeActiveObject(dwRegisterActiveObject, NULL);
    OleUninitialize();
}
```

Creating a Type Library

Type information is the OLE Automation standard for describing the objects, properties, and methods that your OLE Automation server exposes. Browsers and compilers use the type information to display and access the exposed objects.

Most OLE Automation servers create type libraries. Type libraries contain type information, Help filenames and contexts, and function-specific documentation strings, and enable access at both compile time and run time. Type libraries are described in Object Description Language (ODL) and are compiled by MkTypLib, as the following figure illustrates:

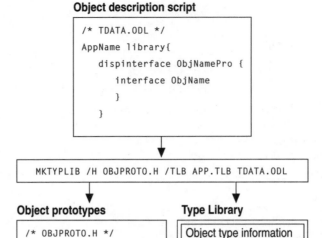

Object description script

```
/* TDATA.ODL */
AppName library{
    dispinterface ObjNamePro {
        interface ObjName
        }
    }
```

```
MKTYPLIB /H OBJPROTO.H /TLB APP.TLB TDATA.ODL
```

Object prototypes

```
/* OBJPROTO.H */
ObjectCF : IClassFactory
Object : IDispatch
```

Type Library

| Object type information |
| Object type information |
| ... |

OLE Automation also supports the creation of alternative tools that compile and access type information. Chapter 9, "Type Building Interfaces," describes interfaces for creating these tools.

A type library stores complete type information for all of an application's exposed objects. It may be included as a resource in a DLL or remain as a stand-alone file (.TLB).

▶   **To create a type library**

1.   Write an object description script (.ODL file) for the objects you expose.

2.   Build the type library (.TLB) and class description header file (.H) from the script using MkTypLib.

Writing an Object Description Script

An object description script is essentially an annotated header file, written in Object Description Language (ODL). The following example shows a portion of LINES.ODL, the object description script for the Lines sample.

```
[
    uuid(3C591B20-1F13-101B-B826-00DD01103DE1),      // LIBID_Lines
    helpstring("Lines 1.0 Type Library"),
    lcid(0x0409),
    version(1.0)
]
```

```
library Lines
{
    importlib("stdole.tlb");
    #define DISPID_NEWENUM -4
.
.
.
```

The preceding entry describes the type library (LINES.TLB) created by the sample. The items in square brackets are attributes, which provide additional information about the library. In the example, the attributes give the library's universally unique identifier (UUID), a Help string, a locale identifier, and a version number.

The **importlib** directive is similar to the C or C++ #include directive. It allows access to the type descriptions in STDOLE.TLB from the Lines library. However, it doesn't copy those types into LINES.TLB. Therefore, to use LINES.TLB, both LINES.TLB and STDOLE.TLB must be available.

By default, ODL files are preprocessed with the C preprocessor, so the #include and #define directives may be used.

The ODL script continues with information on the objects in the type library:

```
[
    uuid(3C591B25-1F13-101B-B826-00DD01103DE1),      // IID_IPoint
    helpstring("Point object."),
    oleautomation,
    dual
]
interface IPoint : IDispatch
{
    [propget, helpstring("Returns and sets x coordinate.")]
    HRESULT x( [out, retval] int* retval);
    [propput, helpstring("Returns and sets x coordinate.")]
    HRESULT x([in] int Value);

    [propget, helpstring("Returns and sets y coordinate.")]
    HRESULT y( [out, retval] int* retval);
    [propput, helpstring("Returns and sets y coordinate.")]
    HRESULT y([in] int Value);
}
// .
// . Additional definitions omitted
// .
}
```

This entry describes the IPoint interface. The interface has the attributes **oleautomation** and **dual**, indicating that the types of all its properties and methods are compatible with OLE Automation, and that it supports binding through both **IDispatch** and VTBLs. IPoint has two pairs of property accessor functions, which set and return the X and Y properties.

The Value parameter of both the X and Y properties has the **in** attribute. These parameters supply a value and are read-only. Conversely, the retval parameter of each property has the **out** and **retval** attributes, indicating that it returns the value of the property.

Because IPoint supports VTBL binding and rich error information, its properties return HRESULTs and pass their function return values through **retval** parameters. For more information, see Chapter 7, "MkTypLib and Object Description Language."

```
[
        uuid(3C591B21-1F13-101B-B826-00DD01103DE1),        // CLSID_Lines
        helpstring("Lines Class"),
        appobject
    ]
    coclass Lines
    {
        [default] interface IApplication;
            interface IDispatch;
    }
}
```

The file concludes with the description of the Lines Application object, as specified by the **appobject** attribute. The **default** attribute applies to the IApplication interface, indicating that this interface will be returned by default.

Building the Type Library

The MkTypLib tool builds type libraries. MkTypLib is described in detail in Chapter 7, "MkTypLib and Object Description Language."

▶ **To create a type library from an object description script**

From Windows, run the MkTypLib tool on the script. For example:

```
MKTYPLIB /TLB output.tlb /H output.h inscript.odl
```

The example creates a type library named OUTPUT.TLB and a header file named OUTPUT.H, based on the object description script INSCRIPT.ODL.

Note that MkTypLib requires Windows. If you run it from NMAKE, you must use the WX server support provided with OLE. For example, start WXSRVR in Windows and use the following command line in your NMAKE script:

```
MKTYPLIB /o odlscrip.err /TLB output.tlb /h output.h inscript.odl
```

Alternatively, you can add MkTypLib to the Tools menu in the Microsoft Visual C++ programming environment. If you do this, be sure to check the "Ask for Arguments" check box, so the programming environment will prompt you for the options and input file before running the tool.

After creating the type library (.TLB), you can include it in the resource step of building your application or leave it as a stand-alone file. In either case, be sure to specify the filename and path of the library in the application's registration file (.REG), so that OLE Automation can find the type library when necessary. See the following section for information on registering the type library.

▶ **To build an application that uses a type library**

1. Include the header file output by MkTypLib in your project.

2. Compile the project.

3. Optionally, use the Resource Compiler to bind the type library with your compiled project. You can bind the type library with DLLs or with .EXE files. For example, to bind a type library named OUTPUT.TLB with a DLL, use the following statement in the .RC file for the DLL:

```
1 typelib output.tlb
```

A DLL that contains a typelib resource usually has the .OLB (object library) extension.

The following figure illustrates the process.

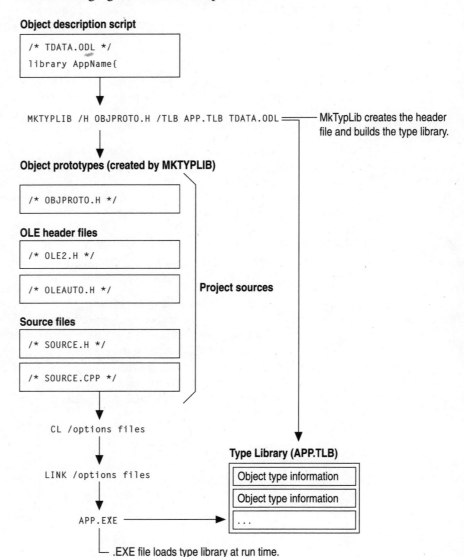

Object description script

```
/* TDATA.ODL */
library AppName{
```

```
MKTYPLIB /H OBJPROTO.H /TLB APP.TLB TDATA.ODL
```
MkTypLib creates the header file and builds the type library.

Object prototypes (created by MKTYPLIB)

```
/* OBJPROTO.H */
```

OLE header files

```
/* OLE2.H */
```

```
/* OLEAUTO.H */
```
Project sources

Source files

```
/* SOURCE.H */
```

```
/* SOURCE.CPP */
```

```
CL /options files
```

```
LINK /options files
```

Type Library (APP.TLB)

| Object type information |
| Object type information |
| ... |

```
APP.EXE
```
.EXE file loads type library at run time.

Creating a Registration File

Before an application can use OLE and OLE Automation, the OLE objects must be registered with the user's system registration database. Registration makes the following possible:

- OLE Automation controllers can create instances of the OLE Automation objects through **CoCreateInstance.**

- OLE Automation tools can find the type libraries that are installed on the user's computer.

- OLE can find remoting code for the interfaces.

OLE provides sample registration files to perform this task for the OLE objects and the sample applications.

▶ **To create a registration file**

1. Copy LINES.REG.

2. Rename and edit the file, adding entries for your application.

The registration file provides information about the application, Application object, classes of objects, type libraries, and interfaces. Entries for objects and interfaces start with the constant HKEY_CLASSES_ROOT, which represents the root key of the entire registration database. Entries for type libraries start with HKEY_TYPELIB_ROOT. After the constant, each entry supplies specific information about an object, type library, or interface.

The following sections give a brief overview of the syntax used in registering OLE Automation objects. For detailed information, refer to the *OLE Programmer's Guide and Reference.*

Note that you can use the **DLLRegisterServer** function to register all the objects implemented by a DLL. This function registers the class IDs for each object, the ProgIDs for each application, and the type library. For details, refer to the description of **DLLRegisterServer** in *Programming with MFC* provided with Microsoft Visual C++, version 4.0.

Registering the Application

Registration maps the programmatic ID (ProgID) of the application to a unique class ID (CLSID), so that you can create instances of the application by name, rather than by CLSID. For example, registering Microsoft Excel associates a CLSID with the ProgID "Excel.Application." In Visual Basic, you use the ProgId to create an instance of the application, as follows:

```
SET x1 = CreateObject("Excel.Application")
```

By passing the ProgID to **CLSIDFromProgID**, you can get the corresponding CLSID for use in **CoCreateInstance**. Only applications that will be used in this way need to be registered.

The registration file uses the following syntax for the application:

\ *AppName.ObjectName*[.*VersionNumber*] = *human_readable_string*
\ *AppName.ObjectName***CLSID** = {*UUID*}

AppName
> The name of the application.

ObjectName
> The name of the object to be registered, in this case, Application.

VersionNumber
> The optional version number of the object.

human_readable_string
> A string that describes the application, as you want it to appear to users. The recommended maximum length is 40 characters.

UUID
> The universally unique ID for the application class (CLSID). To generate a universally unique ID for your class, run the utility GUIDGEN.EXE provided in the \OLE2\BIN directory.

Example

```
REGEDIT
; Registration information for OLE Automation Hello 2.0 Application

; Version independent registration. Points to Version 2.0
HKEY_CLASSES_ROOT\Hello.Application = OLE Automation Hello Application
HKEY_CLASSES_ROOT\Hello.Application\Clsid = {F37C8061-4AD5-101B-B826-00DD01103DE1}

; Version 2.0 registration
HKEY_CLASSES_ROOT\Hello.Application.2 = OLE Automation Hello 2.0 Application
HKEY_CLASSES_ROOT\Hello.Application.2\Clsid = {F37C8061-4AD5-101B-B826-00DD01103DE1}
```

Registering Classes

Objects that can be created with **CoCreateInstance** must also be registered with the system. For these objects, registration maps a CLSID to the OLE Automation server file (.DLL or .EXE) in which the object resides. The CLSID also maps an OLE Automation object back to its application and ProgID. The following figure shows how registration connects ProgIDs, CLSIDs, and OLE Automation servers:

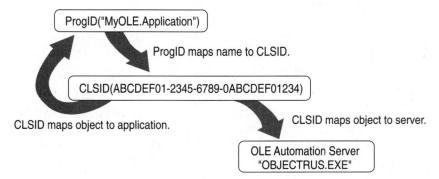

The registration file uses the following syntax for each class of each object your application exposes:

\CLSID\\{*UUID*} = *human_readable_string*
\CLSID\\{*UUID*}**ProgID** = *AppName.ObjectName.VersionNumber*
\CLSID\\{*UUID*}**VersionIndependentProgID** = *AppName.ObjectName*
\CLSID\\{*UUID*}**LocalServer**[**32**] = *filepath*[/**Automation**]
\CLSID\\{*UUID*}**InProcServer**[**32**] = *filepath*[/**Automation**]

human_readable_string
   A string that describes the object, as you want it to appear to users. The recommended maximum length is 40 characters.

AppName
   The name of the application, as specified previously in the application registration string.

ObjectName
   The name of the object to be registered.

VersionNumber

The version number of the object.

UUID

The universally unique ID for the application class (CLSID). To generate a universally unique ID for your class, run the utility GUIDGEN.EXE provided in the \OLE2\BIN directory.

filepath

The full path and name of the file that contains the object. The optional **/Automation** switch tells the application it was launched for OLE Automation purposes. The switch should be specified for the Application object's class. For more information on **/Automation**, see the section "Initializing the Active Object" earlier in this chapter.

The programmatic IDs (ProgID and VersionIndependentProgID) are used by other programmers to gain access to the objects you expose. These IDs should follow consistent naming guidelines across all your applications. They may contain up to 39 characters, must not contain any punctuation (except for the period), and must not start with a digit.

Version-independent names consist of an *AppName.ObjectName*, without a version number; for example, Word.Document or Excel.Chart.

Version-dependent names consist of an *AppName.ObjectName.VersionNumber*, such as Excel.Application.5.

LocalServer indicates that the OLE Automation server is an EXE file and runs in a separate process from the OLE Automation controller. **InProcServer** indicates that the server is a DLL and runs in the same process as the OLE Automation controller. The optional **32** specifies a server intended for use on 32-bit Windows systems.

The *filepath* you register should give the full path and name, so that applications need not rely on the MS-DOS PATH variable to find the object.

Example

```
HKEY_CLASSES_ROOT\CLSID\{F37C8061-4AD5-101B-B826-00DD01103DE1} = Hello 2.0 Application
HKEY_CLASSES_ROOT\CLSID\{F37C8061-4AD5-101B-B826-00DD01103DE1}\ProgID = Hello.Application.2
HKEY_CLASSES_ROOT\CLSID\{F37C8061-4AD5-101B-B826-00DD01103DE1}\VersionIndependentProgID =
Hello.Application
HKEY_CLASSES_ROOT\CLSID\{F37C8061-4AD5-101B-B826-00DD01103DE1}\LocalServer = hello.exe
/Automation
```

Registering Type Library Information

Tools and applications that expose type information must register the information so that it is available to type browsers and programming tools. You can generate the correct registration entries for a type library by calling the **RegisterTypeLib** function on the type library. You can then use REGEDIT, supplied with the Win32 SDK, to write the registration entries to a text file from your system registration database.

The following information is registered for a type library:

\TypeLib\\{*libUUID***}**
\TypeLib\\{*libUUID***}***major.minor* = *human_readable_string*
\TypeLib\\{*libUUID***}***major.minor***\HELPDIR** = [*helpfile_path*]
\TypeLib\\{*libUUID***}***major.minor***\Flags** = *typelib_flags*
\TypeLib\\{*libUUID***}***major.minor******lcid******platform* = *localized_typelib_filename*

libUUID
> The universally unique ID of the type library.

major.minor
> The two-part version number of the type library. If only the minor version number increases, all the features of the previous type library are supported in a compatible way. If the major version number changes, code that compiled against the type library must be recompiled. The version number of the type library may differ from the version number of the application.

human_readable_string
> A string that describes the type library, as you want it to appear to users. The recommended maximum length is 40 characters.

helpfile_path
> The directory where the Help file for the types in the type library is located. Note that if the application supports type libraries for multiple languages, the libraries may refer to different filenames in the Help file directory.

typelib_flags
> The hexadecimal representation of the type library flags for this type library. These are the values of the LIBFLAGS enumeration, and are the same flags specified in the *uLibFlags* parameter to **ICreateTypeLib::SetLibFlags**. They can't have leading zeros or the 0x prefix.

lcid
> The hexadecimal string representation of the locale ID (LCID). It is one to four hexadecimal digits with no 0x prefix and no leading zeros. The LCID may have a neutral sublanguage.

platform
> The target operating system platform: 16-bit Windows, 32-bit Windows, or Mac.

localized_typelib_filename
> The full name of the localized type library.

Using the LCID specifier, an application can explicitly register the filenames of type libraries for different languages. This allows the application to find the desired language without having to open all type libraries with a given name. To find the type library for Australian English (309), the application would first look for it and, if that fails, look for an entry for Standard English (9). If there is no entry for Standard English, the application looks for the LANG_SYSTEM_DEFAULT (0). For more information on locale support, refer to your operating system documentation for the NLS interface; for 16-bit systems, see Appendix A.

Example

```
; Type library registration information
HKEY_CLASSES_ROOT\TypeLib\{F37C8060-4AD5-101B-B826-00DD01103DE1}
HKEY_CLASSES_ROOT\TypeLib\{F37C8060-4AD5-101B-B826-00DD01103DE1}\2.0 = OLE Automation Hello
2.0 Type Library
HKEY_CLASSES_ROOT\TypeLib\{F37C8060-4AD5-101B-B826-00DD01103DE1}\2.0\HELPDIR =
;US english
HKEY_CLASSES_ROOT\TypeLib\{F37C8060-4AD5-101B-B826-00DD01103DE1}\2.0\409\win16 = hello.tlb
```

Registering Interfaces

Applications that add interfaces need to register the interfaces, so that OLE can find the appropriate remoting code for interprocess communication. By default, OLE Automation registers dispinterfaces that appear in the ODL file. It also registers remote OLE Automation-compatible interfaces that are not registered elsewhere under the ProxyStubClsid for PSAutomation.

The information registered for an interface is as follows:

\Interface\{*IID***}** = *InterfaceName*
\Interface\{*IID***}\Typelib** = *LIBID*
\Interface\{*IID***}\ProxyStubClsid[32]** = *CLSID*

IID
> The universally unique ID of the interface.

InterfaceName
> The name of the interface.

LIBID

> The UUID associated with the type library in which the interface is described.

CLSID

> The UUID associated with the proxy/stub implementation of the interface, used internally by OLE for interprocess communication. OLE Automation objects use the proxy/stub implementation of **IDispatch**.

Example

The following lines from HELLO.REG register the interface for VTBL binding. The ProxyStubClsid in the example refers to the proxy/stub implementation of **IDispatch**.

```
HKEY_CLASSES_ROOT\Interface\{F37C8062-4AD5-101B-B826-00DD01103DE1} = IHello
HKEY_CLASSES_ROOT\Interface\{F37C8060-4AD5-101B-B826-00DD01103DE1}\TypeLib = {F37C8060-
4AD5-101B-B826-00DD01103DE1}
HKEY_CLASSES_ROOT\Interface\{F37C8060-4AD5-101B-B826-00DD01103DE1}\ProxyStubClsid =
{00020424-0000-0000-C000-000000000046}
```

Registration File Example

Lines uses the following entries to register its Application object (Lines.Application) and its type library with the system (LINES.REG):

```
REGEDIT
; Registration information for the Lines Automation Object application

; Version independent registration
HKEY_CLASSES_ROOT\Lines.Application = Lines
HKEY_CLASSES_ROOT\Lines.Application\Clsid = {3C591B21-1F13-101B-B826-00DD01103DE1}

; Version 1.0 registration
HKEY_CLASSES_ROOT\Lines.Application.1 = Lines 1.0
HKEY_CLASSES_ROOT\Lines.Application.1\Clsid = {3C591B21-1F13-101B-B826-00DD01103DE1}
HKEY_CLASSES_ROOT\CLSID\{3C591B21-1F13-101B-B826-00DD01103DE1} = Lines 1.0
HKEY_CLASSES_ROOT\CLSID\{3C591B21-1F13-101B-B826-00DD01103DE1}\ProgID = Lines.Application.1
HKEY_CLASSES_ROOT\CLSID\{3C591B21-1F13-101B-B826-00DD01103DE1}\VersionIndependentProgID =
Lines.Application
HKEY_CLASSES_ROOT\CLSID\{3C591B21-1F13-101B-B826-00DD01103DE1}\LocalServer = lines.exe
/Automation

; Type library registration information
HKEY_CLASSES_ROOT\TypeLib\{3C591B20-1F13-101B-B826-00DD01103DE1}
HKEY_CLASSES_ROOT\TypeLib\{3C591B20-1F13-101B-B826-00DD01103DE1}\1.0 = Lines 1.0 Type
Library
HKEY_CLASSES_ROOT\TypeLib\{3C591B20-1F13-101B-B826-00DD01103DE1}\1.0\HELPDIR =
;US english
HKEY_CLASSES_ROOT\TypeLib\{3C591B20-1F13-101B-B826-00DD01103DE1}\1.0\409\win16 = lines.tlb
```

```
; Interface registration. All interfaces that support vtable binding must be
; registered as follows. RegisterTypeLib & LoadTypeLib will do this automatically.

; LIBID_Lines = {3C591B20-1F13-101B-B826-00DD01103DE1}

; IID_IPoint = {3C591B25-1F13-101B-B826-00DD01103DE1}
HKEY_CLASSES_ROOT\Interface\{3C591B25-1F13-101B-B826-00DD01103DE1} = IPoint
HKEY_CLASSES_ROOT\Interface\{3C591B25-1F13-101B-B826-00DD01103DE1}\TypeLib = {3C591B20-
1F13-101B-B826-00DD01103DE1}
HKEY_CLASSES_ROOT\Interface\{3C591B25-1F13-101B-B826-00DD01103DE1}\ProxyStubClsid =
{00020424-0000-0000-C000-000000000046}

; IID_ILine = {3C591B24-1F13-101B-B826-00DD01103DE1}
HKEY_CLASSES_ROOT\Interface\{3C591B24-1F13-101B-B826-00DD01103DE1} = ILine
HKEY_CLASSES_ROOT\Interface\{3C591B24-1F13-101B-B826-00DD01103DE1}\TypeLib = {3C591B20-
1F13-101B-B826-00DD01103DE1}
HKEY_CLASSES_ROOT\Interface\{3C591B24-1F13-101B-B826-00DD01103DE1}\ProxyStubClsid =
{00020424-0000-0000-C000-000000000046}

; IID_ILines = {3C591B26-1F13-101B-B826-00DD01103DE1}
HKEY_CLASSES_ROOT\Interface\{3C591B26-1F13-101B-B826-00DD01103DE1} = ILines
HKEY_CLASSES_ROOT\Interface\{3C591B26-1F13-101B-B826-00DD01103DE1}\TypeLib = {3C591B20-
1F13-101B-B826-00DD01103DE1}
HKEY_CLASSES_ROOT\Interface\{3C591B26-1F13-101B-B826-00DD01103DE1}\ProxyStubClsid =
{00020424-0000-0000-C000-000000000046}

; IID_IPoints = {3C591B27-1F13-101B-B826-00DD01103DE1}
HKEY_CLASSES_ROOT\Interface\{3C591B27-1F13-101B-B826-00DD01103DE1} = IPoints
HKEY_CLASSES_ROOT\Interface\{3C591B27-1F13-101B-B826-00DD01103DE1}\TypeLib = {3C591B20-
1F13-101B-B826-00DD01103DE1}
HKEY_CLASSES_ROOT\Interface\{3C591B27-1F13-101B-B826-00DD01103DE1}\ProxyStubClsid =
{00020424-0000-0000-C000-000000000046}

; IID_IPane = {3C591B23-1F13-101B-B826-00DD01103DE1}
HKEY_CLASSES_ROOT\Interface\{3C591B23-1F13-101B-B826-00DD01103DE1} = IPane
HKEY_CLASSES_ROOT\Interface\{3C591B23-1F13-101B-B826-00DD01103DE1}\TypeLib = {3C591B20-
1F13-101B-B826-00DD01103DE1}
HKEY_CLASSES_ROOT\Interface\{3C591B23-1F13-101B-B826-00DD01103DE1}\ProxyStubClsid =
{00020424-0000-0000-C000-000000000046}

; IID_IApplication = {3C591B22-1F13-101B-B826-00DD01103DE1}
HKEY_CLASSES_ROOT\Interface\{3C591B22-1F13-101B-B826-00DD01103DE1} = IApplication
HKEY_CLASSES_ROOT\Interface\{3C591B22-1F13-101B-B826-00DD01103DE1}\TypeLib = {3C591B20-
1F13-101B-B826-00DD01103DE1}
HKEY_CLASSES_ROOT\Interface\{3C591B22-1F13-101B-B826-00DD01103DE1}\ProxyStubClsid =
{00020424-0000-0000-C000-000000000046}
```

Supporting Multiple National Languages

Applications sometimes need to expose objects with names that differ across localized versions of the product. The names pose a problem for programming languages that need to access these objects, because late binding will be sensitive to the locale of the application. The **IDispatch** interface provides a range of solutions that vary in cost of implementation and quality of language support. All methods of the **IDispatch** interface that are potentially sensitive to language are passed a locale ID (LCID), which identifies the local language context.

The following are some of the approaches a class implementation may take:

- Accept any LCID and use the same member names in all locales. This is acceptable if the exposed interface will typically be accessed only by very advanced users. For example, the member names for OLE interfaces will never be localized.

- Accept all LCIDs supported by all versions of the product. In this case, the implementation of **GetIDsOfNames** would need to interpret the passed array of names based on the given LCID. This is the most acceptable solution because it allows users to write code in their natural language and run the code on any localized version of the application.

- Simply return an error (DISP_E_UNKNOWNLCID) from **GetIDsOfNames** if the caller's LCID doesn't match the localized version of the class. This would prevent your customers from being able to write late-bound code that runs on machines with different localized implementations of the class.

- Recognize the particular version's localized names, as well as one language that is recognized in all versions. For example, a French version might accept French and English names, where English is the language supported in all versions. Users who want to write code that runs in all countries would have to use English.

However, to provide general language support, the application should check the LCID before interpreting member names. Because **Invoke** is passed an LCID, methods can properly interpret parameters whose meaning varies by locale. The following sections provide examples and guidelines of how to create multilingual applications.

Implementing IDispatch for Multilingual Applications

When creating applications that will support multiple languages, you need to create separate type libraries for each supported language and write versions of the IDispatch member functions that include dependencies for each language. In the following example, the Hello example code is modified to define locale IDs for both US English and German.

Write a separate type library for each supported language

The type libraries use the same DISPIDs and GUIDs but localize names and Help strings based on the language. The following registration file example includes entries for US English and German.

```
; Type library registration information
HKEY_CLASSES_ROOT\TypeLib\{F37C8060-4AD5-101B-B826-00DD01103DE1}
HKEY_CLASSES_ROOT\TypeLib\{F37C8060-4AD5-101B-B826-00DD01103DE1}\2.0 =
Hello 2.0 Type Library
HKEY_CLASSES_ROOT\TypeLib\{F37C8060-4AD5-101B-B826-00DD01103DE1}\2.0\HELPDIR
=
;US english
HKEY_CLASSES_ROOT\TypeLib\{F37C8060-4AD5-101B-B826-00DD01103DE1}\2.0\409\win16 =
helloeng.tlb
;German
HKEY_CLASSES_ROOT\TypeLib\{F37C8060-4AD5-101B-B826-00DD01103DE1}\2.0\407\win16 =
helloger.tlb
```

Define the locale IDs for the supported languages

Refer to the next section to obtain the language IDs for your supported languages.

```
// Locale IDs for the languages that are supported
#define LCID_ENGLISH MAKELCID(MAKELANGID(0x09, 0x01))
#define LCID_GERMAN  MAKELCID(MAKELANGID(0x07, 0x01))
```

Using the Hello code example, you define member variables that will be used to hold English and German type information.

```
class FAR CHello : public IHello
{
public:
    :

private:
    LPTYPEINFO m_ptinfoEnglish;    // English type information of Hello
                                      application interface.
    LPTYPEINFO m_ptinfoGerman;     // German type information of Hello
                                      application interface.
    :
};
```

Load type information for each supported language

The following example uses the LoadTypeInfo function to load locale-specific type library information when the Hello object is created.

```
LoadTypeInfo(&phello->m_ptinfoEnglish, IID_IHello, LCID_ENGLISH);
LoadTypeInfo(&phello->m_ptinfoGerman, IID_IHello, LCID_GERMAN);

/* LoadTypeInfo - Gets type information of an object's interface from
 * the type library.
 *
 * Parameters:
 *   ppunkStdDispatch      Returns type information.
 *   clsid                 Interface id of object in type library.
 *   lcid                  Locale ID of typeinfo to be loaded.
 *
 * Return Value:
 *   HRESULT
 *
 */
HRESULT LoadTypeInfo(ITypeInfo FAR* FAR* pptinfo, REFCLSID clsid,
LCID lcid)
{
    HRESULT hr;
    LPTYPELIB ptlib = NULL;
    LPTYPEINFO ptinfo = NULL;

    *pptinfo = NULL;

    // Load Type Library.
    hr = LoadRegTypeLib(LIBID_Hello, 2, 0, lcid, &ptlib);
    if (FAILED(hr))
        return hr;

    // Get type information for interface of the object.
    hr = ptlib->GetTypeInfoOfGuid(clsid, &ptinfo);
    if (FAILED(hr))
    {
        ptlib->Release();
        return hr;
    }

    ptlib->Release();
    *pptinfo = ptinfo;
    return NOERROR;
}
```

Implement the IDispatch member functions

The following code implements language-sensitive versions of **GetTypeInfoCount**, **GetIDsOfNames**, and **Invoke**. Note that Invoke doesn't check the locale ID, but merely passes it to **DispInvoke**.

```
STDMETHODIMP
CHello::GetTypeInfoCount(UINT FAR* pctinfo)
{
    *pctinfo = 1;
    return NOERROR;
}

STDMETHODIMP
CHello::GetTypeInfo(
        UINT itinfo,
        LCID lcid,
        ITypeInfo FAR* FAR* pptinfo)
{
    LPTYPEINFO ptinfo;
    *pptinfo = NULL;

    if(itinfo != 0)
        return ResultFromScode(DISP_E_BADINDEX);

    if(lcid == LOCALE_SYSTEM_DEFAULT || lcid == 0)
        lcid = GettSystemDefaultLCID();

    if(lcid == LOCALE_USER_DEFAULT)
        lcid = GetUserDefaultLCID();

    switch(lcid)
    {
        case LCID_GERMAN:
            ptinfo = m_ptinfoGerman;
            break;

        case LCID_ENGLISH:
            ptinfo = m_ptinfoEnglish;
            break;

        default:
            return ResultFromScode(DISP_E_UNKNOWNLCID);
    }

    ptinfo->AddRef();
    *pptinfo = ptinfo;
    return NOERROR;
}
```

```
STDMETHODIMP
CHello::GetIDsOfNames(
        REFIID riid,
        OLECHAR FAR* FAR* rgszNames,
        UINT cNames,
        LCID lcid,
        DISPID FAR* rgdispid)
{
    LPTYPEINFO ptinfo;

    if(lcid == LOCALE_SYSTEM_DEFAULT || lcid == 0)
        lcid = GetSystemDefaultLCID();

    if(lcid == LOCALE_USER_DEFAULT)
        lcid = GetUserDefaultLCID();

    switch(lcid)
    {
        case LCID_GERMAN:
            ptinfo = m_ptinfoGerman;
            break;

        case LCID_ENGLISH:
            ptinfo = m_ptinfoEnglish;
            break;

        default:
            return ResultFromScode(DISP_E_UNKNOWNLCID);
    }
    return DispGetIDsOfNames(ptinfo, rgszNames, cNames, rgdispid);
}

STDMETHODIMP
CHello::Invoke(
        DISPID dispidMember,
        REFIID riid,
        LCID lcid,
        WORD wFlags,
        DISPPARAMS FAR* pdispparams,
        VARIANT FAR* pvarResult,
        EXCEPINFO FAR* pexcepinfo,
        UINT FAR* puArgErr)
{
    HRESULT hr;
    m_bRaiseException = FALSE;
    hr = DispInvoke(
        this, m_ptinfoEnglish,
        dispidMember, wFlags, pdispparams,
        pvarResult, pexcepinfo, puArgErr);
```

```
        if (m_bRaiseException)
        {
            if (NULL != pexcepinfo)
                _fmemcpy(pexcepinfo, &m_excepinfo, sizeof(EXCEPINFO));
            return ResultFromScode(DISP_E_EXCEPTION);
        }
        else return hr;
}
```

Interpreting Arguments and Strings Based on LCID

Some methods or properties need to interpret arguments based on the LCID. Such methods or properties can require that an LCID be passed as an argument.

The following code example implements a property that takes an LCID. In this example, **get_CheckingBalance** returns a currency string that contains the amount of money in the checking account. The currency string should be correctly formated depending on the locale that is passed in. **ConvertCurrency** is a private function that converts the checking balance to the currency of the country described by **llcid**. The string form of converted currency is placed in **m_szBalance**. **GetCurrencyFormat** is a 32-bit Windows function that that formats a currency string for the given locale.

The following represents the .ODLfile:

```
[
uuid(83219430-CB36-11cd-B774-00DD01103DE1),
helpstring("Bank Account object."),
oleautomation,
dual
]
interface IBankAccount : IDispatch
{
    [propget, helpstring("Returns account balance formatted for the
        country described by localeID.")]
    HRESULT CheckingBalance([in, lcid] long localeID, [out, retval]
    BSTR* retval);
    :
}
```

The following represents the .H file:

```
class FAR CBankAccount : public IBankAccount
{
    public:
    // IUnknown methods
        :
```

```
    // IDispatch methods
        :

    // IBankAccount methods
    STDMETHOD(get_CheckingBalance)(long llcid, BSTR FAR* pbstr);
        :
}
```

The following represents the .CPP file:

```
STDMETHODIMP
CBankAccount::get_CheckingBalance(long llcid, BSTR FAR* pbstr)
{
    TCHAR ach[100];
    ConvertCurrency(llcid);
        GetCurrencyFormat(llcid, 0, m_szBalance, NULL, ach,
        sizeof(ach));
        *pbstr = SysAllocString(ach); // Return currency string formated
                                      // according to locale id.
        return NOERROR;
}
```

The LCID is commonly used to parse strings that contain locale-dependent information. For example, a function that takes a string such as "6/11/59" needs the LCID to determine whether the month is June (6) or November (11). The LCID should not be used for output strings, including error strings; these should always be displayed in the current system language.

Locale, Language, and Sublanguage IDs

The following macro is defined for creating LCIDs (WINNT.H for 32-bit systems; OLENLS.H for 16-bit systems):

```
/*
 * LCID creation/extraction macros:
 *
 *   MAKELCID - construct locale ID from language ID and
 *                  country code.
 */
#define MAKELCID(1) ((DWORD)(((WORD)(1)) | (((DWORD)((WORD)(0))) <<
16)))
```

There are two predefined LCID values: LOCALE_SYSTEM_DEFAULT is the system default locale, and LOCALE_USER_DEFAULT is the current user's locale.

Another macro constructs a language ID:

```
/*
 * Language ID creation/extraction macros:
 *
 *      MAKELANGID - construct language ID from primary language ID and
 *                   sublanguage ID
 */
#define MAKELANGID(p, s)        (((((USHORT)(s)) << 10) | (USHORT)(p))
```

The following three combinations of primary language ID and sublanguage ID have special meanings:

PRIMARYLANGID	SUBLANGID	Result
LANG_NEUTRAL	SUBLANG_NEUTRAL	Language neutral
LANG_NEUTRAL	SUBLANG_SYS_DEFAULT	System default language
LANG_NEUTRAL	SUBLANG_DEFAULT	User default language

For primary language IDs, the range 0x200 to 0x3ff is user definable. The range 0x000 to 0x1ff is reserved for system use. For sublanguage IDs, the range 0x20 to 0x3f is user definable. The range 0x00 to 0x1f is reserved for system use.

Language tables

The following table lists the primary language IDs supported by OLE Automation. For more information on national language support for 16-bit Windows systems, refer to Appendix A, "National Language Support Functions." On 32-bit Windows systems, see your operating system documentation.

Language	PRIMARYLANGID
Neutral	0x00
Chinese	0x04
Czech	0x05
Danish	0x06
Dutch	0x13
English	0x09
Finnish	0x0b
French	0x0c
German	0x07
Greek	0x08
Hungarian	0x0e
Icelandic	0x0F
Italian	0x10

Language	PRIMARYLANGID
Japanese	0x11
Korean	0x12
Norwegian	0x14
Polish	0x15
Portuguese	0x16
Russian	0x19
Slovak	0x1b
Spanish	0x0a
Swedish	0x1d
Turkish	0x1F

The following table lists the sublanguage IDs supported by OLE Automation. For more information on national language support for 16-bit systems, refer to Appendix B, "National Language Support Functions." On 32-bit Windows systems, see your operating system documentation.

Sublanguage	SUBLANGID
Neutral	0x00
Default	0x01
System Default	0x02
Chinese (Simplified)	0x02
Chinese (Traditional)	0x01
Czech	0x01
Danish	0x01
Dutch	0x01
Dutch (Belgian)	0x02
English (US)	0x01
English (UK)	0x02
English (Australian)	0x03
English (Canadian)	0x04
English (Irish)	0x06
English (New Zealand)	0x05
Finnish	0x01
French	0x01
French (Belgian)	0x02
French (Canadian)	0x03
French (Swiss)	0x04

Sublanguage	SUBLANGID
German	0x01
German (Swiss)	0x02
German (Austrian)	0x03
Greek	0x01
Hungarian	0x01
Icelandic	0x01
Italian	0x01
Italian (Swiss)	0x02
Japanese	0x01
Korean	0x01
Norwegian (Bokmal)	0x01
Norwegian (Nynorsk)	0x02
Polish	0x01
Portuguese	0x02
Portuguese (Brazilian)	0x01
Russian	0x01
Slovak	0x01
Spanish (Castilian)[1]	0x01
Spanish (Mexican)	0x02
Spanish (Modern)[1]	0x03
Swedish	0x01
Turkish	0x01

[1] The only difference between Spanish (Castilian) and Spanish (Modern) is the sort ordering. The LCType values are all the same.

CHAPTER 3

Accessing OLE Automation Objects

To access exposed objects, you can create OLE Automation controllers using Microsoft Visual Basic™, Microsoft Visual C++™, Microsoft Excel, Microsoft Project, and other applications and programming languages that support OLE. This chapter discusses several strategies for accessing exposed objects:

- Creating scripts with Microsoft Visual Basic
- Creating your own controllers that manipulate objects
- Creating type information browsers

Regardless of the strategy you choose, your OLE Automation controller needs to follow these steps:

▶ **To initialize and create the object**

1. Initialize OLE.
2. Create an instance of the exposed object.

▶ **To manipulate methods and properties**

1. Get information about the object's methods and properties.
2. Invoke the methods and properties.

▶ **To release OLE when your application or programming tool terminates**

1. Revoke the active object.
2. Unitialize OLE.

Packaging Scripts Using Visual Basic

Microsoft Visual Basic provides a complete programming environment for creating Windows applications.

Visual Basic can manipulate the exposed OLE objects of other applications. Internally, it fully supports OLE Automation **dual** interfaces. For the syntax and semantics of the OLE Automation features, see the Visual Basic Help file, VB.HLP. Appendix C lists how the Visual Basic statements translate into OLE application programming interfaces (APIs).

Note You don't need Visual Basic in order to use OLE Automation. It is presented here as an example of a programming tool that supports OLE Automation and is convenient for packaging OLE Automation scripts. Optionally, you can use a different OLE Automation controller for your testing.

You can call exposed objects directly from programs written with Visual Basic. This figure shows how this was done for the sample program HELLO.EXE:

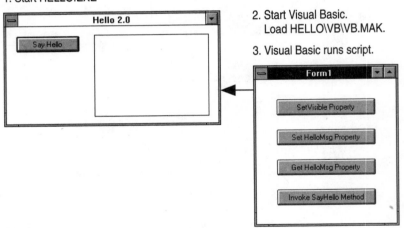

1. Start HELLO.EXE

2. Start Visual Basic.
   Load HELLO\VB\VB.MAK.

3. Visual Basic runs script.

▶ **To access an exposed object**

1. Start Visual Basic. Initialization and release of OLE is handled automatically by Visual Basic.

2. Use the Tools/References menu to select the type library of the object.

3. Add code to declare a variable of the interface type. For example:

```
Dim HelloObj As IHello
```

4. Add code in event procedures to create an instance of the object and to manipulate the object using its properties and methods. For example:

```
Sub Form_Load ( )
    Set HelloObj = New Hello.Hello
End Sub
Sub SetVisible_Click ( )
    HelloObj.Visible = True
End Sub
```

5. From the Run menu, choose Start and trigger the event by clicking the form.

The following figure shows the interfaces you use when accessing exposed objects through Visual Basic.

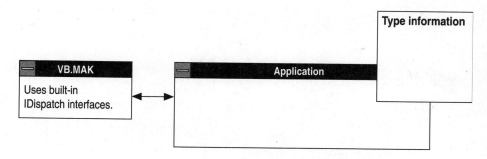

Accessing a Remote Object

With Visual Basic, accessing the remote object requires only that the program declare an object variable and assign the return of a **New** statement to the variable. The following is the syntax for the statements:

Dim *ObjectVar* **As** *InterfaceName*
Set *ObjectVar* = **New** *CoClassName*

The **Dim** statement declares a variable of an interface type. The **New** keyword creates an instance of an object. Used together, the two declare and create an instance of an OLE Automation object. For example:

```
Dim MyLines As ILines
Set MyLines = New Lines.Lines
```

The **Dim** statement declares the object variable MyLines of the interface type ILines. The **Set** statement assigns a new object of the *component object class* (coclass) Lines to the variable MyLines. When you use the **Dim** statement to set a variable to an interface type, susbsequent uses of the variable execute faster than with the generic **Object** syntax.

The **New** keyword applies only to creating coclasses of interface or dispinterface types. To create other types of objects, you must declare the variable with the **Dim** statement, and then use the **CreateObject** function as follows:

Set *ObjectVar* = **CreateObject**(*ProgID*)

CreateObject creates an OLE Automation object, based on the specified *ProgID*. The *ProgID* has the form:

"*AppName.ObjectName*"

The *AppName* is the name of the application, and the *ObjectName* identifies the type of object to create. See "Registering the Application" in Chapter 2 for more information on ProgIDs.

The **GetObject** function can be used to re-establish the reference to the most recently used object that corresponds to the *Filename* and *AppName.ObjectName* specification.

Set *ObjectVar* = **GetObject**("*Filename*", *ProgID*)

For example, if the OLE Automation controller needs an existing instance of an object instead of a new instance, it could use **GetObject**.

The Hello sample application included in the Win32 SDK displays a Hello message in response to a mouse click. You can add a simple form that accesses the Hello application's exposed object from another process.

▶ **To add a form**

1. Start Visual Basic.

2. Choose Open Project from the File menu.

3. In the dialog box, select VB.MAK from the \OLE2\SAMPLE\HELLO\VB directory.

4. In the Forms box, choose View Form to see the form, or choose View Code to see the Visual Basic code.

```
'Module-level declarations
Dim HelloObj As IHello

Sub Form_load ( )
    Set HelloObj = New Hello.Hello
End Sub

Sub Invoke_SayHello_Method_Click ( )
    HelloObj.SayHello
End Sub
```

```
Sub Get_HelloMsg_Property_Click ()
    Debug.Print HelloObj.HelloMessage
End Sub

Sub Set_HelloMsg_Property_Click ( )
    HelloObj.HelloMessage = "Hello Universe"
End Sub

Sub SetVisible_Click ( )
    HelloObj.Visible = True
End Sub
```

The Form_Load subroutine creates the Hello Application object, and the other subroutines manipulate Hello's Application object through the Visible and HelloMessage properties and the SayHello method.

To program an object in Visual Basic, you need its class name and the names and parameters of its properties and methods. For the Hello sample, you need to know the exact names of the SayHello method and the Visible and HelloMsg properties, and the types of their arguments. This information is published as documentation for many objects, such as those exposed by Microsoft Excel. You can also obtain the information by viewing the object's type library with an object browser like the one included in Visual Basic. A sample browser, BROWSE, is provided in the Win32 SDK.

Creating an Invisible Object

In the preceding section, Visual Basic was used to access and program a form-based interface for Hello. The Hello Application object was started as invisible and was later displayed when its Visible property was set to True. Some objects are not visible, and some objects are never displayed to the user. For example, a word processing application may expose its spelling checker engine as an object. This object supports a method called CheckWord that takes a string as an argument. If the string is spelled correctly, the method returns True; otherwise, the method returns False. If the string is spelled incorrectly, you could pass it to another (hypothetical) method called SuggestWord that returns a suggestion for its correct spelling. The code might look something like this:

```
Sub CheckSpelling ()
    Dim ObjVar As New SpellChecker
    Dim MyWord, Result

    MyWord = "potatoe"

    ' Check the spelling.
    Result = ObjVar.CheckWord MyWord
```

```
        ' If False, get suggestion.
        If Not Result Then
            MyWord = ObjVar.SuggestWord MyWord
        End If
End Sub
```

In this example, the spelling checker is never displayed to the user. Its capabilities are exposed through the properties and methods of the spelling checker object.

As shown in the example, you create and reference invisible objects the same way as any other type of object.

Activating an Object from a File

Many OLE Automation applications allow the user to save objects in files. For example, a spreadsheet application that supports Worksheet objects allows the user to save the worksheet in a file. The same application may also support a chart object that the user can save in a file. To activate an object that has been saved in a file, you use the **GetObject** function.

To activate an object from a file, first declare an object variable, then call the **GetObject** function using the following syntax:

GetObject (*filename*[, *ProgID*])

The *filename* argument is a string containing the full path and name of the file you want to activate. For example, an application named SPDSHEET.EXE creates an object that was saved in a file called REVENUE.SPD. The following code invokes SPDSHEET.EXE, loads the file REVENUE.SPD, and assigns REVENUE.SPD to an object variable:

```
Dim Ss As Spreadsheet
Set Ss = GetObject("C:\ACCOUNTS\REVENUE.SPD")
```

If the *filename* argument is omitted, **GetObject** returns the currently active object of the specified *ProgID*. For example:

```
Set Ss = GetObject (,"SpdSheet.Application")
```

If there is no active object of the class SpdSheet.Application, an error occurs.

In addition to activating an entire file, some applications let you activate part of a file. To activate part of a file, add an exclamation point (!) or a backslash (\) to the end of the filename, followed by a string that identifies the part of the file you want to activate. Refer to the object's documentation for information on how to create this string.

For example, if SPDSHEET.EXE is a spreadsheet application that uses R1C1 syntax, the following code could be used to activate a range of cells within REVENUE.SPD:

```
Set Ss = GetObject("C:\ACCOUNTS\REVENUE.SPD!R1C1:R10C20")
```

These examples invoke an application and activate an object. Notice that in these examples the application name (SPDSHEET.EXE) is never specified. When you use **GetObject** to activate an object, the registry files determine the application to invoke and the object to activate based on the filename or ProgID you provide. If you do not include a ProgID, OLE Automation activates the default object of the specified file.

Some OLE Automation servers, however, support more than one class of object. Suppose the spreadsheet file, REVENUE.SPD, supports three different classes of objects: an Application object, a Worksheet object, and a Toolbar object, all of which are part of the same file. To specify which object to activate, you must supply an argument for the optional *ProgID* parameter. For example:

```
Set Ss = GetObject("C:\REVENUE.SPD", "SPDSHEET.TOOLBAR")
```

This statement activates the Spdsheet.Toolbar object in the file REVENUE.SPD.

Accessing Linked and Embedded Objects

Some applications that supply objects support linking and embedding as well as OLE Automation. Using the OLE custom control (MSOLE2.VBX) from the OLE toolkit, you can create and display linked and embedded objects in a Visual Basic application. If the objects also support OLE Automation, you can access their properties and methods using the Object property. The Object property returns the object in the OLE control. This property refers to an OLE object in the same way an object variable created using the **New**, **CreateObject**, or **GetObject** functions refers to the object.

For example, an OLE control named Ole1 contains an object that supports OLE Automation. This object has an Insert method, a Select method, and a Bold property. In this case, you could write the following code to manipulate the OLE control's object:

```
' Insert text in the object.
Ole1.Object.Insert "Hello, world."
' Select the text.
Ole1.Object.Select
' Format the text as bold.
Ole1.Object.Bold = True
```

Manipulating Objects

Once you have created a variable that references an OLE object, the object can be manipulated in the same way as any other Visual Basic object. To get and set an object's properties or to perform an object's methods, you use the *object.property* or *object.method* syntax. You can include multiple objects, properties, and methods on the same line of code using the following syntax:

```
ObjVar.Cell(1,1).FontBold = True
```

Accessing an Object's Properties

To assign a value to a property of an object, put the object variable and property name on the left side of an assignment and the desired property setting on the right side. For example:

```
Dim ObjVar As IMyInterface
Dim RowPos, ColPos
Set ObjVar = New MyObject

ObjVar.Text = "Hello, world"
ObjVar.Cell(RowPos, ColPos) = "This property accepts two arguments."
' Sets the font for ObjVar.Selection.
ObjVar.Selection.Font = 12
```

You can also retrieve property values from an object:

```
Dim X As Object

X = ObjVar.Text
X = ObjVar.Range(12, 32)
```

Invoking Methods

In addition to getting and setting properties, you can manipulate an object using the methods it supports. Some methods may return a value, as in the following example:

```
X = ObjVar.Calculate(1,2,3)
```

Methods that do not return a value behave like subroutines. For example:

```
' This method requires two arguments.
ObjVar.Move XPos, YPos
```

If you assign such a method to a variable, an error occurs.

Creating Applications and Tools That Access Objects

OLE Automation provides interfaces for accessing exposed objects from an application or programming tool written in C or C++. The following sections show C++ code that uses the same type of access method as the Visual Basic code described earlier in this chapter. Although the process is more complicated than with Visual Basic, the approach is similar. Note, however, that this section shows the minimum code necessary to access and manipulate a remote object.

You can use the **IDispatch** interface to access OLE Automation objects, or you can access objects directly through the VTBL. Because VTBL references can be bound at compile time, VTBL access is generally faster than access through **IDispatch**. Whenever possible, you should use the **ITypeInfo** interface to get information about an object, including the VTBL addresses of the object's members. Then use this information to access OLE Automation objects through the VTBL.

To create compilers and other programming tools that use information from type libraries, you use the **ITypeComp** interface. This interface binds to exposed objects at compile time. For details on **ITypeComp**, see Chapter 8, "Type Description Interfaces."

Accessing Members through VTBLs

For objects that have dual interfaces, the first seven members of the VTBL are the members of **IUnknown** and **IDispatch**, and the subsequent members are standard OLE Component Object Model (COM) entries for the interface's member functions. You can call these entries directly from C++.

▶ **To access a method or property through the VTBL**

1. Initialize OLE.
2. Create an instance of the exposed object.
3. Manipulate the properties and methods of the object.
4. Uninitialize OLE.

The code excerpt that follows shows how to access a property of the Hello object. Error handling has been omitted for brevity.

```
HRESULT hr;
CLSID clsid;                      //CLSID of Hello object
LPUNKNOWN punk = NULL;            //IUnknown of Hello object
IHello* phello = NULL;           //IHello interface of Hello object

//Initialize OLE.
hr = OleInitialize(NULL);
```

```
// Retrieve CLSID from the progID for Hello.
hr = CLSIDFromProgID("Hello.Application", &clsid);

// Create an instance of the Hello object and ask for its
// IDispatch interface.
hr = CoCreateInstance(clsid, NULL, CLSCTX_SERVER,
                          IID_IUnknown, (void FAR* FAR*)&punk);

hr = punk->QueryInterface(IID_IHello, (void FAR* FAR*)&pHello);

punk->Release();     //Release when no longer needed.

hr = pHello->put_Visible (TRUE);

//Additional code to work with other methods and properties.
// .
// .
// .

OleUninitialize();
```

The example initializes OLE, then calls the **CLSIDFromProgID** function to obtain the CLSID for the Hello application. With the CLSID, the example can call **CoCreateInstance** to create an instance of the Hello Application object. **CoCreateInstance** returns a pointer to the object's IUnknown interface (`punk`), and this, in turn, is used to call **QueryInterface** to get `pHello`, a pointer to the IID_IHello dual interface. The `punk` is no longer needed, so the example releases it. The example then sets the value of the Visible property to True.

If the function returns an error HRESULT, you can get detailed, contextual information through the **IErrorInfo** interface. See Chapter 10, "Error Handling Interfaces," for details.

Accessing Members through IDispatch

To bind to exposed objects at run time, you use **IDispatch**.

▶ **To create an OLE Automation controller using IDispatch**

1. Initialize OLE.
2. Create an instance of the object you want to access. The object's OLE Automation server creates the object.
3. Obtain a reference to the object's **IDispatch** interface (if it has implemented one).

4. Manipulate the object through the methods and properties exposed in its **IDispatch** interface.

5. Terminate the object by invoking the appropriate method in its **IDispatch** interface or by releasing all references to the object.

6. Uninitialize OLE.

The following table shows minimum set of functions necessary to manipulate a remote object.

Function	Purpose	Interface
OleInitialize	Initializes OLE	OLE API function
CoCreateInstance	Creates an instance of the class represented by the specified class ID, and returns a pointer to the object's **IUnknown** interface.	Component object API function
QueryInterface	Checks whether **IDispatch** has been implemented for the object. If so, returns a pointer to the IDispatch implementation.	IUnknown
GetIDsOfNames	Returns DISPIDs for properties and methods and their parameters.	IDispatch
Invoke	Invokes a method, or sets or gets a property of the remote object.	IDispatch
Release	Decrements the reference count for an **IUnknown** or **IDispatch** object.	IUnknown
OleUninitialize	Uninitializes OLE.	OLE API function

The code that follows is extracted from is a generalized Windows-based OLE Automation controller for the Hello sample. The controller relies on helper functions provided in INVHELP.CPP, available in \OLE2\SAMPLE\BROWSE. Error checking is omitted to save space, but would normally be used where an HRESULT is returned.

The two functions that follow initialize OLE, then create an instance of an object and get a pointer to the object's **IDispatch** interface (INVHELP.CPP):

```
BOOL InitOle(void)
{
    if(OleInitialize(NULL) != 0)
        return FALSE;

    return TRUE;
}
```

```
HRESULT CreateObject(LPSTR pszProgID, IDispatch FAR* FAR* ppdisp)
{
    CLSID clsid;                  // CLSID of OLE Automation object
    HRESULT hr;
    LPUNKNOWN punk = NULL;        // IUnknown of OLE Automation object
    LPDISPATCH pdisp = NULL;      // IDispatch of OLE Automation object

    *ppdisp = NULL;

    // Retrieve CLSID from the progID that the user specified.
    hr = CLSIDFromProgID(pszProgID, &clsid);
    if (FAILED(hr))
        goto error;

    // Create an instance of the OLE Automation object and ask for the
    // IDispatch interface.
    hr = CoCreateInstance(clsid, NULL, CLSCTX_SERVER,
                              IID_IUnknown, (void FAR* FAR*)&punk);
    if (FAILED(hr))
        goto error;

    hr = punk->QueryInterface(IID_IDispatch, (void FAR* FAR*)&pdisp);
    if (FAILED(hr))
        goto error;

    *ppdisp = pdisp;
    punk->Release();
    return NOERROR;

error:
    if (punk) punk->Release();
    if (pdisp) pdisp->Release();
    return hr;
}
```

The CreateObject function is passed a ProgID and returns a pointer to the
IDispatch implementation of the specified object. CreateObject calls the OLE API
CLSIDFromProgID to get the CLSID that corresponds to the requested object,
then passes the CLSID to **CoCreateInstance** to create an instance of the object and
get a pointer to the object's **IUnknown** interface. (The **CLSIDFromProgID**
function is described in the *OLE Programmer's Guide and Reference*). With this
pointer, CreateObject calls **IUnknown::QueryInterface**, specifying
IID_IDispatch, to get a pointer to the object's **IDispatch** interface.

```
HRESULT FAR
Invoke(LPDISPATCH pdisp,
    WORD wFlags,
    LPVARIANT pvRet,
    EXCEPINFO FAR* pexcepinfo,
    UINT FAR* pnArgErr,
    LPSTR pszName,
    char *pszFmt,
    ...)
{
    va_list argList;
    va_start(argList, pszFmt);
    DISPID dispid;
    HRESULT hr;
    VARIANTARG* pvarg = NULL;

    if (pdisp == NULL)
        return ResultFromScode(E_INVALIDARG);

    // Get DISPID of property/method
    hr = pdisp->GetIDsOfNames(IID_NULL, &pszName, 1,
        LOCALE_SYSTEM_DEFAULT, &dispid);
    if(FAILED(hr))
        return hr;

    DISPPARAMS dispparams;
    _fmemset(&dispparams, 0, sizeof dispparams);

    // Determine number of arguments.
    if (pszFmt != NULL)
        CountArgsInFormat(pszFmt, &dispparams.cArgs);

    // Property puts have a named argument that represents the value
    // being assigned to the property.
    DISPID dispidNamed = DISPID_PROPERTYPUT;
    if (wFlags & DISPATCH_PROPERTYPUT)
    {
        if (dispparams.cArgs == 0)
            return ResultFromScode(E_INVALIDARG);
        dispparams.cNamedArgs = 1;
        dispparams.rgdispidNamedArgs = &dispidNamed;
    }
```

```
if (dispparams.cArgs != 0)
{
    // Allocate memory for all VARIANTARG parameters.
    pvarg = new VARIANTARG[dispparams.cArgs];
    if(pvarg == NULL)
        return ResultFromScode(E_OUTOFMEMORY);
    dispparams.rgvarg = pvarg;
    _fmemset(pvarg, 0, sizeof(VARIANTARG) * dispparams.cArgs);

    // Get ready to walk vararg list.
    LPSTR psz = pszFmt;
    pvarg += dispparams.cArgs - 1;    // Params go in opposite order.

    while (psz = GetNextVarType(psz, &pvarg->vt))
    {
        if (pvarg < dispparams.rgvarg)
        {
            hr = ResultFromScode(E_INVALIDARG);
            goto cleanup;
        }
        switch (pvarg->vt)
        {
        case VT_I2:
            V_I2(pvarg) = va_arg(argList, short);
            break;
        case VT_I4:
            V_I4(pvarg) = va_arg(argList, long);
            break;
        // Additional cases omitted to save space...
        default:
            {
                hr = ResultFromScode(E_INVALIDARG);
                goto cleanup;
            }
            break;
        }
        --pvarg; // Get ready to fill next argument.
    } //while
} //if

// Initialize return variant, in case caller forgot. Caller can pass
// NULL if no return value is expected.
if (pvRet)
    VariantInit(pvRet);
// Make the call.
hr = pdisp->Invoke(dispid, IID_NULL, LOCALE_SYSTEM_DEFAULT, wFlags,
    &dispparams, pvRet, pexcepinfo, pnArgErr);
```

```
cleanup:
    // Clean up any arguments that need it.
    if (dispparams.cArgs != 0)
    {
        VARIANTARG FAR* pvarg = dispparams.rgvarg;
        UINT cArgs = dispparams.cArgs;
        while (cArgs--)
        {
            switch (pvarg->vt)
            {
            case VT_BSTR:
                VariantClear(pvarg);
                break;
            }
            ++pvarg;
        }
    }
    delete dispparams.rgvarg;
    va_end(argList);
    return hr;
}
```

The Invoke function in the example is a general-purpose function that calls
IDispatch::Invoke to invoke a property or method of an OLE Automation object.
As arguments, it accepts the object's IDispatch implementation, the name of the
member to invoke, flags that control the invocation, and a variable list of the
member's arguments.

Using the object's IDispatch implementation and the name of the member, it calls
GetIDsOfNames to get the DISPID of the requested member. The member's
DISPID must be used later, in the call to **IDispatch::Invoke**.

The invocation flags specify whether a method, property put, or property get
function is being invoked. The helper function simply passes these flags directly to
IDispatch::Invoke.

The helper function next fills in the DISPPARAMS structure with the parameters of
the member. DISPPARAMS structures have the following form:

```
typedef struct FARSTRUCT tagDISPPARAMS{
    VARIANTARG FAR* rgvarg;              // Array of arguments
    DISPID FAR* rgdispidNamedArgs;       // Dispids of named arguments
    UINT cArgs;                          // Number of arguments
    UINT cNamedArgs;                     // Number of named arguments
} DISPPARAMS;
```

The *rgvarg* field is a pointer to an array of VARIANTARG structures. Each element of the array specifies an argument, whose position in the array corresponds to its position in the parameter list of the method definition. The *cArgs* field specifies the total number of arguments, and the *cNamedArgs* field specifies the number of named arguments. For methods and property get functions, all arguments may be accessed as positional, or they may be accessed as named arguments. Property put functions have a named argument that is the new value for the property. The DISPID of this argument is DISPID_PROPERTYPUT.

To build the *rgvarg* array, the Invoke helper function retrieves the parameter values and types from its own argument list, and constructs a VARIANTARG structure for each one. (See INVHELP.CPP for a description of the format string that specifies the types of the parameters.) Parameters are put in the array in reverse order, so that the last parameter is in *rgvarg*[0] and so forth. Although VARIANTARG has the following five fields, only the first and fifth are used:

```
typedef struct FARSTRUCT tagVARIANT VARIANTARG;

struct FARSTRUCT tagVARIANT{
    VARTYPE vt;
    unsigned short wReserved1;
    unsigned short wReserved2;
    unsigned short wReserved3;
    union {
        short        iVal;      /* VT_I2    */
    .
    .   // The rest of this union specifies numerous other types.
    .

    };
} VARIANTARG;
```

The first field contains the argument's type, and the fifth contains its value. To pass a long integer, for example, the *vt* and *iVal* fields of the VARIANTARG structure would be filled with VT_I4 (long integer) and the actual value of the long integer.

In addition, for property put functions, the first element of the *rgdispidNamedArgs* array must contain DISPID_PROPERTYPUT.

After filling the DISPPARAMS structure, the Invoke helper function initializes *pvRet*, a VARIANT in which **IDispatch::Invoke** returns a value from the method or property. The following is the actual call to **IDispatch::Invoke**:

```
hr = pdisp->Invoke(dispid, IID_NULL, LOCALE_SYSTEM_DEFAULT, wFlags,
        &dispparams, pvRet, pexcepinfo, pnArgErr);
```

The variable `pdisp` is a pointer to the object's IDispatch interface. The `dispid` is the DISPID of the method or property being invoked. The value IID_NULL must be specified for all **IDispatch::Invoke** calls, and LOCALE_SYSTEM_DEFAULT is a constant denoting the default LCID for this system. The `wFlags`, `dispparams`, and `pvRet` arguments have already been discussed. In the final two arguments, `pexcepinfo` and `pnArgErr`, **IDispatch::Invoke** can return error information. If the invoked member has defined an exception handler, it returns exception information in `pexcepinfo`. If certain errors occur in the argument vector, `pnArgErr` points to the errant argument. The function return value `hr` is an HRESULT that indicates success or various types of failure.

For more information, including how to pass optional arguments, see "IDispatch::Invoke" in Chapter 5, "Dispatch Interfaces."

Creating Type Information Browsers

Type information browsers allow you and your customers to scan type libraries to determine what types of objects are available. The following figure shows the interfaces you use when you create compilers or browsers that access type libraries.

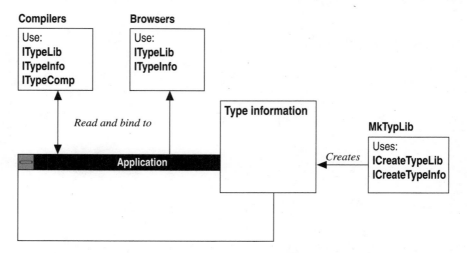

The Browse sample in \OLE2\SAMPLE\BROWSE shows how a browser might access a type library. The Browse sample is a Windows-based type browser that presents a dialog box from which you can select the type information items to display. This function prompts you for the name of the type library, opens the library, and gathers and displays information.

C H A P T E R 4

Standards and Guidelines

This chapter describes the standard OLE Automation objects and discusses naming guidelines for creating objects that are unique to applications, especially user-interactive applications that support a multiple-document interface (MDI). However, if your OLE Automation object is not user interactive or supports only a single-document interface (SDI), you should adapt the standards and guidelines as appropriate.

- *Standard objects* comprise a standard set of objects defined by OLE. They should be used as appropriate to your application. The objects described in this chapter are oriented toward document-based, user-interactive applications. Other applications (such as noninteractive database servers) may have different requirements.

- *Naming guidelines* are recommendations meant to improve consistency across applications.

This chapter covers each of these points in turn. Examples are shown in a hypothetical syntax derived from Visual Basic.

Note These standards and guidelines are subject to change.

Standard Objects

The following table lists the OLE Automation standard objects. Although none of these objects is required, user-interactive applications with subordinate objects should include an Application object.

Object name	Description
Application	Top-level object; provides a standard way for OLE Automation controllers to retrieve and navigate an application's subordinate objects.
Document	Provides a way to open, print, change, and save an application document.
Documents	Provides a way to iterate over and select open documents in multiple-document interface (MDI) applications.
Font	Describes fonts that are used to display or print text.

The following figure shows how the standard objects fit into the organization of the objects an application provides.

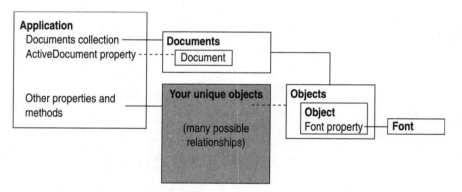

The following sections describe the standard properties and methods for all objects, all collection objects, and each of the standard objects. These sections list only the standard methods and properties for each object, as well as the standard arguments for those properties and methods.

Note You may define additional application-specific properties and methods for each object. You may also provide additional optional arguments for any of the listed properties or methods; however, the optional arguments should follow the standard arguments in a positional argument list.

All Objects

All objects, including the Application object and collection objects, must provide the following properties:

Property name	Return type	Description
Application	VT_DISPATCH	Returns the Application object; read only.
Parent	VT_DISPATCH	Returns the creator of the object; read only.

Note The Application and Parent properties of the Application object return the Application object.

All Collection Objects

A collection provides a set of objects over which iteration can be performed. All collection objects must provide the following properties:

Property name	Return type	Description
Count	VT_I4	Returns the number of items in the collection; read only. Required.
_NewEnum	VT_DISPATCH	A special property that returns an enumerator object that implements **IEnumVARIANT**. Required.

Collection Methods

Methods for collections are described in the following table. The Item method is required; other methods are optional.

Method name	Return type	Description
Add	VT_DISPATCH or VT_EMPTY	Adds an item to a collection. Returns VT_DISPATCH if object is created (object can't exist outside the collection) or VT_EMPTY if no object is created (object can exist outside the collection).
Item	Varies with type of collection	Returns the indicated item in the collection. Required. The Item method may take one or more arguments to indicate the element within the collection to return. This method is the default member (DISPID_VALUE) for the collection object.
Remove	VT_EMPTY	Removes an item from a collection. Uses indexing arguments in the same way as the Item method.

All collection objects must provide at least one form of indexing through the Item method. The dispatch ID of the Item method is DISPID_VALUE. Because it is the default member, it can be used in the following convenient form:

```
ThirdDef = MyWords(3).Definition    ' Equivalent to
                                    ' MyWords.Item(3).Definition
```

The Item method takes one or more arguments to indicate the index. Indexes may be numbers, strings, or other types. For example:

```
DogDef = MyWords("dog").Definition
```

Important   Within the application's type library, the _NewEnum property has a special dispatch ID: DISPID_NEWENUM. The name "_NewEnum" should not be localized.

The Add method may take one or more arguments. For example, if MyWord is an object with the properties Letters and Definition:

```
Dim MyWord As New Word
Dim MyDictionary as Words
MyWord = "dog"
MyWord.Letters = "Dog"
MyWord.Definition = "My best friend."
MyDictionary.Add MyWord
MyDictionary.Remove("Dog")
```

For more information on creating collection objects, see Chapter 2, "Exposing OLE Automation Objects."

Kinds of Collections

The standard for collections allows you to describe two kinds of collections, depending on whether it makes sense for the collected objects to exist outside the collection.

In some cases, it isn't logical for an object to exist independently of its collection. For example, an application's Documents collection contains all currently open Document objects. Opening a document means adding it to the collection, and closing the document means removing it from the collection. All open documents are, therefore, part of the collection; the application can't have open documents that aren't part of the collection. The relationship between the collection and the members of the collection can be shown in the following ways:

- Documents.Add creates an object (an open document) and adds it to the collection. Since an object is created, a reference to it is returned:

  ```
  Set MyDoc = Documents.Add
  ```

- Document.Close removes an object from the collection:

  ```
  Set SomeDoc = Documents(3)
  SomeDoc.Close
  ```

In other cases, it is logical for the objects to exist outside the collection. For example, a Mail application might have Name objects, and many collections of these Name objects. Each Name object would have a user's email name, full name, and possibly other information. The email name and full name would likely be properties named EmailName and FullName.

Additionally, the application might have the following collections of Name objects:

- A collection for the "to" list on each piece of mail
- A collection of the names of all of the people to whom a user has sent mail

The collections of Name objects could be indexed by using either EmailName or FullName.

For these collections, the Add method doesn't create an object because the object already exists. Therefore, the Add method should take an object as an argument and should not return a value. Assuming the existence of two collections (AddressBook and ToList), a user might execute the following code to add a Name object to the ToList collection:

```
Dim Message as Object
Dim AddressBook as Object
Dim NameRef as Object
.
.
.

Set NameRef = AddressBook.Names("Fred Funk")
Message.ToList.Add    NameRef
```

The Name object already exists and is contained in the AddressBook collection. The first line of code gets a reference to the Name object for "Fred Funk" and makes NameRef point to it. The second line of code adds a reference to the object to the ToList collection. No new object is created, so no reference is returned from the Add method. Unlike the relationship between Documents and Document, there is no way for the collected object (the Name) to know how to remove itself from the collections in which it is contained. Thus, to remove an item from a collection, the Remove method is used:

```
Message.ToList.Remove("Fred Funk")
```

This line of code removes the Name object that has the FullName "Fred Funk." The "Fred Funk" object may exist in other collections. These other collections will be unaffected.

Application Object

If a type library is used, the Application object should be the object that has the **appobject** attribute. Because some OLE Automation controllers use the type information to allow unqualified access to the Application object's members, it is important to avoid overloading the Application object with too many members.

The Application object should have the properties listed in the following table. The Application, FullName, Name, Parent, and Visible properties are required; other properties are optional.

Property name	Return type	Description
ActiveDocument	VT_DISPATCH, VT_EMPTY	Returns the active document object or VT_EMPTY if none; read only.
Application	VT_DISPATCH	Returns the Application object; read only. Required.
Caption	VT_BSTR	Sets or returns the title of the application window; read/write. Setting the Caption to VT_EMPTY returns control to the application.
DefaultFilePath	VT_BSTR	Sets or returns the default path specification used by the application for opening files; read/write.
Documents	VT_DISPATCH	Returns a collection object for the open documents; read only.
FullName	VT_BSTR	Returns the file specification for the application, including path; read only. For example, `C:\DRAWDIR\SCRIBBLE`. Required.
Height	VT_R4	Sets or returns the distance between the top and bottom edge of the main application window; read/write.
Interactive	VT_BOOL	Sets or returns True if the application accepts actions from the user, and False otherwise; read/write.
Left	VT_R4	Sets or returns the distance between the left edge of the physical screen and the main application window; read/write.
Name	VT_BSTR	Returns the name of the application, such as "Microsoft Excel"; read only. The Name property is the default member (DISPID_VALUE) for the Application object. Required.
Parent	VT_DISPATCH	Returns the Application object; read only. Required.

Property name	Return type	Description
Path	VT_BSTR	Returns the path specification for the application's executable file; read only. For example, C:\DRAWDIR if the executable is C:\DRAWDIR\SCRIBBLE.EXE.
StatusBar	VT_BSTR	Sets or returns the text displayed in the status bar; read/write.
Top	VT_R4	Sets or returns the distance between the top edge of the physical screen and main application window; read/write.
Visible	VT_BOOL	Sets or returns whether the application is visible to the user; read/write. The default is False when the application is started with **/Automation** command-line switch. Required.
Width	VT_R4	Sets or returns the distance between the left and right edges of the main application window; read/write.

The Application object should have the following methods. The Quit method is required; other methods are optional.

Method name	Return type	Description
Help	VT_EMPTY	Displays online Help. May take three optional arguments: *helpfile* (VT_BSTR), *helpcontextID* (VT_I4), and *helpstring* (VT_BSTR). The *helpfile* argument specifies the Help file to display; if omitted, the main Help file for the application is displayed. The *helpcontextID* and *helpstring* arguments specify a Help context to display, and only one of them may be supplied; if both are omitted, the default Help topic is displayed.
Quit	VT_EMPTY	Exits the application and closes all open documents. Required.
Repeat	VT_EMPTY	Repeats the previous action in the user interface.
Undo	VT_EMPTY	Reverses the previous action in the user interface.

Document Object

If your application is document-based, it should provide a Document object named "Document." Use a different name only if "Document" is inappropriate, for example, if your application uses highly technical or otherwise specialized terminology within its user interface.

The Document object should have the properties listed in the table that follows. The Application, FullName, Name, Parent, Path, and Saved properties are required; other properties are optional.

Property name	Return type	Description
Application	VT_DISPATCH	Returns the Application object; read only. Required.
Author	VT_BSTR	Sets or returns the summary information about the document's author; read/write.
Comments	VT_BSTR	Sets or returns summary information comments for the document; read/write.
FullName	VT_BSTR	Returns the file specification of the document, including path; read only. Required.
Keywords	VT_BSTR	Sets or returns summary information keywords associated with the document; read/write.
Name	VT_BSTR	Returns the filename of the document, not including the file's path specification; read only.
Parent	VT_DISPATCH	Returns the parent of the Document object; read only. Required.
Path	VT_BSTR	Returns the path specification for the document, not including the filename or filename extension; read only. Required.
ReadOnly	VT_BOOL	Returns True if the file is read only and False otherwise; read only.
Saved	VT_BOOL	Returns True if the document has never been saved, but has not changed since it was created. Returns True if it has been saved and has not changed since last saved. Returns False if it has never been saved and has changed since it was created; or if it was saved, but has changed since last saved. Read only; required.
Subject	VT_BSTR	Sets or returns the summary information about the subject of the document; read/write.
Title	VT_BSTR	Sets or returns the summary information about the title of the document; read/write.

The Document object should have the following methods. The Activate, Close, Print, Save, and SaveAs methods are required; other methods are optional.

Method name	Return type	Description
Activate	VT_EMPTY	Activates the first window associated with the document. Required.
Close	VT_EMPTY	Closes all windows associated with the document and removes the document from the Documents collection. Required. Takes two optional arguments, *saveChanges* (VT_BOOL) and *fileName* (VT_BSTR). The *fileName* argument specifies the name of the file in which to save the document.
NewWindow	VT_EMPTY	Creates a new window for the document.
Print	VT_EMPTY	Prints the document. Required. Takes three optional arguments: *from* (VT_I2), *to* (VT_I2), and *copies* (VT_I2). The *from* and *to* arguments specify the page range to print. The *copies* argument specifies the number of copies to print.
PrintOut	VT_EMPTY	Same as Print method, but provides an easier way to use the method in Visual Basic version 3.0, because Print is a Visual Basic keyword.
PrintPreview	VT_EMPTY	Previews the pages and page breaks of the document. Equivalent to choosing Print Preview from the File menu.
RevertToSaved	VT_EMPTY	Reverts to the last saved copy of the document, discarding any changes.
Save	VT_EMPTY	Saves changes to the file specified in the document's FullName property. Required.
SaveAs	VT_EMPTY	Saves changes to a file. Required. Takes one optional argument, *filename* (VT_BSTR). The *filename* argument may optionally include a path specification.

Documents Collection Object

If your application supports a multiple-document interface (MDI), you should provide a Documents collection object. Use the name "Documents" for this collection unless the name is inappropriate for your application.

The Documents collection object should have all of the following properties.

Property name	Return type	Description
Application	VT_DISPATCH	Returns the Application object; read only. Required.
Count	VT_I4	Returns the number of items in the collection; read only. Required.
_NewEnum	VT_DISPATCH	A special property that returns an enumerator object that implements **IEnumVARIANT**. Required.
Parent	VT_DISPATCH	Returns the parent of the Documents collection object; read only. Required.

The Documents collection object should have all of the following methods.

Method name	Return type	Description
Add	VT_DISPATCH	Creates a new document and adds it to the collection. Returns the document that was created. Required.
Close	VT_EMPTY	Closes all documents in the collection. Required.
Item	VT_DISPATCH or VT_EMPTY	Returns a Document object from the collection or returns VT_EMPTY if the document does not exist. Takes an optional argument, *index*, which may be a string (VT_BSTR) indicating the document name, a number (VT_I4) indicating the ordered position within the collection, or either (VT_VARIANT). If *index* is omitted, returns the Document collection. The Item method is the default member (DISPID_VALUE). Required.
Open	VT_DISPATCH or VT_EMPTY	Opens an existing document and adds it to the collection. Returns the document that was opened or VT_EMPTY if the object could not be opened. Takes one required argument, *filename*, and one optional argument, *password*. Both arguments have type VT_BSTR. Required.

Font Object

The Font object may be appropriate for some applications. It should have the following properties. The Application, Bold, Italic, Parent, and Size properties are required; other properties are optional.

Property name	Return type	Description
Application	VT_DISPATCH	Returns the Application object; read only. Required.
Bold	VT_BOOL	Sets or returns True if the font is boldface, and False otherwise; read/write. Required.
Color	VT_I4	Sets or returns the RGB color of the font; read/write.
Italic	VT_BOOL	Sets or returns True if the font is italic, and False otherwise; read/write. Required.
Name	VT_BSTR	Returns the name of the font; read only.
OutlineFont	VT_BOOL	Sets or returns True if the font is scaleable, and False otherwise. For example, bitmapped fonts are not scaleable, whereas TrueType fonts are scaleable; read/write.
Parent	VT_DISPATCH	Returns the parent of the Font object; read only. Required.
Shadow	VT_BOOL	Sets or returns True if the font appears with a shadow, and False otherwise; read/write.
Size	VT_R4	Sets or returns the size of the font in points; read/write. Required.
Strikethrough	VT_BOOL	Sets or returns True if the font appears with a line running through it, and False otherwise; read/write.
Subscript	VT_BOOL	Sets or returns True if the font is subscripted, and False otherwise; read/write.
Superscript	VT_BOOL	Sets or returns True if the font is superscripted and False otherwise; read/write.

Naming Conventions

Choose names for exposed objects, properties, and methods that can be easily understood by the users of your application. The guidelines in this section apply to all the items you expose:

- Objects (implemented as classes in your application)
- Properties and methods (implemented as members of a class)
- Named arguments (implemented as named parameters in a member function)
- Constants and enumerations (implemented as settings for properties and methods)

Use entire words or syllables

It is easier for users to remember complete words than to remember whether you abbreviated Window as Wind, Wn, or Wnd.

When you need to abbreviate because an identifier would be too long, try to use complete initial syllables. For example, use AltExpEval instead of AlternateExpressionEvaluation.

Use	Don't use
Application	App
Window	Wnd

Use mixed case

All identifiers should use mixed case, rather than underscores, to separate words.

Use	Don't use
ShortcutMenus	Shortcut_Menus, Shortcutmenus, SHORTCUTMENUS, SHORTCUT_MENUS
BasedOn	basedOn

Use the same word you use in the interface

Use consistent terminology; don't use names like HWND that are based on Hungarian notation. Try to use the same word your users would use to describe a concept.

Use	Don't use
Name	Lbl

Use the correct plural for the class name

Collection classes should use the correct plural for the class name. For example, if you have a class named Axis, you should store the collection of Axis objects in an Axes class. Similarly, a collection of Vertex objects is stored in a Vertices class. In cases where English uses the same word for the plural, append the word "Collection."

Use	Don't use
Axes	Axiss
SeriesCollection	CollectionSeries
Windows	ColWindow

Using plurals rather than inventing new names for collections reduces the number of items a user must remember. It also simplifies the selection of names for collections.

Note, however, that for some collections this may not be appropriate, especially where a set of objects exists independently of the collection. For example, a Mail program might have a Name object that exists in several collections, such as ToList, CCList, and GroupList. In this case, you might specify the individual name collections as ToNames, CCNames, and GroupNames.

P A R T 2

Reference Information

C H A P T E R 5

Dispatch Interfaces

The dispatch interfaces provide a way to expose and access objects within an application. OLE Automation defines the following dispatch interfaces and functions:

- **IDispatch** interface—Exposes objects, methods, and properties to OLE Automation programming tools and other applications.

- Dispatch functions—Simplify the implementation of an **IDispatch** interface. You can use these functions to automatically generate an **IDispatch** interface.

- **IEnumVARIANT** interface—Provides a way for OLE Automation controllers to iterate over collection objects.

Overview of Interfaces

The following table describes the member functions of each of the dispatch interfaces.

Interface	Member name	Purpose
IDispatch	**Invoke**	Provides access to properties and methods exposed by the object.
	GetIDsOfNames	Maps a single member name and an optional set of argument names to a corresponding set of integer DISPIDs, which may then be used on subsequent calls to **Invoke**.
	GetTypeInfo	Retrieves the type information for an object.
	GetTypeInfoCount	Retrieves the number of type information interfaces that an object provides (either 0 or 1).

Interface	Member name	Purpose
IEnumVARIANT	Clone	Creates a copy of the current enumeration state.
	Next	Gets the next item or items in the enumeration sequence and returns them through an array.
	Reset	Resets the enumeration sequence to the beginning.
	Skip	Skips over the next item or items in the enumeration sequence.

Overview of Functions

The dispatch functions are summarized in the following table. For 32-bit systems, these functions are provided in OLEAUT32.DLL; the header file is OLEAUTO.H, and the import library is OLEAUT32.LIB. For 16-bit systems, these functions are provided in OLE2DISP.DLL; the header file is DISPATCH.H, and the import library is OLE2DISP.LIB.

Category	Function name	Purpose
Dispatch interface creation	CreateDispTypeInfo	Creates simplified type information for an object.
	CreateStdDispatch	Creates a standard IDispatch implementation for an object.
	DispGetIDsOfNames	Converts a set of names to DISPIDs.
	DispGetParam	Retrieves and coerces elements from a DISPPARAMS structure.
	DispInvoke	Calls a member function of an IDispatch interface.
Active object initialization	GetActiveObject	Retrieves an instance of an object that is initialized with OLE.
	RegisterActiveObject	Initializes a running object with OLE. (Use when application starts.)
	RevokeActiveObject	Revokes a running application's initialization with OLE. (Use when application ends.)

IDispatch Interface

Implemented by	Used by	Header filename
Applications that expose programmable objects.	Applications that access programmable objects.	OLEAUTO.H (32-bit systems) DISPATCH.H (16-bit systems)

OLE Automation objects may implement the **IDispatch** interface for access by OLE Automation controllers, such as Visual Basic. The object's properties and methods can be accessed using **IDispatch::GetIDsOfNames** and **IDispatch::Invoke**.

The following examples show how to access an OLE Automation object through the **IDispatch** interface. Note that the code is abbreviated and omits error handling.

```
// Declarations of variables used
    DEFINE_GUID(CLSID_Hello,    //...portions omitted for brevity...

    HRESULT hresult;
    IUnknown * punk;
    IDispatch * pdisp;
    OLECHAR FAR* szMember = "SayHello";
    DISPID dispid;
    DISPPARAMS dispparamsNoArgs = {NULL, NULL, 0, 0};
    EXCEPINFO excepinfo;
    UINT nArgErr;
```

In the following lines, **OleInitialize** loads the OLE DLLs and **CoCreateInstance** initializes the OLE Automation object's class factory. For more information on these two functions, see the *OLE Programmer's Guide and Reference*.

```
// Initialize OLE DLLs
hresult = OleInitialize(NULL);

// OLE function CoCreateInstance starts application using GUID
hresult = CoCreateInstance(CLSID_Hello, &punk);
```

QueryInterface checks whether the object supports **IDispatch**. (As with any call to **QueryInterface**, the returned pointer must be released when it is no longer needed.)

```
// QueryInterface to see if it supports IDispatch.
hresult = punk->QueryInterface(IID_IDispatch, &pdisp);
```

GetIDsOfNames retrieves the dispatch identifier (DISPID) for the indicated method or property, in this case, `szMember`.

```
// Retrieve the dispatch identifier for the SayHello method.
// Use defaults where possible.
hresult = pdisp->GetIDsOfNames(
                    IID_NULL,
                    &szMember,
                    1,
                    LOCALE_SYSTEM_DEFAULT,
                    &dispid);
```

In the following call to **Invoke**, the dispatch identifier (`dispid`) indicates the property or method to invoke. The **SayHello** method takes no parameters, so the fifth argument (`&dispparamsNoArgs`), contains NULL and 0, as initialized at declaration. To invoke a property or method that requires parameters, you would need to supply the parameters in the DISPPARAMS structure.

```
// Invoke the method. Use defaults where possible.
hresult = pdisp->Invoke(
                    dispid,
                    IID_NULL,
                    LOCALE_SYSTEM_DEFAULT,
                    DISPATCH_METHOD,
                    &dispparamsNoArgs,
                    NULL,
                    NULL,
                    NULL);
```

Data Types, Structures, and Enumerations

The **IDispatch** interface uses these data types and structures:

Name	Purpose
BSTR	A length-prefixed string.
CALLCONV	Identifies the calling convention used by a member function.
CURRENCY	Provides a precise data type of monetary data.
DISPID	Identifies a method, property, or argument to **Invoke**.
DISPPARAMS	Contains arguments passed to a method or property.
EXCEPINFO	Describes an error that occurred during **Invoke**.
INTERFACEDATA	Describes the members of an interface.

Name	Purpose
LCID	Provides locale information for international string comparisons and localized member names.
METHODDATA	Describes a method or property.
PARAMDATA	Describes a parameter to a method.
VARIANT	Describes a VARIANTARG that can't have the VT_BYREF bit set. Because VT_BYREF is not set, data of type VARIANT can't be passed within DISPPARAMS.
VARIANTARG	Describes arguments that may be passed within DISPPARAMS.
VARTYPE	Identifies the available variant types.

BSTR

A length-prefixed string used by OLE Automation data manipulation functions.

```
typedef OLECHAR *BSTR;
```

For details on this data type, see Chapter 6, "Data Manipulation Functions."

CALLCONV

Identifies the calling convention used by a member function described in METHODDATA.

```
typedef enum tagCALLCONV {
      CC_CDECL = 1
    , CC_MSCPASCAL
    , CC_PASCAL = CC_MSCPASCAL
    , CC_MACPASCAL
    , CC_STDCALL
    , CC_RESERVED
    , CC_SYSCALL
    , CC_MPWCDECL
    , CC_MPWPASCAL
    , CC_MAX          /* end of enum marker */
} CALLCONV;
```

On 16-bit Windows systems, functions implemented with the CC_CDECL calling convention can't have return type **float** or **double**. This includes functions returning DATE, which is a floating-point type.

CURRENCY

A currency number is stored as an 8-byte, two's complement integer, scaled by 10,000 to give a fixed-point number with 15 digits to the left of the decimal point and 4 digits to the right. This representation provides a range of ±922337203685477.5807. The currency data type is useful for calculations involving money, or for any fixed-point calculation where accuracy is particularly important.

```
typedef CY CURRENCY;
```

The data type is defined as a structure for working with currency more conveniently:

```
typedef struct tagCY
    {
    unsigned long Lo;
    long Hi;
    }
CY;
```

DISPID

Used by **IDispatch::Invoke** to identify methods, properties, and arguments.

```
typedef LONG DISPID;
```

The following DISPIDs have special meaning:

DISPID	Description
DISPID_VALUE	The default member for the object. This property or method is invoked when an OLE Automation controller specifies the object name without a property or method.
DISPID_NEWENUM	The _NewEnum property. This special, restricted property is required for collection objects. It returns an enumerator object that supports **IEnumVariant** and should have the **restricted** attribute specified in ODL.
DISPID_EVALUATE	The Evaluate method. This method is implicitly invoked when the OLE Automation controller encloses the arguments in square brackets. For example, the following two lines are equivalent:

```
x.[A1:C1].value = 10
x.Evaluate("A1:C1").value = 10
```

The Evaluate method has the dispatch ID DISPID_EVALUATE.

DISPID	Description
DISPID_PROPERTYPUT	The parameter that receives the value of an assignment in a property "put."
DISPID_CONSTRUCTOR	The C++ constructor function for the object.
DISPID_DESTRUCTOR	The C++ destructor function for the object.
DISPID_UNKNOWN	Value returned by **IDispatch::GetIDsOfNames** to indicate that a member or parameter name was not found.

DISPPARAMS

Used by **IDispatch::Invoke** to contain the arguments passed to a method or property. For more information, see "**IDispatch::Invoke**" later in this chapter.

```
typedef struct FARSTRUCT tagDISPPARAMS{
VARIANTARG FAR* rgvarg;              // Array of arguments
    DISPID FAR* rgdispidNamedArgs;   // Dispatch IDs of named arguments
    unsigned int cArgs;              // Number of arguments
    unsigned int cNamedArgs;         // Number of named arguments
} DISPPARAMS;
```

EXCEPINFO

Describes an exception that occurred during **IDispatch::Invoke**. See the section "**IDispatch::Invoke**" for more information on exceptions.

```
typedef struct FARSTRUCT tagEXCEPINFO {
    unsigned short wCode;        // An error code describing the error.
    unsigned short wReserved;
    BSTR bstrSource;             // Source of the exception.
    BSTR bstrDescription;        // Textual description of the error.
    BSTR bstrHelpFile;           // Help file path.
    unsigned long dwHelpContext; // Help context ID.
    void FAR* pvReserved;
    /* Pointer to function that fills in Help and description info */
    HRESULT (STDAPICALLTYPE FAR* pfnDeferredFillIn)
            (struct tagEXCEPINFO FAR*);
    SCODE scode;                 // An SCODE describing the error.
} EXCEPINFO, FAR* LPEXCEPINFO;
```

The following table describes the fields of the EXCEPINFO structure:

Name	Type	Description
wCode	**unsigned short**	An error code identifying the error. Error codes should be greater than 1000. Either this field or the *scode* field must be filled in; the other must be set to 0.
wReserved	**unsigned short**	Reserved; should be set to 0.
bstrSource	BSTR	A textual, human-readable name of the source of the exception. Typically this will be an application name. This field should be filled in by the implementor of **IDispatch.**
bstrDescription	BSTR	A textual, human-readable description of the error intended for the customer. If no description is available, use NULL.
bstrHelpFile	BSTR	The fully qualified drive, path, and filename of a Help file with more information about the error. If no Help is available, use NULL.
dwHelpContext	**unsigned long**	The Help context of the topic within the Help file. This field should be filled in if and only if the *bstrHelpFile* field is not NULL.
pvReserved	**void FAR***	Must be set to NULL.
pfnDeferredFillIn	HRESULT (STDAPICALLTYPE FAR* pfnDeferredFillIn) (struct tagEXCEPINFO FAR*)	Pointer to a function that takes an EXCEPINFO structure as an argument and returns an HRESULT value. If deferred fill-in is not desired, this field should be set to NULL.
scode	SCODE	An SCODE describing the error. Either this field or *wCode* (but not both) must be filled in; the other must be set to 0.

Use the *pfnDeferredFillIn* field to allow an object to defer filling in the *bstrDescription*, *bstrHelpFile*, and *dwHelpContext* fields until they are needed. This field might be used, for example, if loading the string for the error is a time-consuming operation. To use deferred fill-in, the object puts a function pointer in this slot and does not fill any of the other fields except *wCode* (which is required in any case). To get additional information, the caller passes the EXCEPINFO structure back to the pexcepinfo callback function, which fills in the additional information. When the OLE Automation object and the OLE Automation controller are in different processes, the OLE Automation object calls *pfnDeferredFillIn* before returning to the controller.

INTERFACEDATA

Describes the OLE Automation object's properties and methods.

```
typedef struct FARSTRUCT tagINTERFACEDATA {
    METHODDATA FAR* pmethdata;   // Pointer to an array of METHODDATAs
    unsigned int cMembers;       // Count of members
} INTERFACEDATA;
```

LCID

Identifies a locale for national language support. Locale information is used for international string comparisons and localized member names. For information on LCIDs, see "Supporting Multiple Languages" in Chapter 2.

```
typedef unsigned long LCID;
```

METHODDATA

Used to describe a method or property.

```
typedef struct FARSTRUCT tagMETHODDATA {
    OLECHAR FAR* szName;       // Member name
    PARAMDATA FAR* ppdata;     // Pointer to array of PARAMDATAs
    DISPID dispid;             // Member ID
    unsigned int iMeth;        // Method index
    CALLCONV cc;               // Calling convention
    unsigned int cArgs;        // Count of arguments
    unsigned short wFlags;     // Whether this is a method or
                               // a property get, put, or putref
    VARTYPE vtReturn;          // Return type
} METHODDATA;
```

The following table describes the fields of the METHODDATA structure:

Name	Type	Description
szName	OLECHAR FAR*	The method name.
ppdata	PARAMDATA FAR*	The parameters for the method. The first parameter is *ppdata*[0], and so on.
dispid	DISPID	The ID of the method as used in **IDispatch**.
iMeth	unsigned int	The index of the method in the interface's VTBL. The indexes start with 0.
cc	CALLCONV	The calling convention. The CDECL and Pascal calling conventions are supported by the dispatch interface creation functions, such as **CreateStdDispatch**.

Name	Type	Description
cArgs	unsigned int	The number of arguments for the method.
wFlags	unsigned short	Flags that indicate whether the method is used for getting or setting a property. The flags are the same as in **IDispatch::Invoke**. DISPATCH_METHOD indicates this is not used for a property. DISPATCH_PROPERTYGET indicates the method is used to get a property value. DISPATCH_PROPERTYPUT indicates the method is used to set the value of a property. DISPATCH_PROPERTYPUTREF indicates the method is used to make the property refer to a passed-in object.
vtReturn	VARTYPE	Return type for the method.

PARAMDATA

Used to describe a parameter accepted by a method or property.

```
typedef struct FARSTRUCT tagPARAMDATA {
    OLECHAR FAR* szName;     // Parameter name
    VARTYPE vt;              // Parameter type
} PARAMDATA;
```

The following table describes the fields of the PARAMDATA structure:

Name	Type	Description
szName	OLECHAR FAR *	The parameter name. Names should follow standard conventions for programming language access; that is, no embedded spaces or control characters, and 32 or fewer characters. This name should be localized, because each type description describes names for a particular locale.
vt	VARTYPE	The VARTYPE that will be used by the receiver. If more than one parameter type is accepted, VT_VARIANT should be specified.

VARIANT and VARIANTARG

Use VARIANTARG to describe arguments passed within DISPPARAMS. Use VARIANT to specify variant data that can't be passed by reference; the VARIANT type can't have the VT_BYREF bit set. Note that VARIANTs can be passed by value even if VARIANTARGs cannot.

```
typedef struct FARSTRUCT tagVARIANT VARIANT;
typedef struct FARSTRUCT tagVARIANT VARIANTARG;

typedef struct tagVARIANT  {
    VARTYPE vt;
    unsigned short wReserved1;
    unsigned short wReserved2;
    unsigned short wReserved3;
    union {
        unsigned char    bVal;          /* VT_UI1                    */
        short            iVal;          /* VT_I2                     */
        long             lVal;          /* VT_I4                     */
        float            fltVal;        /* VT_R4                     */
        double           dblVal;        /* VT_R8                     */
        VARIANT_BOOL     bool;          /* VT_BOOL                   */
        SCODE            scode;         /* VT_ERROR                  */
        CY               cyVal;         /* VT_CY                     */
        DATE             date;          /* VT_DATE                   */
        BSTR             bstrVal;       /* VT_BSTR                   */
        Iunknown    FAR* punkVal;       /* VT_UNKNOWN                */
        Idispatch   FAR* pdispVal;      /* VT_DISPATCH               */
        SAFEARRAY   FAR* parray;        /* VT_ARRAY|*                */
        unsigned char FAR *pbVal;       /* VT_BYREF|VT_UI1           */
        short       FAR* piVal;         /* VT_BYREF|VT_I2            */
        long        FAR* plVal;         /* VT_BYREF|VT_I4            */
        float       FAR* pfltVal;       /* VT_BYREF|VT_R4            */
        double      FAR* pdblVal;       /* VT_BYREF|VT_R8            */
        VARIANT_BOOL FAR* pbool;        /* VT_BYREF|VT_BOOL          */
        SCODE       FAR* pscode;        /* VT_BYREF|VT_ERROR         */
        CY          FAR* pcyVal;        /* VT_BYREF|VT_CY            */
        DATE        FAR* pdate;         /* VT_BYREF|VT_DATE          */
        BSTR        FAR* pbstrVal;      /* VT_BYREF|VT_BSTR          */
        IUnknown FAR*  FAR* ppunkVal;   /* VT_BYREF|VT_UNKNOWN       */
        IDispatch FAR* FAR* ppdispVal;  /* VT_BYREF|VT_DISPATCH      */
        SAFEARRAY FAR* FAR* parray;     /* VT_ARRAY|*                */
        VARIANT     FAR* pvarVal;       /* VT_BYREF|VT_VARIANT       */
        void        FAR* byref;         /* Generic ByRef             */
    };
};
```

To simplify extracting values from VARIANTARGs, OLE Automation provides a
set of functions for manipulating this type. Use of these functions is strongly
recommended to ensure that applications apply consistent coercion rules. The
functions are described in Chapter 6, "Data Manipulation Functions."

The *vt* value governs the interpretation of the union as follows:

Value	Description
VT_EMPTY	No value was specified. If an argument is left blank, you should **not** return VT_EMPTY for the argument. Instead, you should return the VT_ERROR value: DISP_E_MEMBERNOTFOUND.
VT_EMPTY | VT_BYREF	Illegal.
VT_UI1	An unsigned 1-byte character is stored in *bVal*.
VT_UI1 | VT_BYREF	A reference to an unsigned 1-byte character was passed; a pointer to the value is in *pbVal*.
VT_I2	A 2-byte integer value is stored in *iVal*.
VT_I2 | VT_BYREF	A reference to a 2-byte integer was passed; a pointer to the value is in *piVal*.
VT_I4	A 4-byte integer value is stored in *lVal*.
VT_I4 | VT_BYREF	A reference to a 4-byte integer was passed; a pointer to the value is in *plVal*.
VT_R4	An IEEE 4-byte real value is stored in *fltVal*.
VT_R4 | VT_BYREF	A reference to an IEEE 4-byte real was passed; a pointer to the value is in *pfltVal*.
VT_R8	An 8-byte IEEE real value is stored in *dblVal*.
VT_R8 | VT_BYREF	A reference to an 8-byte IEEE real was passed; a pointer to its value is in *pdblVal*.
VT_CY	A currency value was specified. A currency number is stored as an 8-byte, two's complement integer, scaled by 10,000 to give a fixed-point number with 15 digits to the left of the decimal point and 4 digits to the right. The value is in *cyVal*.
VT_CY | VT_BYREF	A reference to a currency value was passed; a pointer to the value is in *pcyVal*.
VT_BSTR	A string was passed; it is stored in *bstrVal*. This pointer must be obtained and freed via the BSTR functions, which are described in Chapter 6, "Data Manipulation Functions."
VT_BSTR | VT_BYREF	A reference to a string was passed. A BSTR* which points to a BSTR is in *pbstrVal*. The referenced pointer must be obtained or freed via the BSTR functions.
VT_NULL	A propagating NULL value was specified. This should not be confused with the NULL pointer. The NULL value is used for tri-state logic as with SQL.

Value	Description
VT_NULL I VT_BYREF	Illegal.
VT_ERROR	An SCODE was specified. The type of the error is specified in *scode*. Generally, operations on error values should raise an exception or propagate the error to the return value, as appropriate.
VT_ERROR I VT_BYREF	A reference to an SCODE was passed. A pointer to the value is in *pscode*.
VT_BOOL	A Boolean (True/False) value was specified. A value of 0xFFFF (all bits one) indicates True; a value of 0 (all bits zero) indicates False. No other values are legal.
VT_BOOL I VT_BYREF	A reference to a Boolean value. A pointer to the Boolean value is in *pbool*.
VT_DATE	A value denoting a date and time was specified. Dates are represented as double-precision numbers, where midnight, January 1, 1900 is 2.0, January 2, 1900 is 3.0, and so on. The value is passed in *date*.
	This is the same numbering system used by most spreadsheet programs, although some incorrectly believe that February 29, 1900 existed, and thus set January 1, 1900 to 1.0. The date can be converted to and from an MS-DOS representation using **VariantTimeToDosDateTime**, discussed in Chapter 6, "Data Manipulation Functions."
VT_DATE I VT_BYREF	A reference to a date was passed. A pointer to the value is in *pdate*.
VT_DISPATCH	A pointer to an object was specified. The pointer is in *pdispVal*. This object is only known to implement **IDispatch**; the object can be queried as to whether it supports any other desired interface by calling **QueryInterface** on the object. Objects that do not implement **IDispatch** should be passed using VT_UNKNOWN.
VT_DISPATCH I VT_BYREF	A pointer to a pointer to an object was specified. The pointer to the object is stored in the location referred to by *ppdispVal*.
VT_VARIANT	Illegal. VARIANTARGs must be passed by reference.
VT_VARIANT I VT_BYREF	A pointer to another VARIANTARG is passed in *pvarVal*. This referenced VARIANTARG will never have the VT_BYREF bit set in *vt*, so only one level of indirection can ever be present. This value can be used to support languages that allow functions to change the types of variables passed by reference.

Value	Description
VT_UNKNOWN	A pointer to an object that implements the **IUnknown** interface is passed in *punkVal*.
VT_UNKNOWN | VT_BYREF	A pointer to a pointer to the **IUnknown** interface is passed in *ppunkVal*. The pointer to the interface is stored in the location referred to by *ppunkVal*.
VT_ARRAY | <anything>	An array of data type <anything> was passed. (VT_EMPTY and VT_NULL are illegal types to combine with VT_ARRAY). The pointer in *pByrefVal* points to an array descriptor, which describes the dimensions, size, and in-memory location of the array. The array descriptor is never accessed directly, but instead is read and modified using the functions described in Chapter 6, "Data Manipulation Functions."

VARTYPE

VARTYPE is an enumeration type used in VARIANT, TYPEDESC, OLE property sets, and safe arrays. The enumeration constants listed below are valid in the *vt* field of a VARIANT structure.

```
typedef unsigned short VARTYPE;
enum VARENUM{
    VT_EMPTY    = 0,        // Not specified
    VT_NULL     = 1,        // Null
    VT_I2       = 2,        // 2-byte signed int
    VT_I4       = 3,        // 4-byte signed int
    VT_R4       = 4,        // 4-byte real
    VT_R8       = 5,        // 8-byte real
    VT_CY       = 6,        // Currency
    VT_DATE     = 7,        // Date
    VT_BSTR     = 8,        // Binary string
    VT_DISPATCH = 9,        // IDispatch FAR*
    VT_ERROR    = 10,       // SCODE
    VT_BOOL     = 11,       // Boolean; True=-1, False=0
    VT_VARIANT  = 12,       // VARIANT FAR*
    VT_UNKNOWN  = 13,       // IUnknown FAR*
    VT_UI1      = 17,       // Unsigned char
    .
    .    //Other constants that are not valid in VARIANTs
    .
};
    VT_RESERVED = (int) 0x8000
    // By reference: a pointer to the data is passed
    VT_BYREF    = (int) 0x4000
    VT_ARRAY    = (int) 0x2000   // A safe array of the data is passed
```

IDispatch::GetIDsOfNames

HRESULT IDispatch::GetIDsOfNames(*riid, rgszNames, cNames, lcid, rgdispid***)**
REFIID *riid*
OLECHAR FAR* FAR* *rgszNames*
unsigned int *cNames*
LCID *lcid*
DISPID FAR* *rgdispid*

Maps a single member and an optional set of argument names to a corresponding set of integer DISPIDs, which may be used on subsequent calls to **IDispatch::Invoke**. The dispatch function **DispGetIDsOfNames** provides a standard implementation of **GetIDsOfNames**.

Parameters

riid
Reserved for future use. Must be NULL.

rgszNames
Passed-in array of names to be mapped.

cNames
Count of the names to be mapped.

lcid
The locale context in which to interpret the names.

rgdispid
Caller-allocated array, each element of which contains an ID corresponding to one of the names passed in the *rgszNames* array. The first element represents the member name; the subsequent elements represent each of the member's parameters.

Return Value

The SCODE obtained from the returned HRESULT is one of the following:

SCODE	Meaning
S_OK	Success.
E_OUTOFMEMORY	Out of memory.
DISP_E_UNKNOWNNAME	One or more of the names were not known. The returned array of DISPIDs contains DISPID_UNKNOWN for each entry that corresponds to an unknown name.
DISP_E_UNKNOWNLCID	The LCID was not recognized.

Comments

An **IDispatch** implementation may choose to associate any positive integer ID value with a given name. Zero is reserved for the default, or Value property; −1 is reserved to indicate an unknown name; and other negative values are defined for other purposes. For example, if **GetIDsOfNames** is called and the implementation does not recognize one or more of the names, it will return DISP_E_UNKNOWNNAME and the *rgdispid* array will contain DISPID_UNKNOWN for the entries that correspond to the unknown names.

The member and parameter DISPIDs must remain constant for the lifetime of the object. This allows a client to obtain the DISPIDs once and cache them for later use.

When **GetIDsOfNames** is called with more than one name, the first name (*rgszNames*[0]) corresponds to the member name, and subsequent names correspond to the names of the member's parameters.

The same name may map to different DISPIDs, depending on context. For example, a name may have a DISPID when it is used as a member name with a particular interface, a different DISPID as a member of a different interface, and different mapping for each time it appears as a parameter.

The **IDispatch** interface binds to names at run time. To bind at compile time instead, an **IDispatch** client can map names to DISPIDs using the type information interfaces described in Chapter 8, "Type Description Interfaces." This allows a client to bind to members at compile time and avoid calling **GetIDsOfNames** at run time.

The implementation of **GetIDsOfNames** must be case insensitive. Clients that need case-sensitive name mapping should use the type information interfaces to map names to DISPIDs, rather than calling **GetIDsOfNames**.

Examples

The following code from the Lines sample file LINE.CPP implements the **GetIDsOfNames** member function for the CLine class. The OLE Automation object uses the standard implementation, **DispGetIDsOfNames**.

```
STDMETHODIMP
CLine::GetIDsOfNames(
        REFIID riid,
        OLECHAR FAR* FAR* rgszNames,
        UINT cNames,
        LCID lcid,
        DISPID FAR* rgdispid)
{
        return DispGetIDsOfNames(m_ptinfo, rgszNames, cNames, rgdispid);
}
```

The following code might appear in an OLE Automation controller that calls **GetIDsOfNames** to get the DISPID of the CLine Color property.

```
HRESULT hresult;
IDispatch FAR* pdisp = (IDispatch FAR*)NULL;
DISPID dispid;
OLECHAR FAR* szMember = "color";

// Omitted code that sets pdisp...
hresult = pdisp->GetIDsOfNames(
    IID_NULL,
    &szMember,
    1, LOCALE_SYSTEM_DEFAULT,
    &dispid);
```

See Also   **CreateStdDispatch, DispGetIDsOfNames, ITypeInfo::GetIDsOfNames**

IDispatch::GetTypeInfo

HRESULT IDispatch::GetTypeInfo(*itinfo, lcid, pptinfo*)
unsigned int *itinfo*
LCID *lcid*
ITypeInfo FAR* FAR* *pptinfo*

Retrieves a type information object, which can be used to get the type information for an interface.

Parameters   *itinfo*

The type information to return. Pass 0 to retrieve type information for the **IDispatch** implementation.

lcid

The locale ID for the type information. An object may be able to return different type information for different languages. This is important for classes that support localized member names. For classes that don't support localized member names, this parameter can be ignored.

pptinfo

Receives a pointer to the type information object requested.

Return Value   The SCODE obtained from the returned HRESULT is one of the following:

SCODE	Meaning
S_OK	Success; the TypeInfo element exists.
DISP_E_BADINDEX	Failure; *itinfo* argument was not 0.
TYPE_E_ELEMENTNOTFOUND	Failure; *itinfo* argument was not 0.

Example   The following code from the sample file LINES.CPP loads information from the type library and implements the member function **GetTypeInfo**:

```
// These lines from CLines::Create load type information for the
// Lines collection from the type library.
    hr = LoadTypeInfo(&pLines->m_ptinfo, IID_ILines);
    if (FAILED(hr))
        goto error;

// Additional code omitted...

// This function implements GetTypeInfo for the CLines collection.
STDMETHODIMP
CLines::GetTypeInfo(
        UINT itinfo,
        LCID lcid,
        ITypeInfo FAR* FAR* pptinfo)
{
    *pptinfo = NULL;

    if(itinfo != 0)
        return ResultFromScode(DISP_E_BADINDEX);

    m_ptinfo->AddRef();
    *pptinfo = m_ptinfo;

    return NOERROR;
}
```

IDispatch::GetTypeInfoCount

HRESULT IDispatch::GetTypeInfoCount(*pctinfo***)**
unsigned int FAR* *pctinfo*

Retrieves the number of type information interfaces that an object provides (either 0 or 1).

Parameters

pctinfo

Points to location that receives the number of type information interfaces that the object provides. If the object provides type information, this number is 1; otherwise the number is 0.

Return Value

The SCODE obtained from the returned HRESULT is one of the following:

SCODE	Meaning
S_OK	Success
E_NOTIMPL	Failure

Comments

The function may return zero, which indicates that the object does not provide any type information. In this case, the object may still be programmable through **IDispatch**, but does not provide type information for browsers, compilers, or other programming tools that access type information. This may be useful for hiding an object from browsers or for preventing early binding on an object.

Example

This code from the Lines sample file LINES.CPP implements the **GetTypeInfoCount** member function for the CLines class. (OLE Automation object.)

```
STDMETHODIMP
CLines::GetTypeInfoCount(UINT FAR* pctinfo)
{
    *pctinfo = 1;
    return NOERROR;
}
```

See Also

CreateStdDispatch

IDispatch::Invoke

HRESULT IDispatch::Invoke(*dispidMember*, *riid*, *lcid*, *wFlags*, *pdispparams*, *pvarResult*, *pexcepinfo*, *puArgErr*)
DISPID *dispidMember*
REFIID *riid*
LCID *lcid*
unsigned short *wFlags*
DISPPARAMS FAR* *pdispparams*
VARIANT FAR* *pvarResult*
EXCEPINFO FAR* *pexcepinfo*
unsigned int FAR* *puArgErr*

Provides access to properties and methods exposed by an object. The dispatch function **DispInvoke** provides a standard implementation of **IDispatch::Invoke**.

Parameters

dispidMember

Identifies the member. Use **GetIDsOfNames** or the object's documentation to obtain the dispatch identifier.

riid

Reserved for future use. Must be IID_NULL.

lcid

The locale context in which to interpret arguments. The *lcid* is used by the **GetIDsOfNames** function, and is also passed to **Invoke** to allow the object to interpret its arguments in a locale-specific way. Applications that don't support multiple national languages can ignore this parameter. See "Supporting Multiple National Languages," in Chapter 2, for more information.

wFlags

Flags describing the context of the **Invoke** call, as follows:

Value	Description
DISPATCH_METHOD	The member is being invoked as a method. If a property has the same name, both this and the DISPATCH_PROPERTYGET flag may be set.
DISPATCH_PROPERTYGET	The member is being retrieved as a property or data member.
DISPATCH_PROPERTYPUT	The member is being changed as a property or data member.
DISPATCH_PROPERTYPUTREF	The member is being changed via a reference assignment, rather than a value assignment. This flag is valid only when the property accepts a reference to an object.

pdispparams

Pointer to a structure containing an array of arguments, array of argument dispatch IDs for named arguments, and counts for number of elements in the arrays. See the Comments section for a description of the DISPPARAMS structure.

pvarResult

Pointer to where the result is to be stored, or NULL if the caller expects no result. This argument is ignored if DISPATCH_PROPERTYPUT or DISPATCH_PROPERTYPUTREF is specified.

pexcepinfo

Pointer to a structure containing exception information. This structure should be filled in if DISP_E_EXCEPTION is returned. Can be NULL.

puArgErr
> The index within *rgvarg* of the first argument that has an error. Arguments are stored in *pdispparams->rgvarg* in reverse order, so the first argument is the one with the highest index in the array. This parameter is returned only when the resulting SCODE is DISP_E_TYPEMISMATCH or DISP_E_PARAMNOTFOUND; see "Returning Errors" for details. Can be NULL.

Return Value

The SCODE obtained from the returned HRESULT is one of the following:

SCODE	Meaning
S_OK	Success.
DISP_E_BADPARAMCOUNT	The number of elements provided DISPPARAMS is different from the number of arguments accepted by the method or property.
DISP_E_BADVARTYPE	One of the arguments in *rgvarg* is not a valid variant type.
DISP_E_EXCEPTION	The application needs to raise an exception. In this case the structure passed in *pexcepinfo* should be filled in.
DISP_E_MEMBERNOTFOUND	The requested member does not exist, or the call to **Invoke** tried to set the value of a read-only property.
DISP_E_NONAMEDARGS	This implementation of **IDispatch** does not support named arguments.
DISP_E_OVERFLOW	One of the arguments in *rgvarg* could not be coerced to the specified type.
DISP_E_PARAMNOTFOUND	One of the parameter dispatch IDs does not correspond to a parameter on the method. In this case *puArgErr* should be set to the first argument that contains the error.
DISP_E_TYPEMISMATCH	One or more of the arguments could not be coerced. The index within *rgvarg* of the first parameter with the incorrect type is returned in the *puArgErr* parameter.
DISP_E_UNKNOWNINTERFACE	The interface ID passed in *riid* is not IID_NULL.
DISP_E_UNKNOWNLCID	The member being invoked interprets string arguments according to the locale ID (LCID), and the LCID is not recognized. If the LCID is not needed to interpret arguments, this error should not be returned.
DISP_E_PARAMNOTOPTIONAL	A required parameter was omitted.

To return other errors, you can define your own errors using the MAKE_SCODE macro.

Comments   Generally, you should not implement **Invoke** directly; instead, you should use the dispatch interface creation functions **CreateStdDispatch** and **DispInvoke**. For details, refer to "**CreateStdDispatch**" and "**DispInvoke**" in this chapter, and "Creating the IDispatch Interface" in Chapter 2.

However, if you need to perform some application-specific processing before calling a member, your code should perform the necessary actions and then call **ITypeInfo::Invoke** to invoke the member. **ITypeInfo::Invoke** acts exactly like **IDispatch::Invoke**. In fact, the standard implementations of **IDispatch::Invoke** that are created by **CreateStdDispatch** and **DispInvoke** defer to **ITypeInfo::Invoke**.

In an OLE Automation controller, use **IDispatch::Invoke** to get and set the values of properties or to call a method of an OLE Automation object. The *dispidMember* argument identifies the member to invoke. The dispatch IDs that identify members are defined by the implementor of the object, and can be determined by using the object's documentation, the **IDispatch::GetIDsOfNames** function, or the **ITypeInfo** interface.

Except as noted, the information that follows addresses developers of OLE Automation controllers. Nevertheless, if you're writing code that exposes OLE Automation objects, you should be familiar with all this information, because it describes the behavior that users of your exposed objects will expect.

Calling a Method with No Arguments

The simplest use of **Invoke** is to call a method that has no arguments. You need only pass the dispatch ID of the method, a locale ID, the DISPATCH_METHOD flag, and an empty DISPPARAMS stucture. For example:

```
HRESULT hresult;
IUnknown FAR* punk;
IDispatch FAR* pdisp = (IDispatch FAR*)NULL;
OLECHAR FAR* szMember = "simple";
DISPID dispid;
DISPPARAMS dispparamsNoArgs = {NULL, NULL, 0, 0};

hresult = CoCreateInstance(CLSID_CMyObject, NULL, CLSCTX_SERVER,
                           IID_Unknown, (void FAR* FAR*)&punk);

hresult = punk->QueryInterface(IID_IDispatch,
                (void FAR* FAR*)&pdisp);

hresult = pdisp->GetIDsOfNames(IID_NULL, &szMember, 1,
                               LOCALE_SYSTEM_DEFAULT, &dispid) ;
```

```
hresult = pdisp->Invoke(
        dispid,
        IID_NULL,
        LOCALE_SYSTEM_DEFAULT,
        DISPATCH_METHOD,
        &dispparamsNoArgs, NULL, NULL, NULL);
```

The example invokes a method named Simple on an object of the class CMyObject. First, it calls **CoCreateInstance**, which instantiates the object and returns a pointer to the object's **IUnknown** interface (punk). Next, it calls **QueryInterface**, receiving a pointer to the object's **IDispatch** interface (pdisp), and then uses pdisp to call the object's **GetIDsOfNames** function, passing the string 'Simple' in szMember to get the dispatch ID for the Simple method. With the dispatch ID for Simple in dispid, it calls **Invoke** to invoke the method, specifying DISPATCH_METHOD for the wFlags parameter, and using the system default locale.

To further simplify the code, the example declares a DISPPARAMS structure named dispparamsNoArgs appropriate to an **Invoke** call with no arguments.

Because the Simple method takes no arguments and returns no result, the puArgErr and pvarResult parameters are NULL. In addition, the example passes NULL for pexcepinfo, indicating that it is not prepared to handle exceptions and will handle only HRESULT errors.

Most methods, however, take one or more arguments. To invoke these methods, you must fill in the DISPPARAMS structure, as described in "Passing Parameters."

OLE Automation defines special dispatch IDs for invoking an object's Value (default), _NewEnum, and Evaluate members. See "DISPID" in this chapter for details.

Getting and Setting Properties

Properties are accessed the same way as methods, except that DISPATCH_PROPERTYGET or DISPATCH_PROPERTYPUT is specified instead of DISPATCH_METHOD. Note that some languages can't distinguish between retrieving a property and calling a method; both the DISPATCH_PROPERTYGET and DISPATCH_METHOD flags should be set in this case.

The following example gets the value of a property named On. Assume that the object has been created and its interfaces queried as in the previous example:

```
VARIANT FAR *pvarResult;
//...code omitted for brevity...
szMember = "On";
hresult = pdisp->GetIDsOfNames(IID_NULL, &szMember, 1,
                              LOCALE_SYSTEM_DEFAULT, &dispid) ;
```

```
hresult = pdisp->Invoke(
        dispid,
        IID_NULL,
        LOCALE_SYSTEM_DEFAULT,
        DISPATCH_PROPERTYGET,
        &dispparamsNoArgs, pvarResult, NULL, NULL);
```

As in the previous example, the code calls **GetIDsOfNames** for the dispatch ID of
the On property, then passes the ID to **Invoke**. **Invoke** returns the property's value
in pvarResult. In general, the return value does not have VT_BYREF set.
However, implementors may set this bit and return a pointer to the return value, if
the lifetime of the return value is the same as that of the object.

To change the property's value, the call looks like this:

```
VARIANT FAR *pvarResult;
DISPPARAMS dispparams;

//...Code omitted for brevity...

szMember = "On";
dispparams.rgvarg[0].vt = VT_BOOL;
dispparams.rgvarg[0].bool = FALSE;
dispparams.rgdispidNamedArgs = DISPID_PROPERTYPUT;
dispparams.cArgs = 1;
disparams.cNamedArgs = 1;
hresult = pdisp->GetIDsOfNames(IID_NULL, &szMember, 1,
                                LOCALE_SYSTEM_DEFAULT, &dispid) ;

hresult = pdisp->Invoke(
        dispid,
        IID_NULL,
        LOCALE_SYSTEM_DEFAULT,
        DISPATCH_PROPERTYPUT,
        &dispparams, NULL, NULL, NULL);
```

The new value for the property (the Boolean value False) is passed as an argument
when the On property's put function is invoked. Note that the dispatch ID for the
argument is DISPID_PROPERTYPUT. This special dispatch ID is defined by OLE
Automation to designate the parameter that contains the new value for a property's
put function. The remaining details of the DISPPARAMS structure are described in
the next section, "Passing Parameters."

The DISPATCH_PROPERTYPUT flag in the example above indicates that a property is being set by value. In Visual Basic, the following statement assigns the Value (default) property of YourObj to the property Prop:

```
MyObj.Prop = YourObj
```

This statement should be flagged as a DISPATCH_PROPERTYPUT. Similarly, statements like the following assign the Value property of one object to the Value property of another object:

```
Worksheet.Cell(1,1) = Worksheet.Cell(6,6)
MyDoc.Text1 = YourDoc.Text1
```

These statements result in a PROPERTY_PUT operation on Worksheet.Cell(1,1) and MyDoc.Text1.

Use the DISPATCH_PROPERTYPUTREF flag to indicate a property or data member that should be set by reference. For example, the following Visual Basic statement assigns the pointer to YourObj to the property Prop, and should be flagged as DISPATCH_PROPERTYPUTREF:

```
Set MyObj.Prop = YourObj
```

The Set statement causes a reference assignment, rather than a value assignment.

Note that the right side parameter is always passed by name, and should not be accessed positionally.

Passing Parameters

Arguments to the method or property being invoked are passed in the DISPPARAMS structure. This structure consists of a pointer to an array of arguments represented as variants, a pointer to an array of dispatch IDs for named arguments, and the number of arguments in each array.

```
typedef struct FARSTRUCT tagDISPPARAMS{
    VARIANTARG FAR* rgvarg;            // Array of arguments
    DISPID FAR* rgdispidNamedArgs;    // Dispatch IDs of named arguments
    unsigned int cArgs;               // Number of arguments
    unsigned int cNamedArgs;          // Number of named arguments
} DISPPARAMS;
```

The arguments are passed in the array *rgvarg*[ ], with the number of arguments passed in *cArgs*. Place the arguments in the array from last to first, so *rgvarg*[0] has the last argument and *rgvarg*[*cArgs* −1] has the first argument. The method or property may change the values of elements within the array *rgvarg* only if they have the VT_BYREF flag set; otherwise they should be considered read only.

A dispatch invocation can have named arguments as well as positional arguments. If *cNamedArgs* is 0, all the elements of *rgvarg*[ ] represent positional arguments. If *cNamedArgs* is nonzero, each element of *rgdispidNamedArgs*[ ] contains the DISPID of a named argument, and the value of the argument is in the matching element of *rgvarg*[ ]. The dispatch IDs of the named arguments are always contiguous in *rgdispidNamedArgs*, and their values are in the first *cNamedArgs* elements of *rgvarg*. Named arguments can't be accessed positionally and vice versa.

The DISPID of an argument is its zero-based position in the argument list. For example, the following method takes three arguments:

```
BOOL _export CDECL
CCredit::CheckCredit(BSTR bstrCustomerID,    // DISPID = 0
                     BSTR bstrLenderID,      // DISPID = 1
                     CURRENCY cLoanAmt)      // DISPID = 2
{
... // Code omitted.
}
```

If you include the DISPID with each named argument, you may pass the named arguments to **Invoke** in any order. For example, if a method is to be invoked with two positional arguments, followed by three named arguments (A, B, and C), using the following hypothetical syntax, then *cArgs* would be 5, and *cNamedArgs* would be 3:

object.method("arg1", "arg2", A := "argA", B := "argB", C: = "argC")

The first positional argument would be in *rgvarg*[4]. The second positional argument would be in *rgvarg*[3]. The ordering of named arguments should be immaterial to the **IDispatch** implementation, but these are also generally passed in reverse order. The argument named A would be in *rgvarg*[2], with the DISPID of A in *rgdispidNamedArgs*[2]. The argument named B would be in *rgvarg*[1], with the corresponding DISPID in *rgdispidNamedArgs*[1]. The argument named C would be in *rgvarg*[0], with the DISPID corresponding to C in *rgdispidNamedArgs*[0]. The following diagram illustrates the arrays and their contents.

	0	1	2	3	4
rgvarg	"argC"	"argB"	"argA"	"arg2"	"arg1"
rgdispidNamedArgs	ID of C	ID of B	ID of A		

You can also use **Invoke** on members with optional arguments, but all the optional arguments must be of type VARIANT. As with required arguments, the contents of the argument vector depend on whether the arguments are positional or named. The invoked member must ensure that the arguments are valid; **Invoke** merely passes the DISPPARAMS structure it receives.

Omitting named arguments is straightforward. You simply pass the arguments in *rgvarg* and their DISPIDs in *rgdispidNamedArgs*. To omit the argument named B, in the preceding example, you would set *rgvarg*[0] to the value of C, with its DISPID in *rgdispidNamedArgs*[0]; and *rgvarg*[1] to the value of A, with its DISPID in *rgdispidNamedArgs*[1]. The subsequent positional arguments would occupy elements 2 and 3 of the arrays. In this case, *cArgs* is 4, and *cNamedArgs* is 2.

If the arguments are positional (unnamed), set *cArgs* to the total number of possible arguments, *cNamedArgs* to zero, and pass VT_ERROR as the type of the omitted arguments, and DISP_E_PARAMNOTFOUND as the value. For example, the following code invokes ShowMe (,1):

```
VARIANT FAR *pvarResult;
EXCEPINFO FAR *pExcepinfo;
unsigned int FAR *puArgErr;
DISPPARAMS dispparams;

//...Code omitted for brevity...

szMember = "ShowMe";
hresult = pdisp->GetIDsOfNames(IID_NULL, &szMember, 1,
                               LOCALE_SYSTEM_DEFAULT, &dispid) ;
dispparams.rgvarg[0].vt = VT_I2;
dispparams.rgvarg[0].ival = 1;
dispparams.rgvarg[1].vt = VT_ERROR;
dispparams.rgvarg[1].scode = DISP_E_PARAMNOTFOUND;
dispparams.cArgs = 2;
disparams.cNamedArgs = 0;

hresult = pdisp->Invoke(
        dispid,
        IID_NULL,
        LOCALE_SYSTEM_DEFAULT,
        DISPATCH_METHOD,
        &dispparams, pvarResult, pExcepinfo, puArgErr);
```

The example takes two positional arguments, but omits the first. Therefore, *rgvarg*[0] contains 1, the value of the last argument in the argument list, and *rgvarg*[1] contains VT_ERROR and the error scode, indicating the omitted first argument.

The calling code is responsible for releasing all strings and objects referred to by *rgvarg*[ ] or placed in **pvarResult*. As with other parameters that are passed by value, if the invoked member must maintain access to a string after returning, the string should be copied. Similarly, if the member needs access to a passed object pointer after returning, it must call **AddRef** on the object. A common example occurs when an object property is changed to refer to a new object, using the DISPATCH_PROPERTYPUTREF flag.

For those implementing **IDispatch::Invoke**, OLE Automation provides the **DispGetParam** function to retrieve parameters from the argument vector and coerce them to the proper type. See "**DispGetParam**," later in this chapter, for details.

Indexed Properties

When you invoke indexed properties of any dimension, you need to pass the indexes as additional arguments. To set an indexed property, place the new value in the first element of the *rgvarg*[ ] vector, and the indexes in the subsequent elements. To get an indexed property, pass the indexes in the first *n* elements of *rgvarg* and the number of indexes in *cArg*. **Invoke** returns the value of the property in *pvarResult*.

OLE Automation stores array data in column-major order, which is the same ordering scheme used by Visual Basic and FORTRAN, but different from C, C++, and Pascal. If you're programming in C, C++, or Pascal, you need to pass the indexes in the reverse order. The following example shows how to fill the DISPPARAMS structure in C++:

```
dispparams.rgvarg[0].vt = VT_I2;
dispparams.rgvarg[0].iVal = 99;
dispparams.rgvarg[1].vt = VT_I2;
dispparams.rgvarg[1].iVal = 2;
dispparams.rgvarg[2].vt = VT_I2;
dispparams.rgvarg[2].iVal = 1;
dispparams.rgdispidNamedArgs = DISPID_PROPERTYPUT;
dispparams.cArgs = 3;
disparams.cNamedArgs = 1;
```

The example changes the value of Prop[1,2] to 99. The new property value is passed in *rgvarg*[0]. The rightmost index is passed in *rgvarg*[1], and the next index in *rgvarg*[2]. The *cArgs* field specifies the number of elements of *rgvarg*[ ] that contain data, and *cNamedArgs* is 1, indicating the new value for the property.

Property collections are an extension of this feature.

Raising Exceptions During Invoke

When you implement **IDispatch::Invoke**, you can choose to communicate errors either through the normal return value or by raising an exception. An exception is a special situation that is normally dealt with by jumping to the nearest enclosing exception handler.

To raise an exception, **IDispatch::Invoke** returns DISP_E_EXCEPTION and fills the structure passed through *pexcepinfo* with information about the cause of the exception or error. You can use the information to understand the cause of the exception and deal with it as necessary.

The exception information structure includes an error code number which identifies the kind of exception, a string which describes the error in a human-readable way, and a Help file and Help context number which can be passed to Windows Help for details about the error. At a minimum, the error code number must be filled in with a valid number.

If you consider **IDispatch** as another way to call C++ style methods in an interface, EXCEPINFO models the throwing of an exception or **longjmp()** call by such a method.

Returning Errors

Invoke returns DISP_E_MEMBERNOTFOUND if one of the following conditions occurs:

- A member or parameter with the specified DISPID and matching *cArgs* can't be found, and the parameter is not optional.
- The member is a void function and the caller didn't set *pvarResult* to NULL.
- The member is a read-only property and the caller set *wFlags* to DISPATCH_PROPERTYPUT or DISPATCH_PROPERTYPUTREF.

If **Invoke** finds the member, but uncovers errors in the argument list, it returns one of several other errors. DISP_E_BAD_PARAMCOUNT means that the DISPPARAMS structure contains an incorrect number of parameters for the property or method. DISP_E_NONAMEDARGS means that **Invoke** received named arguments, but they are not supported by this member.

DISP_E_PARAMNOTFOUND means that the correct number of parameters was passed, but the dispatch ID for one or more parameters was incorrect. If **Invoke** can't convert one of the arguments to the desired type, it returns DISP_E_TYPEMISMATCH. In these two cases, if it can identify which argument is incorrect, **Invoke** sets **puArgErr* to the index within *rgvarg* of the argument with the error. For example, if an OLE Automation method expects a reference to a double-precision number as an argument, but receives a reference to an integer, the argument should be coerced. However, if the method receives a date, **IDispatch::Invoke** returns DISP_E_TYPEMISMATCH and sets **puArgErr* to the index of the integer in the argument array.

OLE Automation provides functions to perform standard conversions of VARIANT, and these should be used for consistent operation. Only when these functions fail is DISP_E_TYPEMISMATCH returned. For more information on converting arguments, see Chapter 6, "Data Manipulation Functions."

Example   This code from the Lines sample file LINES.CPP implements the **Invoke** member function for the CLines class:

```
STDMETHODIMP
CLines::Invoke(
        DISPID dispidMember,
        REFIID riid,
        LCID lcid,
        WORD wFlags,
        DISPPARAMS FAR* pdispparams,
        VARIANT FAR* pvarResult,
        EXCEPINFO FAR* pexcepinfo,
        UINT FAR* puArgErr)
{
    HRESULT hr;

    m_bRaiseException = FALSE;
    hr = DispInvoke(
        this, m_ptinfo,
        dispidMember, wFlags, pdispparams,
        pvarResult, pexcepinfo, puArgErr);
    if (m_bRaiseException)
    {
        if (NULL != pexcepinfo)
        _fmemcpy(pexcepinfo, &m_excepinfo, sizeof(EXCEPINFO));
        return ResultFromScode(DISP_E_EXCEPTION);
    }
    else return hr;
}
```

This code calls the CLine **Invoke** member function to get the value of the Color property:

```
HRESULT hr;
EXCEPINFO excepinfo;
UINT nArgErr;
VARIANT vRet;
DISPPARAMS FAR * pdisp;
OLECHAR FAR* szMember;
DISPPARAMS dispparamsNoArgs = {NULL, NULL, 0, 0};

// Initialization code omitted for brevity.
szMember = "Color";
hr = pdisp->GetIDsOfNames(IID_NULL, &szMember, 1, LOCALE_SYSTEM_DEFAULT,
    &dispid);
```

```
// Get Color property.
hr = pdisp->Invoke(dispid, IID_NULL, LOCALE_SYSTEM_DEFAULT,
    DISPATCH_PROPERTYGET, &dispparams, &vRet, &excepinfo, &nArgErr);
```

See Also   **CreateStdDispatch, DispInvoke, DispGetParam, ITypeInfo::Invoke**

Dispatch Interface Creation Functions

Implemented by	Used by	Header filename	Import library name
OLEAUT32.DLL (32-bit systems)	Applications that expose programmable objects.	OLEAUTO.H	OLEAUT32.LIB
OLE2DISP.DLL (16-bit systems)		DISPATCH.H	OLE2DISP.LIB

These functions simplify the creation of IDispatch interfaces.

CreateDispTypeInfo

HRESULT CreateDispTypeInfo (*pInterfacedata, lcid, pptinfo*)
INTERFACEDATA *pInterfacedata*
LCID *lcid*
ITypeInfo FAR* FAR* *pptinfo*

Creates simplified type information for use in an implementation of **IDispatch**.

Parameters   *pInterfacedata*
      The interface description that this type information describes.

lcid
      The locale ID (LCID) for the names used in the type information.

pptinfo
      On return, pointer to a pointer to a type information implementation for use in
      DispGetIDsOfNames and **DispInvoke**.

Return Value   The SCODE obtained from the returned HRESULT is one of the following:

SCODE	Meaning
S_OK	The interface is supported.
E_INVALIDARG	Either the interface description or the locale ID is invalid.
E_OUTOFMEMORY	Insufficient memory to complete operation.

Comments

Type information may be constructed at run time using **CreateDispTypeInfo** and an INTERFACEDATA structure that describes the object being exposed.

The type information returned by this function is primarily designed to automate the implementation of **IDispatch**. **CreateDispTypeInfo** doesn't return all the type information described in Chapter 9, "Type Building Interfaces." The argument *pInterfaceData* is not a complete description of an interface. It does not include Help information, comments, optional parameters, and other type information that is useful in different contexts.

The recommended method for providing type information about an object is to describe the object using the Object Description Language (ODL) and to compile the object description into a type library using MkTypLib.

To use type information from a type library, use the **LoadTypeLib** and **GetTypeInfoOfGuid** functions instead of **CreateDispTypeInfo**. For more information, see Chapter 8, "Type Description Interfaces."

Example

The code that follows creates type information from the INTERFACEDATA shown to expose the CCalc object.

```
static METHODDATA NEARDATA rgmdataCCalc[] =
{
      PROPERTY(VALUE,    IMETH_ACCUM,    IDMEMBER_ACCUM,    VT_I4)
    , PROPERTY(ACCUM,    IMETH_ACCUM,    IDMEMBER_ACCUM,    VT_I4)
    , PROPERTY(OPND,     IMETH_OPERAND,  IDMEMBER_OPERAND,  VT_I4)
    , PROPERTY(OP,       IMETH_OPERATOR, IDMEMBER_OPERATOR, VT_I2)
    , METHOD0(EVAL,      IMETH_EVAL,     IDMEMBER_EVAL,     VT_BOOL)
    , METHOD0(CLEAR,     IMETH_CLEAR,    IDMEMBER_CLEAR,    VT_EMPTY)
    , METHOD0(DISPLAY,   IMETH_DISPLAY,  IDMEMBER_DISPLAY,  VT_EMPTY)
    , METHOD0(QUIT,      IMETH_QUIT,     IDMEMBER_QUIT,     VT_EMPTY)
    , METHOD1(BUTTON,    IMETH_BUTTON,   IDMEMBER_BUTTON,   VT_BOOL)
};

INTERFACEDATA NEARDATA g_idataCCalc =
{
    rgmdataCCalc, DIM(rgmdataCCalc)
};

// Use Dispatch Interface creation functions to implement IDispatch
CCalc FAR*
CCalc::Create()
{
    HRESULT hresult;
    CCalc FAR* pcalc;
    CArith FAR* parith;
    ITypeInfo FAR* ptinfo;
    IUnknown FAR* punkStdDisp;
extern INTERFACEDATA NEARDATA g_idataCCalc;
```

```
        if((pcalc = new FAR CCalc()) == NULL)
            return NULL;
        pcalc->AddRef();

        parith = &(pcalc->m_arith);

        // Build a TypeInfo for the functionality on this object that
        // is being exposed for external programmability.
        hresult = CreateDispTypeInfo(
            &g_idataCCalc, LOCALE_SYSTEM_DEFAULT, &ptinfo);
        if(hresult != NOERROR)
            goto LError0;

        // Create an aggregate with an instance of the default
        // implementation of IDispatch that is initialized with our
        // TypeInfo.
        hresult = CreateStdDispatch(
            pcalc,                  // controlling unknown
            parith,            // instance to dispatch on
            ptinfo,            // typeinfo describing the instance
            &punkStdDisp);

        ptinfo->Release();

        if(hresult != NOERROR)
            goto LError0;

        pcalc->m_punkStdDisp = punkStdDisp;

        return pcalc;

LError0:;
    pcalc->Release();
    return NULL;
}
```

CreateStdDispatch

HRESULT CreateStdDispatch (*punkOuter, pvThis, ptinfo, ppunkStdDisp*)
IUnknown FAR* *punkOuter*
void FAR* *pvThis*
ITypeInfo FAR* *ptinfo*
IUnknown FAR* FAR* *ppunkStdDisp*

Creates a standard implementation of the **IDispatch** interface through a single function call. This simplifies exposing objects through OLE Automation.

Parameters

punkOuter
    Pointer to the object's **IUnknown** implementation.

pvThis
    Pointer to the object to expose.

ptinfo
    Pointer to the type information that describes the exposed object.

ppunkStdDisp
    Pointer to the location where the implementation of the **IDispatch** interface for this object is returned. This pointer is NULL if the function fails.

Return Value

The SCODE obtained from the returned HRESULT is one of the following:

SCODE	Meaning
S_OK	Success.
E_INVALIDARG	One of the first three arguments is invalid.
E_OUTOFMEMORY	There was insufficient memory to complete the operation.

Comments

You can use **CreateStdDispatch** when you create an object instead of implementing the **IDispatch** member functions for the object. The implementation that **CreateStdDispatch** creates has these limitations:

- Supports only one national language
- Supports only dispatch-defined exception codes returned from **Invoke**

LoadTypeLib, **GetTypeInfoOfGuid**, and **CreateStdDispatch** comprise the minimum set of functions you need to cal l to expose an object using a type library. For more information on **LoadTypeLib** and **GetTypeInfoOfGuid**, see Chapter 8, "Type Description Interfaces."

CreateDispTypeInfo and **CreateStdDispatch** comprise the minimum set of dispatch components you need to call to expose an object using type information provided by the INTERFACEDATA structure.

Example

The following code implements the **IDispatch** interface for the CCalc class using **CreateStdDispatch**.

```
CCalc FAR*
CCalc::Create()
{
    HRESULT hresult;
    CCalc FAR* pcalc;
    CArith FAR* parith;
    ITypeInfo FAR* ptinfo;
    IUnknown FAR* punkStdDisp;
```

```
        extern INTERFACEDATA NEARDATA g_idataCCalc;

    if((pcalc = new FAR CCalc()) == NULL)
        return NULL;
    pcalc->AddRef();

    parith = &(pcalc->m_arith);

    // Build a TypeInfo for the functionality on this object that
    // is being exposing for external programmability.
    hresult = CreateDispTypeInfo(
        &g_idataCCalc, LOCALE_SYSTEM_DEFAULT, &ptinfo);
    if(hresult != NOERROR)
        goto LError0;

    // Create an aggregate with an instance of the default
    // implementation of IDispatch that is initialized with our
    // TypeInfo.
    hresult = CreateStdDispatch(
        pcalc,                  // controlling unknown
        parith,              // instance to dispatch on
        ptinfo,              // typeinfo describing the instance
    &punkStdDisp);

    ptinfo->Release();

    if(hresult != NOERROR)
        goto LError0;

    pcalc->m_punkStdDisp = punkStdDisp;

    return pcalc;

LError0:;
    pcalc->Release();
    return NULL;
}
```

DispGetIDsOfNames

HRESULT DispGetIDsOfNames (*ptinfo, rgszNames, cNames, rgdispid*)
ITypeInfo * *ptinfo*
OLECHAR FAR* FAR* *rgszNames*
unsigned int *cNames*
DISPID FAR* *rgdispid*

Uses type information to convert a set of names to DISPIDs. This is the recommended implementation of **IDispatch::GetIDsOfNames**.

Parameters

ptinfo

Pointer to the type information for an interface. Note that this type information is specific to one interface and language code, so it is not necessary to pass an IID or LCID to this function.

rgszNames

An array of name strings, which can be the same array passed to **DispInvoke** in the DISPPARAMS structure. If *cNames* is greater than one, the first name is interpreted as a method name and subsequent names are interpreted as parameters to that method.

cNames

The number of elements in *rgszNames*.

rgdispid

Pointer to an array of DISPIDs to be filled in by this function. The first ID corresponds to the method name; subsequent IDs are interpreted as parameters to the method.

Return Value

The SCODE obtained from the returned HRESULT is one of the following:

SCODE	Meaning
S_OK	The interface is supported.
E_INVALIDARG	One of the arguments is invalid.
DISP_E_UNKNOWNNAME	One or more of the given names were not known. The returned array of DISPIDs will contain DISPID_UNKNOWN for each entry that corresponds to an unknown name.
Other returns	Any of the **ITypeInfo::Invoke** errors may also be returned.

Example

This code from the Lines sample file POINTS.CPP implements the member function **GetIDsOfNames** for the CPoints class using **DispGetIDsOfNames**.

```
STDMETHODIMP
CPoints::GetIDsOfNames(
        REFIID riid,
        char FAR* FAR* rgszNames,
        UINT cNames,
        LCID lcid,
        DISPID FAR* rgdispid)
{
    return DispGetIDsOfNames(m_ptinfo, rgszNames, cNames, rgdispid);
}
```

See Also

CreateStdDispatch, **IDispatch::GetIDsOfNames**

DispGetParam

HRESULT DispGetParam(*dispparams, iPosition, vt, pvarResult, puArgErr*)
DISPPARAMS FAR* *dispparams*
unsigned int *iPosition*
VARTYPE *vt*
VARIANT FAR* *pvarResult*
unsigned int FAR* *puArgErr*

Retrieves a parameter from the DISPPARAMS structure, checking both named parameters and positional parameters, and coerces it to the specified type.

Parameters

dispparams
Pointer to the parameters passed to **IDispatch::Invoke**.

iPosition
The position of the parameter in the parameter list. **DispGetParam** starts at the end of the array, so if *iPosition* is 0, the last parameter in the array is returned.

vt
The type to which the argument should be coerced.

pvarResult
Pointer to the variant into which to pass the parameter.

puArgErr
On return, pointer to the index of the argument that caused a DISP_E_TYPEMISMATCH error. This pointer should be returned to **Invoke** to indicate the position of the argument in DISPPARAMS that caused the error.

Return Value

The SCODE obtained from the HRESULT is one of the following:

SCODE	Meaning
S_OK	Success.
DISP_E_BADVARTYPE	The variant type *vt* is not supported.
DISP_E_OVERFLOW	The retrieved parameter could not be coerced to the specified type.
DISP_E_PARAMNOTFOUND	The parameter indicated by *iPosition* could not be found.
DISP_E_TYPEMISMATCH	The argument could not be coerced to the specified type.
E_INVALIDARG	One of the arguments was invalid.
E_OUTOFMEMORY	Insufficient memory to complete operation.

Comments

The output parameter *pvarResult* must be a valid VARIANT; any existing contents will be released in the standard way. The contents of the VARIANT should be freed with **VariantFree**.

If **DispGetParam** is used to get the right side of a property put operation, the second parameter should be DISPID_PROPERTYPUT. For example:

```
DispGetParam(&dispparams, DISPID_PROPERTYPUT, VT_BOOL, &varResult)
```

Note also that named parameters can't be accessed positionally, and vice versa.

Example

The following example uses **DispGetParam** to set X and Y properties:

```
STDMETHODIMP
CPoint::Invoke(
    DISPID dispidMember,
    REFIID riid,
    LCID lcid,
    unsigned short wFlags,
    DISPPARAMS FAR* pdispparams,
    VARIANT FAR* pvarResult,
    EXCEPINFO FAR* pexcepinfo,
    unsigned int FAR* puArgErr)
{
    unsigned int uArgErr;
    HRESULT hresult;
    VARIANTARG varg0;
    VARIANT varResultDummy;

    UNUSED(lcid);
    UNUSED(pexcepinfo);

    // Make sure the wFlags are legal
    if(wFlags & ~(DISPATCH_METHOD | DISPATCH_PROPERTYGET |
        DISPATCH_PROPERTYPUT | DISPATCH_PROPERTYPUTREF))
        return ResultFromScode(E_INVALIDARG);

    // This object only exposes a "default" interface.
    if(!IsEqualIID(riid, IID_NULL))
        return ResultFromScode(DISP_E_UNKNOWNINTERFACE);
```

```
                    // It simplifies the following code if the caller
                    // ignores the return value.
                    if(puArgErr == NULL)
                        puArgErr = &uArgErr;
                    if(pvarResult == NULL)
                        pvarResult = &varResultDummy;

                    VariantInit(&varg0);

                    // Assume the return type is void, unless we find otherwise.
                    VariantInit(pvarResult);

                    switch(dispidMember){
                    case IDMEMBER_CPOINT_GETX:
                        V_VT(pvarResult) = VT_I2;
                        V_I2(pvarResult) = GetX();
                        break;

                    case IDMEMBER_CPOINT_SETX:
                        hresult = DispGetParam(pdispparams, 0, VT_I2, &varg0, puArgErr);
                        if(hresult != NOERROR)
                            return hresult;
                        SetX(V_I2(&varg0));
                        break;

                    case IDMEMBER_CPOINT_GETY:
                        V_VT(pvarResult) = VT_I2;
                        V_I2(pvarResult) = GetY();
                        break;

                    case IDMEMBER_CPOINT_SETY:
                        hresult = DispGetParam(pdispparams, 0, VT_I2, &varg0, puArgErr);
                        if(hresult != NOERROR)
                        return hresult;
                        SetY(V_I2(&varg0));
                        break;

                    default:
                        return ResultFromScode(DISP_E_MEMBERNOTFOUND);
                    }
                    return NOERROR;
                }
```

See Also   **CreateStdDispatch, IDispatch::Invoke**

DispInvoke

HRESULT DispInvoke(_this, ptinfo, dispidMember, wFlags, pparams, pvarResult, pexcepinfo, puArgErr**)**
void FAR* _this
ITypeInfo FAR* ptinfo
DISPID dispidMember
unsigned short wFlags
DISPPARAMS FAR* pparams
VARIANT FAR* pvarResult
EXCEPINFO pexcepinfo
unsigned int FAR* puArgErr

Automatically calls member functions on an interface, given type information for the interface. You can describe an interface with type information and implement **IDispatch::Invoke** for the interface using this single call.

Parameters

_this
Pointer to an implementation of the **IDispatch** interface described by ptinfo.

ptinfo
Pointer to the type information describing the interface.

dispidMember
Identifies the member. Use **GetIDsOfNames** or the object's documentation to obtain the dispatch ID.

wFlags
Flags describing the context of the **Invoke** call, as follows:

Value	Description
DISPATCH_METHOD	The member is being invoked as a method. If a property has the same name, both this and the DISPATCH_PROPERTYGET flag may be set.
DISPATCH_PROPERTYGET	The member is being retrieved as a property or data member.
DISPATCH_PROPERTYPUT	The member is being changed as a property or data member.
DISPATCH_PROPERTYPUTREF	The member is being changed via a reference assignment, rather than a value assignment. This flag is valid only when the property accepts a reference to an object.

pparams
> Pointer to a structure containing an array of arguments, an array of argument dispatch IDs for named arguments, and counts for number of elements in the arrays.

pvarResult
> Pointer to where the result is to be stored, or NULL if the caller expects no result. This argument is ignored if DISPATCH_PROPERTYPUT or DISPATCH_PROPERTYPUTREF is specified.

pexcepinfo
> Pointer to a structure containing exception information. This structure should be filled in if DISP_E_EXCEPTION is returned.

puArgErr
> The index within *rgvarg* of the first argument that has an error. Arguments are stored in *pdispparams->rgvarg* in reverse order, so the first argument is the one with the highest index in the array. This parameter is returned only when the resulting SCODE is DISP_E_TYPEMISMATCH or DISP_E_PARAMNOTFOUND.

Return Value

The SCODE obtained from the returned HRESULT is one of the following:

SCODE	Meaning
S_OK	Success.
DISP_E_BADPARAMCOUNT	The number of elements provided in DISPPARAMS is different from the number of arguments accepted by the method or property.
DISP_E_BADVARTYPE	One of the arguments in DISPPARAMS is not a valid variant type.
DISP_E_EXCEPTION	The application needs to raise an exception. In this case, the structure passed in *pexcepinfo* should be filled in.
DISP_E_MEMBERNOTFOUND	The requested member does not exist.
DISP_E_NONAMEDARGS	This implementation of **IDispatch** does not support named arguments.
DISP_E_OVERFLOW	One of the arguments in DISPPARAMS could not be coerced to the specified type.
DISP_E_PARAMNOTFOUND	One of the parameter IDs does not correspond to a parameter on the method. In this case *puArgErr* is set to the first argument that contains the error.
DISP_E_PARAMNOTOPTIONAL	A required parameter was omitted.

SCODE	Meaning
DISP_E_TYPEMISMATCH	One or more of the arguments could not be coerced. The index within *rgvarg* of the first parameter with the incorrect type is returned in *puArgErr*.
E_INVALIDARG	One of the arguments is invalid.
E_OUTOFMEMORY	Insufficient memory to complete operation.
Other returns	Any of the **ITypeInfo::Invoke** errors may also be returned.

Comments

The parameter _this is a pointer to an implementation of the interface being deferred to. **DispInvoke** builds a stack frame, coerces parameters using standard coercion rules, pushes them on the stack, and calls the correct member function in the virtual function table (VTBL).

Example

The following code from the Lines sample file LINES.CPP implements **IDispatch::Invoke** using **DispInvoke**. This function uses `m_bRaiseException` to signal that an error occurred during the **DispInvoke** call.

```
STDMETHODIMP
CLines::Invoke(
        DISPID dispidMember,
        REFIID riid,
        LCID lcid,
        WORD wFlags,
        DISPPARAMS FAR* pdispparams,
        VARIANT FAR* pvarResult,
        EXCEPINFO FAR* pexcepinfo,
        UINT FAR* puArgErr)
{
    HRESULT hr;

    if (NULL == pexcepinfo)
        return ResultFromScode(E_INVALIDARG);

    m_bRaiseException = FALSE;
    hr = DispInvoke(
        this, m_ptinfo,
        dispidMember, wFlags, pdispparams,
        pvarResult, pexcepinfo, puArgErr);
    if (m_bRaiseException)
    {
        _fmemcpy(pexcepinfo, &m_excepinfo, sizeof(EXCEPINFO));
        return ResultFromScode(DISP_E_EXCEPTION);
    }
    else return hr;
}
```

See Also

CreateStdDispatch, IDispatch::Invoke

Active Object Registration Functions

Implemented by	Used by	Header filename	Import library name
OLEAUT32.DLL (32-bit systems) OLE2DISP.DLL (16-bit systems)	Applications that expose or access programmable objects.	OLEAUTO.H DISPATCH.H	OLEAUT32.LIB OLE2DISP.LIB

These functions let you identify a running instance of an object. Because they use the OLE object table (**GetRunningObjectTable**), they also require either OLE32.DLL (for 32-bit systems) or OLE2.DLL (for 16-bit systems).

When an application is started with the **/Automation** switch, it should initialize its Application object as the active object by calling **RegisterActiveObject** after it initializes OLE.

Applications may also initialize other top-level objects as the active object. For example, an application that exposes a Document object may want to let OLE Automation controllers retrieve and modify the currently active document.

For more information on initializing the active object, see Chapter 2, "Exposing OLE Automation Objects."

GetActiveObject

HRESULT GetActiveObject(*rclsid*, *pvreserved*, *ppunk*)
REFCLSID *rclsid*
void FAR* *pvreserved*
IUnknown FAR* FAR* *ppunk*

Retrieves a pointer to a running application initialized with OLE.

Parameters

rclsid
> Pointer to the class ID of the active object from the OLE registration database.

pvreserved
> Reserved for future use. Must be NULL.

ppunk
> On return, a pointer to the requested active object.

Return Value   The SCODE obtained from the returned HRESULT is one of the following:

SCODE	Meaning
S_OK	Success
Other returns	Failure

RegisterActiveObject

HRESULT RegisterActiveObject (*punk, rclsid, pvreserved, pdwRegister*)
IUnknown FAR* *punk*
REFCLSID *rclsid*
DWORD *dwFlags*
unsigned long FAR* *pdwRegister*

Registers an object as the active object for its class.

Parameters   *punk*
Pointer to the **IUnknown** interface of the active object.

rclsid
Pointer to the class ID of the active object.

dwFlags
Flags controlling registration of the object. Possible values are
ACTIVEOBJECT_STRONG and ACTIVEOBJECT_WEAK.

pdwRegister
On return, pointer to a handle. You must pass this handle to
RevokeActiveObject to end the object's status as active.

Return Value   The SCODE obtained from the returned HRESULT is one of the following:

SCODE	Meaning
S_OK	Success
Other returns	Failure

Comments   The **RegisterActiveObject** function registers the object to which *punk* points as
the active object for the class denoted by *rclsid*. Registration causes the object to be
listed in OLE's running object table, a globally accessible lookup table that keeps
track of the objects that are currently running on your computer. (See the *OLE
Programmer's Guide and Reference* for more information on the running object
table.) The *dwFlags* parameter specifies the strength or weakness of the
registration, which affects the way the object is shut down.

In general, OLE Automation objects should behave in the following manner:

- If the object is visible, it should shut down only in response to an explicit user command (such as the Exit command from the File menu), or to the equivalent command from an OLE Automation controller (invoking the Quit or Exit method on the Application object).

- If the object is not visible, it should shut down only when the last external connection to it disappears.

Strong registration performs an **AddRef** on the object, thereby incrementing the reference count of the object (and its associated stub) in the running object table. A strongly registered object must be explicitly revoked from the table with **RevokeActiveObject**. Strong registration (ACTIVEOBJECT_STRONG) is the default.

Weak registration keeps a pointer to the object in the running object table, but does not increment the reference count. Consequently, when the last external connection to a weakly registered object disappears, OLE releases the object's stub and the object itself is no longer available.

To ensure the desired behavior, you must consider not only OLE's default actions, but also the following:

- Even though your code creates an invisible object, the object may become visible at some later time. Once the object is visible, it should remain visible and active until it receives an explicit command to shut down, which may occur after references from your code disappear.

- Other OLE Automation controllers may be using the object. If so, your code should not force the object to shut down.

To avoid possible conflicts, OLE Automation objects should always register with ACTIVEOBJECT_WEAK, and call **CoLockObjectExternal** when necessary to guarantee that the object remains active. **CoLockObjectExternal** adds a strong lock, thereby preventing the object's reference count from reaching zero. For detailed information on this function, refer to the *OLE Programmer's Guide and Reference*.

Most commonly, objects need to call **CoLockObjectExternal** when they become visible, so that they remain active until the user requests shutdown.

▶ **To shut down correctly, your code should follow these steps**

1. When the object becomes visible, make the following call to add a lock on behalf of the user:

```
CoLockObjectExternal(punk, TRUE, TRUE)
```

The lock should remain in effect until the user explicitly requests shutdown, such as with a Quit or Exit command.

2. When the user requests shutdown, call **CoLockObjectExternal** again to free the lock, as follows:

```
CoLockObjectExternal(punk, FALSE, TRUE)
```

3. Call **RevokeActiveObject** to make the object inactive.

4. To end all connections from remote processes, call **CoDisconnectObject** as follows:

```
CoDisconnectObject(punk, 0)
```

This function is described in the *OLE Programmer's Guide and Reference*.

RevokeActiveObject

HRESULT RevokeActiveObject (*dwRegister, pvreserved*)
unsigned long *dwRegister*
void FAR* *pvreserved*

Ends an object's status as active.

Parameters

dwRegister
A handle previously returned by **RegisterActiveObject**.

pvreserved
Reserved for future use. Must be NULL.

Return Value

The SCODE obtained from the returned HRESULT is one of the following:

SCODE	Meaning
S_OK	Success
Other returns	Failure

IEnumVARIANT Interface

Implemented by	Used by	Header filename
Applications that expose collections of objects.	Applications that access collections of objects.	OLEAUTO.H (32-bit systems) DISPATCH.H (16-bit systems)

The **IEnumVARIANT** interface provides a method for enumerating a collection of variants, including heterogeneous collections of objects and intrinsic types. Callers of this interface need not know the specific type, or types, of the elements in the collection.

The following is the definition that results from expanding the parameterized type **IEnumVARIANT**:

```
interface IEnumVARIANT : IUnknown {
   virtual HRESULT Next(unsigned long celt,
                        VARIANT FAR* rgvar,
                        unsigned long FAR* pceltFetched) = 0;
   virtual HRESULT Skip(unsigned long celt) = 0;
   virtual HRESULT Reset() = 0;
   virtual HRESULT Clone(IEnumVARIANT FAR* FAR* ppenum) = 0;
   };
```

See the sample file ENUMVAR.CPP in the Lines sample to see how to implement a collection of objects using **IEnumVARIANT**.

IEnumVARIANT::Clone

HRESULT IEnumVARIANT::Clone(*ppenum*)
IEnumVARIANT FAR* FAR* *ppenum*

Creates a copy of the current enumeration state.

Parameter

ppenum
   On return, pointer to the location of the clone enumerator.

Return Value

The SCODE obtained from the returned HRESULT is one of the following:

SCODE	Meaning
S_OK	Success.
E_OUTOFMEMORY	Insufficient memory to complete the operation.

Comments

Using this function, you can record a particular point in the enumeration sequence, then return to it at a later time. The enumerator returned is of the same actual interface as the one that is being cloned.

There is no guarantee that exactly the same set of variants will be enumerated the second time as was enumerated the first. Although an exact duplicate is desirable, the outcome depends on the collection being enumerated. Some collections (for example, an enumeration of the files in a directory) will find it impractical to maintain this condition.

Example

The following code implements **IEnumVariant::Clone** for collections in the Lines sample (ENUMVAR.CPP):

```
STDMETHODIMP
CEnumVariant::Clone(IEnumVARIANT FAR* FAR* ppenum)
{
    CEnumVariant FAR* penum = NULL;
    HRESULT hr;

    *ppenum = NULL;

    hr = CEnumVariant::Create(m_psa, m_cElements, &penum);
    if (FAILED(hr))
        goto error;
    penum->AddRef();
    penum->m_lCurrent = m_lCurrent;

    *ppenum = penum;
    return NOERROR;

error:
    if (penum)
        penum->Release();
    return hr;
}
```

IEnumVARIANT::Next

HRESULT IEnumVARIANT::Next(*celt, rgvar, pceltFetched*)
unsigned long *celt*
VARIANT FAR* *rgvar*
unsigned long FAR* *pceltFetched*

Attempts to get the next *celt* items in the enumeration sequence and return them through the array pointed to by *rgvar*.

Parameters

celt
> The number of elements to be returned.

rgvar
> An array of at least size *celt* in which the elements are to be returned.

pceltFetched
> Pointer to the number of elements returned in *rgvar*, or NULL.

Return Value

The SCODE obtained from the returned HRESULT is one of the following:

SCODE	Meaning
S_OK	The number of elements returned is *celt*.
S_FALSE	The number of elements returned is less than *celt*.

Comments

If fewer than the requested number of elements remain in the sequence, return only the remaining elements; the actual number of elements returned is passed through **pceltFetched* (unless it is NULL).

Example

The following code implements **IEnumVariant::Next** for collections in the Lines sample (ENUMVAR.CPP):

```
STDMETHODIMP
CEnumVariant::Next(ULONG cElements, VARIANT FAR* pvar, ULONG FAR*
pcElementFetched)
{
    HRESULT hr;
    ULONG l;
    long l1;
    ULONG l2;

    if (pcElementFetched != NULL)
        *pcElementFetched = 0;

    for (l=0; l<cElements; l++)
        VariantInit(&pvar[l]);

    // Retrieve the next cElements elements.
    for (l1=m_lCurrent, l2=0; l1<(long)(m_lLBound+m_cElements) &&
        l2<cElements; l1++, l2++)
    {
        hr = SafeArrayGetElement(m_psa, &l1, &pvar[l2]);
        if (FAILED(hr))
            goto error;
    }
    // Set count of elements retrieved
    if (pcElementFetched != NULL)
        *pcElementFetched = l2;
    m_lCurrent = l1;
```

```
        return  (12 < cElements) ? ResultFromScode(S_FALSE) : NOERROR;

error:
    for (l=0; l<cElements; l++)
        VariantClear(&pvar[l]);
    return hr;
}
```

IEnumVARIANT::Reset

HRESULT IEnumVARIANT::Reset()

Resets the enumeration sequence to the beginning.

Return Value
The SCODE obtained from the returned HRESULT is one of the following:

SCODE	Meaning
S_OK	Success
S_FALSE	Failure

Comments
There is no guarantee that exactly the same set of variants will be enumerated the second time as was enumerated the first. Although an exact duplicate is desirable, the outcome depends on the collection being enumerated. Some collections (for example, an enumeration of the files in a directory) will find it impractical to maintain this condition.

Example
The following code implements **IEnumVariant::Reset** for collections in the Lines sample (ENUMVAR.CPP):

```
STDMETHODIMP
CEnumVariant::Reset()
{
    m_lCurrent = m_lLBound;
    return NOERROR;
}
```

IEnumVARIANT::Skip

HRESULT IEnumVARIANT::Skip(*celt*)
unsigned long *celt*

Attempts to skip over the next *celt* elements in the enumeration sequence.

Parameter

celt

    The number of elements to skip.

Return Value

The SCODE obtained from the returned HRESULT is one of the following:

SCODE	Meaning
S_OK	The specified number of elements was skipped.
S_FALSE	The end of the sequence was reached before skipping the requested number of elements.

Example

The following code implements **IEnumVariant::Reset** for collections in the Lines sample (ENUMVAR.CPP):

```
STDMETHODIMP
CEnumVariant::Skip(ULONG cElements)
{
    m_lCurrent += cElements;
    if (m_lCurrent > (long)(m_lLBound+m_cElements))
    {
        m_lCurrent = m_lLBound+m_cElements;
        return ResultFromScode(S_FALSE);
    }
    else return NOERROR;
}
```

CHAPTER 6

Data Manipulation Functions

Data manipulation functions access and manipulate the array, string, and variant data types used by OLE Automation.

Overview of Functions

The data manipulation functions are summarized in the following table.

Category	Function name	Purpose
Array manipulation	**SafeArrayAccessData**	Increments the lock count of an array and returns a pointer to array data.
	SafeArrayAllocData	Allocates memory for a safe array based on a descriptor created with **SafeArrayAllocDescriptor**.
	SafeArrayAllocDescriptor	Allocates memory for a safe array descriptor.
	SafeArrayCopy	Copies an existing array.
	SafeArrayCreate	Creates a new array descriptor.
	SafeArrayDestroy	Destroys an array descriptor.
	SafeArrayDestroyData	Frees memory used by the data elements in a safe array.
	SafeArrayDestroyDescriptor	Frees memory used by a safe array descriptor.
	SafeArrayGetDim	Returns the number of dimensions in an array.
	SafeArrayGetElement	Retrieves an element of an array.
	SafeArrayGetElemsize	Returns the size of an element.
	SafeArrayGetLBound	Retrieves the lower bound for a given dimension.

Category	Function name	Purpose
	SafeArrayGetUBound	Retrieves the upper bound for a given dimension.
	SafeArrayLock	Increments the lock count of an array.
	SafeArrayPtrOfIndex	Returns a pointer to an array element.
	SafeArrayPutElement	Assigns an element into an array.
	SafeArrayRedim	Resizes a safe array.
	SafeArrayUnAccessData	Frees a pointer to array data and decrements the lock count of the array.
	SafeArrayUnlock	Decrements the lock count of an array.
String manipulation	**SysAllocString**	Creates and initializes a string.
	SysAllocStringByteLen	Creates a zero-terminated string of a specified length (32-bit only).
	SysAllocStringLen	Creates a string of a specified length.
	SysFreeString	Frees a previously created string.
	SysReAllocString	Changes the size and value of a string.
	SysReAllocStringLen	Changes the size of an existing string.
	SysStringByteLen	Returns the length of a string in bytes (32-bit only).
	SysStringLen	Returns the length of a string.
Variant manipulation	**VariantChangeType**	Converts a variant to another type.
	VariantChangeTypeEx	Converts a variant to another type using a locale ID.
	VariantClear	Releases resources and sets a variant to VT_EMPTY.
	VariantCopy	Copies a variant.
	VariantCopyInd	Copies variants that may contain a pointer.
	VariantInit	Initializes a variant.
	Low-level conversion functions	Converts specific types of variants to other variant types. These functions are called by **VariantChangeType** and **VariantChangeTypeEx**.

Category	Function name	Purpose
Time conversion	**DosDateTimeToVariantTime**	Converts MS-DOS® date and time representations to a variant time.
	VariantTimeToDosDateTime	Converts a variant time to MS-DOS date and time representations.

Array Manipulation Functions

Implemented by	Used by	Header filename	Import library name
OLEAUT32.DLL (32-bit systems) OLE2DISP.DLL (16-bit systems)	Applications that expose or access programmable objects.	OLEAUTO.H DISPATCH.H	OLEAUT32.LIB OLE2DISP.LIB

The arrays passed by IDispatch::Invoke within VARIANTARGs are called *safe arrays*. Safe arrays contain information about the number of dimensions and bounds within them. When an array is an argument or the return value of a function, the *parray* field of VARIANTARG points to an array descriptor. This array descriptor should not be accessed directly unless you are creating arrays containing elements with nonvariant data types. Instead, use the functions SafeArrayAccessData and SafeArrayUnaccessData to access the data.

The base type of the array is indicated by VT_ tag | VT_ARRAY. The data referenced by an array descriptor is stored in column-major order, which is the same ordering scheme used by Visual Basic and FORTRAN, but different from C and Pascal. *Column-major order* means that the leftmost dimension (as specified in a programming language syntax) changes first.

Following are the definitions of the safe array descriptor and the functions to use when accessing the data in the descriptor and the array itself.

Data Types and Structures

SAFEARRAY

```
typedef struct FARSTRUCT tagSAFEARRAY {
    unsigned short cDims;       // Count of dimensions in this array.
    unsigned short fFeatures;   // Flags used by the SafeArray
                                // routines documented below:
```

```
#if defined(WIN32)
    unsigned long cbElements;       // Size of an element of the array;
                                    // Does not include size of
                                    // pointed-to data.
    unsigned long cLocks;           // Number of times the array has been
                                    // locked without corresponding unlock.
#else
    unsigned short cbElements;
    unsigned short cLocks;
    unsigned long handle;           // Unused but kept for compatibility
#endif
    void HUGEP* pvData;             // Pointer to the data.
    SAFEARRAYBOUND rgsabound[1];    // One bound for each dimension.
} SAFEARRAY;
```

Note that the definition varies, depending on the target operating system platform. On 32-bit Windows systems, both the *cbElements* and *cLocks* parameters are unsigned long integers, and the *handle* parameter is omitted. On 16-bit Windows systems, *cbElements* and *cLocks* are unsigned short integers, and the *handle* parameter has been retained for compatibility with earlier software.

The array *rgsabound* is stored with the leftmost dimension in *rgsabound*[0] and the rightmost dimension in *rgsabound*[*cDims* − 1]. If an array were specified in C-like syntax as a[2][5], it would have two elements in the *rgsabound* vector. Element 0 has an *lLbound* of 0 and a *cElements* of 2. Element 1 has an *lLbound* of 0 and a *cElements* of 5.

The *fFeatures* flags describe attributes of an array that may affect how the array is released. This allows freeing the array without referencing its containing variant. The bits are accessed using the following constants:

```
#define FADF_AUTO       0x0001  // Array is allocated on the stack.
#define FADF_STATIC     0x0002  // Array is statically allocated.
#define FADF_EMBEDDED   0x0004  // Array is embedded in a structure.
#define FADF_FIXEDSIZE  0x0010  // Array may not be resized or
                                // reallocated.
#define FADF_BSTR       0x0100  // An array of BSTRs.
#define FADF_UNKNOWN    0x0200  // An array of IUnknown*.
#define FADF_DISPATCH   0x0400  // An array of IDispatch*.
#define FADF_VARIANT    0x0800  // An array of VARIANTs.
#define FADF_RESERVED   0xF0E8  // Bits reserved for future use.
```

SAFEARRAYBOUND

```
typedef struct tagSAFEARRAYBOUND {
    unsigned long cElements;
    long lLbound;
} SAFEARRAYBOUND;
```

This structure represents the bounds of one dimension of the array. The lower bound of the dimension is represented by *lLbound*, and *cElements* represents the number of elements in the dimension.

SafeArrayAccessData

HRESULT SafeArrayAccessData (*psa, ppvdata*)
SAFEARRAY FAR* *psa*
void HUGEP* FAR* *ppvdata*

Increments the lock count of an array and retrieves a pointer to the array data.

Parameters

psa
Pointer to an array descriptor created by **SafeArrayCreate**.

ppvdata
On exit, pointer to a pointer to the array data. Note that arrays may be larger than 64K, so huge pointers must be used in Windows version 3.1 or later.

Return Value

The SCODE obtained from the returned HRESULT is one of the following:

SCODE	Meaning
S_OK	Success.
E_INVALIDARG	The argument *psa* was not a valid safe array descriptor.
E_UNEXPECTED	The array could not be locked.

SafeArrayAllocData

HRESULT SafeArrayAllocData(*psa*)
SAFEARRAY FAR* *psa*

Allocates memory for a safe array based on a descriptor created with
SafeArrayAllocDescriptor.

Parameters

psa
Pointer to an array descriptor created by **SafeArrayAllocDescriptor**.

Return Value

The SCODE obtained from the returned HRESULT is one of the following:

SCODE	Meaning
S_OK	Success.
E_INVALIDARG	The argument *psa* was not a valid safe array descriptor.
E_UNEXPECTED	The array could not be locked.

Example

The following example creates a safe array using the **SafeArrayAllocDescriptor**
and **SafeArrayAllocData** functions.

```
SAFEARRAY FAR* FAR*ppsa;
unsigned int ndim = 2;
HRESULT hresult = SafeArrayAllocDescriptor( ndim, ppsa );
if( FAILED( hresult ) )
    return ERR_OutOfMemory;
(*ppsa)->rgsabound[ 0 ].lLbound = 0;
(*ppsa)->rgsabound[ 0 ].cElements = 5;
(*ppsa)->rgsabound[ 1 ].lLbound = 1;
(*ppsa)->rgsabound[ 1 ].cElements = 4;
hresult = SafeArrayAllocData( *ppsa );
if( FAILED( hresult ) ) {
    SafeArrayDestroyDescriptor( *ppsa )
    return ERR_OutOfMemory;
}
```

See Also

SafeArrayAllocData, SafeArrayDestroyData, SafeArrayDestroyDescriptor

SafeArrayAllocDescriptor

HRESULT SafeArrayAllocDescriptor(*cDims, ppsaOut*)
unsigned int *cDims*
SAFEARRAY FAR* FAR* *ppsaOut*

Allocates memory for a safe array descriptor.

Parameters

cDims
    The number of dimensions of the array.

ppsaOut
    Pointer to a location in which to store the created array descriptor.

Return Value

The SCODE obtained from the returned HRESULT is one of the following:

SCODE	Meaning
S_OK	Success.
E_INVALIDARG	The argument *psa* was not a valid safe array descriptor.
E_UNEXPECTED	The array could not be locked.

Comments

This function lets you create safe arrays containing elements with data types other than those provided by **SafeArrayCreate**. After creating an array descriptor using **SafeArrayAllocDescriptor**, set the element size in the array descriptor and call **SafeArrayAllocData** to allocate memory for the array elements.

Example

The following example creates a safe array using the **SafeArrayAllocDescriptor** and **SafeArrayAllocData** functions.

```
SAFEARRAY FAR* FAR*ppsa;
unsigned int ndim = 2;
HRESULT hresult = SafeArrayAllocDescriptor( ndim, ppsa );
if( FAILED( hresult ) )
    return ERR_OutOfMemory;
(*ppsa)->rgsabound[ 0 ].lLbound = 0;
(*ppsa)->rgsabound[ 0 ].cElements = 5;
(*ppsa)->rgsabound[ 1 ].lLbound = 1;
(*ppsa)->rgsabound[ 1 ].cElements = 4;
hresult = SafeArrayAllocData( *ppsa );
if( FAILED( hresult ) ) {
    SafeArrayDestroyDescriptor( *ppsa )
    return ERR_OutOfMemory;
}
```

See Also

SafeArrayAllocData, SafeArrayDestroyData, SafeArrayDestroyDescriptor

SafeArrayCopy

HRESULT SafeArrayCopy(*psa, ppsaOut*)
SAFEARRAY FAR* *psa*
SAFEARRAY FAR* FAR* *ppsaOut*

Creates a copy of an existing safe array.

Parameters

psa
    Pointer to an array descriptor created by **SafeArrayCreate**.

ppsaOut
    Pointer to a location in which to return the new array descriptor.

Return Value

The SCODE obtained from the returned HRESULT is one of the following:

SCODE	Meaning
S_OK	Success.
E_INVALIDARG	The argument *psa* was not a valid safe array descriptor.
E_OUTOFMEMORY	Insufficient memory to create the copy.

Comments

SafeArrayCopy calls the string or variant manipulation functions if the array to copy contains either of those data types. If the array being copied contains object references, the reference counts for those objects are incremented.

See Also

SysAllocStringLen, **VariantCopy**, **VariantCopyInd**.

SafeArrayCreate

SAFEARRAY * SafeArrayCreate(*vt, cDims, rgsabound*)
VARTYPE *vt*
unsigned int *cDims*
SAFEARRRAYBOUND FAR* *rgsabound*

Creates a new array descriptor, allocates and initializes the data for the array, and returns a pointer to the new array descriptor.

Parameters

vt

The base type of the array (that is, the VARTYPE of each element of the array). The VARTYPE is restricted to a subset of the variant types. Neither the VT_ARRAY nor the VT_BYREF flag can be set. VT_EMPTY and VT_NULL are not valid base types for the array. All other types are legal.

cDims

Number of dimensions in the array. This can't be changed after the array is created.

rgsabound

Pointer to a vector of bounds (one for each dimension) to allocate for the array.

Return Value

Points to the array descriptor, or NULL if the array could not be created.

Example

```
HRESULT PASCAL __export CPoly::EnumPoints(IEnumVARIANT FAR* FAR* ppenum)
{
    unsigned int i;
    HRESULT hresult;
    VARIANT var;
    SAFEARRAY FAR* psa;
    CEnumPoint FAR* penum;
    POINTLINK FAR* ppointlink;
    SAFEARRAYBOUND rgsabound[1];

    rgsabound[0].lLbound = 0;
    rgsabound[0].cElements = m_cPoints;

    psa = SafeArrayCreate(VT_VARIANT, 1, rgsabound);
    if(psa == NULL){
        hresult = ReportResult(0, E_OUTOFMEMORY, 0, 0);
        goto LError0;
    }
    .
    .   // Code omitted here.
    .
LError0:;
    return hresult;
}
```

SafeArrayDestroy

HRESULT SafeArrayDestroy(*psa***)**
SAFEARRAY FAR* *psa*

Destroys an existing array descriptor and all the data in the array. If objects are stored in the array, **Release** is called on each object in the array.

Parameters

psa
> Pointer to an array descriptor created by **SafeArrayCreate**.

Return Value

The SCODE obtained from the returned HRESULT is one of the following:

SCODE	Meaning
S_OK	Success.
DISP_E_ARRAYISLOCKED	The array is currently locked.
E_INVALIDARG	The item pointed to by *psa* is not a safe array descriptor.

Example

```
STDMETHODIMP_(ULONG) CEnumPoint::Release()
{
    if(--m_refs == 0){
        if(m_psa != NULL)
        SafeArrayDestroy(m_psa);
        delete this;
        return 0;
    }
    return m_refs;
}
```

SafeArrayDestroyData

HRESULT SafeArrayDestroyData(*psa***)**
SAFEARRAY FAR* *psa*

Destroys all the data in a safe array. If objects are stored in the array, **Release** is called on each object in the array.

Parameters

psa
> Pointer to an array descriptor.

Return Value   The SCODE obtained from the returned HRESULT is one of the following:

SCODE	Meaning
S_OK	Success.
DISP_E_ARRAYISLOCKED	The array is currently locked.
E_INVALIDARG	The item pointed to by *psa* is not a safe array descriptor.

Comments   This function is typically used when freeing safe arrays that contain elements with data types other than variants.

See Also   **SafeArrayAllocData, SafeArrayAllocDescriptor, SafeArrayDestroyDescriptor**

SafeArrayDestroyDescriptor

HRESULT SafeArrayDestroyDescriptor(*psa*)
SAFEARRAY FAR* *psa*

Destroys a descriptor of a safe array.

Parameters   *psa*
     Pointer to a safe array descriptor.

Return Value   The SCODE obtained from the returned HRESULT is one of the following:

SCODE	Meaning
S_OK	Success.
DISP_E_ARRAYISLOCKED	The array is currently locked.
E_INVALIDARG	The item pointed to by *psa* is not a safe array descriptor.

Comments   This function is typically used to destroy the descriptor of a safe array that contains elements with data types other than variants. Destroying the array descriptor does not destroy the elements in the array. Call **SafeArrayDestroyData** to free the elements before destroying the array descriptor.

See Also   **SafeArrayAllocData, SafeArrayAllocDescriptor, SafeArrayDestroyData**

SafeArrayGetDim

unsigned int SafeArrayGetDim(*psa***)**
SAFEARRAY FAR* *psa*

Returns the number of dimensions in the array.

Parameters   *psa*
　　　　　　　Pointer to an array descriptor created by **SafeArrayCreate**.

Return Value   Returns the number of dimensions in the array.

Example
```
HRESULT
CEnumPoint::Create(SAFEARRAY FAR* psa, CEnumPoint FAR* FAR* ppenum)
{
    long lBound;
    HRESULT hresult;
    CEnumPoint FAR* penum;

    // Verify that the SafeArray is the proper shape.
    //
    if(SafeArrayGetDim(psa) != 1)
        return ReportResult(0, E_INVALIDARG, 0, 0);
.
.   // Code omitted here.
.
}
```

SafeArrayGetElement

HRESULT SafeArrayGetElement(*psa, rgIndices, pvData***)**
SAFEARRAY FAR* *psa*
long FAR* *rgIndices*
void FAR* *pvData*

Retrieves a single element of the array.

Parameters

psa
Pointer to an array descriptor created by **SafeArrayCreate**.

rgIndices
Pointer to a vector of indexes for each dimension of the array. The rightmost (least significant) dimension is *rgIndices*[0]. The leftmost dimension is stored at *rgIndices*[*psa->cDims* − 1].

pvData
Pointer to the location to place the element of the array.

Comments

This function automatically calls **SafeArrayLock** and **SafeArrayUnlock** before and after retrieving the element. The caller must provide a storage area of the correct size to receive the data. If the data element is a string, object, or variant, the function copies the element in the correct way.

Return Value

The SCODE obtained from the returned HRESULT is one of the following:

SCODE	Meaning
S_OK	Success.
DISP_E_BADINDEX	The specified index is invalid.
E_INVALIDARG	One of the arguments is invalid.
E_OUTOFMEMORY	Memory could not be allocated for the element.

Example

```
STDMETHODIMP CEnumPoint::Next(
    ULONG celt,
    VARIANT FAR rgvar[],
    ULONG FAR* pceltFetched)
{
    unsigned int i;
    long ix;
    HRESULT hresult;

    for(i = 0; i < celt; ++i)
        VariantInit(&rgvar[i]);

    for(i = 0; i < celt; ++i){
        if(m_iCurrent == m_celts){
        hresult = ReportResult(0, S_FALSE, 0, 0);
        goto LDone;
    }
```

```
            ix = m_iCurrent++;
            hresult = SafeArrayGetElement(m_psa, &ix, &rgvar[i]);
            if(FAILED(hresult))
            goto LError0;
        }
        hresult = NOERROR;

LDone:;
    *pceltFetched = i;
    return hresult;

LError0:;
    for(i = 0; i < celt; ++i)
        VariantClear(&rgvar[i]);
    return hresult;
}
```

SafeArrayGetElemsize

unsigned int SafeArrayGetElemsize(*psa***)**
SAFEARRAY FAR* *psa*

Returns the size, in bytes, of the elements of a safe array.

Parameters   *psa*
        Pointer to an array descriptor created by **SafeArrayCreate**.

SafeArrayGetLBound

HRESULT SafeArrayGetLBound(*psa, nDim, plLbound***)**
SAFEARRAY FAR* *psa*
unsigned int *nDim*
long FAR* *plLbound*

Returns the lower bound for any dimension of a safe array.

Parameters

psa
> Pointer to an array descriptor created by **SafeArrayCreate**.

nDim
> The array dimension for which to get the lower bound.

plLbound
> Pointer to the location to return the lower bound.

Return Value

The SCODE obtained from the returned HRESULT is one of the following:

SCODE	Meaning
S_OK	Success.
DISP_E_BADINDEX	The specified index is out of bounds.
E_INVALIDARG	One of the arguments is invalid.

Example

```
HRESULT
CEnumPoint::Create(SAFEARRAY FAR* psa, CEnumPoint FAR* FAR* ppenum)
{
    long lBound;
    HRESULT hresult;
    CEnumPoint FAR* penum;


    // Verify that the SafeArray is the proper shape.
    //
    hresult = SafeArrayGetLBound(psa, 1, &lBound);
    if(FAILED(hresult))
        return hresult;
 .
 .   // Code omitted here.
 .

}
```

SafeArrayGetUBound

> **HRESULT SafeArrayGetUBound**(*psa, nDim, plUbound*)
> **SAFEARRAY FAR*** *psa*
> **unsigned int** *nDim*
> **long FAR*** *plUbound*

Returns the upper bound for any dimension of a safe array.

Parameters

psa
Pointer to an array descriptor created by **SafeArrayCreate()**.

nDim
The array dimension for which to get the upper bound.

plUbound
Pointer to the location to return the upper bound.

Return Value

The SCODE obtained from the returned HRESULT is one of the following:

SCODE	Meaning
S_OK	Success.
DISP_E_BADINDEX	The specified index is out of bounds.
E_INVALIDARG	One of the arguments is invalid.

Example

```
HRESULT
CEnumPoint::Create(SAFEARRAY FAR* psa, CEnumPoint FAR* FAR* ppenum)
{
    long lBound;
    HRESULT hresult;
    CEnumPoint FAR* penum;

    // Verify that the SafeArray is the proper shape.
    //
    hresult = SafeArrayGetUBound(psa, 1, &lBound);
    if(FAILED(hresult))
        goto LError0;
    .
    .    // Code omitted
    .
LError0:;
    penum->Release();

    return hresult;
}
```

SafeArrayLock

HRESULT SafeArrayLock(*psa*)
SAFEARRAY FAR* *psa*

Increments the lock count of an array and places a pointer to the array data in *pvData* of the array descriptor.

Parameters

psa

Pointer to an array descriptor created by **SafeArrayCreate**.

Comments

The pointer in the array descriptor is valid until **SafeArrayUnlock** is called. Calls to **SafeArrayLock** can be nested; an equal number of calls to **SafeArrayUnlock** are required.

An array can't be deleted while it is locked.

Return Value

The SCODE obtained from the returned HRESULT is one of the following:

SCODE	Meaning
S_OK	Success.
E_INVALIDARG	The argument *psa* was not a valid safe array descriptor.
E_UNEXPECTED	The array could not be locked.

SafeArrayPtrOfIndex

HRESULT SafeArrayPtrOfIndex(*psa, rgIndices, ppvData***)**
SAFEARRAY FAR* *psa*
long FAR* *rgIndices*
void HUGEP* FAR* *ppvData*

Returns a pointer to an array element.

Parameters

psa

Pointer to an array descriptor created by **SafeArrayCreate**.

rgIndices

An array of index values that identify an element of the array. All indexes for the element must be specified.

ppvData

On return, pointer to the element identified by the values in *rgIndices*.

Comments

The array should be locked before **SafeArrayPtrOfIndex** is called. Failing to lock the array may cause unpredictable results.

Return Value

The SCODE obtained from the returned HRESULT is one of the following:

SCODE	Meaning
S_OK	Success.
E_INVALIDARG	The argument *psa* was not a valid safe array descriptor.
DISP_E_BADINDEX	The specified index was invalid.

SafeArrayPutElement

HRESULT SafeArrayPutElement(*psa, rgIndices, pvData*)
SAFEARRAY FAR* *psa*
long FAR* *rgIndices*
void FAR* *pvData*

Assigns a single element into the array.

Parameters

psa
    Pointer to an array descriptor created by **SafeArrayCreate**.

rgIndices
    Pointer to a vector of indexes for each dimension of the array. The rightmost (least significant) dimension is *rgIndices*[0]. The leftmost dimension is stored at *rgIndices*[*psa->cDims* − 1].

pvData
    Pointer to the data to assign to the array. VT_DISPATCH, VT_UNKNOWN, and VT_BSTR variant types are pointers and don't require another level of indirection.

Comments

This function automatically calls **SafeArrayLock** and **SafeArrayUnlock** before and after assigning the element. If the data element is a string, object, or variant, the function copies it correctly. If the existing element is a string, object or variant, it is cleared correctly.

Note that you can have multiple locks on an array, so you can put elements into an array while the array is locked by other operations.

Return Value

The SCODE obtained from the returned HRESULT is one of the following:

SCODE	Meaning
S_OK	Success.
DISP_E_BADINDEX	The specified index was invalid.
E_INVALIDARG	One of the arguments is invalid.
E_OUTOFMEMORY	Memory could not be allocated for the element.

Example

```
HRESULT PASCAL __export CPoly::EnumPoints(IEnumVARIANT FAR* FAR* ppenum)
{
    unsigned int i;
    HRESULT hresult;
    VARIANT var;
    SAFEARRAY FAR* psa;
    CEnumPoint FAR* penum;
    POINTLINK FAR* ppointlink;
    SAFEARRAYBOUND rgsabound[1];
    rgsabound[0].lLbound = 0;
    rgsabound[0].cElements = m_cPoints;

    psa = SafeArrayCreate(VT_VARIANT, 1, rgsabound);

.   // Code omitted here.
.
.
        V_VT(&var) = VT_DISPATCH;
        hresult = ppointlink->ppoint->QueryInterface(
        IID_IDispatch, (void FAR* FAR*)&V_DISPATCH(&var));
        if(hresult != NOERROR)
            goto LError1;

        ix[0] = i;
        SafeArrayPutElement(psa, ix, &var);

        ppointlink = ppointlink->next;
    }

    hresult = CEnumPoint::Create(psa, &penum);
    if(hresult != NOERROR)
        goto LError1;
    *ppenum = penum;
    return NOERROR;
```

```
LError1:;
    SafeArrayDestroy(psa);

LError0:;
    return hresult;
}
```

SafeArrayRedim

HRESULT SafeArrayRedim(*psa, psaboundNew*)
SAFEARRAY FAR* *psa*
SAFEARRAYBOUND FAR* *psaboundNew*

Changes the least significant (rightmost) bound of a safe array.

Parameters

psa
Pointer to an array descriptor.

psaboundNew
Pointer to a new safe array bound structure containing the new array bound.
Only the least significant dimension of an array may be changed.

Return Value

The SCODE obtained from the returned HRESULT is one of the following:

SCODE	Meaning
S_OK	Success.
DISP_E_ARRAYISLOCKED	The array is currently locked.
E_INVALIDARG	The item pointed to by *psa* is not a safe array descriptor.

Comments

If you reduce the bound of an array, **SafeArrayRedim** deallocates the array
elements outside the new array boundary. If you increase the bound of an array,
SafeArrayRedim allocates and initializes the new array elements. The data is
preserved for elements that exist in both the old and the new array.

SafeArrayUnaccessData

HRESULT SafeArrayUnaccessData(*psa*)
SAFEARRAY FAR* *psa*

Decrements the lock count of an array and invalidates the pointer retrieved by **SafeArrayAccessData**.

Parameters

psa
    Pointer to an array descriptor created by **SafeArrayCreate**.

Return Value

The SCODE obtained from the returned HRESULT is one of the following:

SCODE	Meaning
S_OK	Success.
E_INVALIDARG	The argument *psa* was not a valid safe array descriptor.
E_UNEXPECTED	The array could not be unlocked.

SafeArrayUnlock

HRESULT SafeArrayUnlock(*psa*)
SAFEARRAY FAR* *psa*

Decrements the lock count of an array so it can be freed or resized.

Parameters

psa
    Pointer to an array descriptor created by **SafeArrayCreate**.

Comments

This function is called after access to the data in an array is finished.

Return Value

The SCODE obtained from the returned HRESULT is one of the following:

SCODE	Meaning
S_OK	Success.
E_INVALIDARG	The argument *psa* was not a valid safe array descriptor.
E_UNEXPECTED	The array could not be unlocked.

String Manipulation Functions

Implemented by	Used by	Header filename	Import library name
OLEAUT32.DLL (32-bit systems)	Applications that expose or access programmable objects.	OLEAUTO.H	OLEAUT32.LIB
OLE2DISP.DLL (16-bit systems)		DISPATCH.H	OLE2DISP.LIB

To handle strings that are allocated by one component and freed by another, OLE Automation defines a special set of functions. These functions use the following data type:

```
typedef OLECHAR FAR* BSTR;
```

These strings are zero-terminated, and in most cases they can be treated just like OLECHAR * strings. However, a BSTR can be queried for its length rather than scanned, so it may contain embedded null characters. The length is stored as an integer at the memory location preceding the data in the string. Instead of reading this location directly, applications should use the string manipulation functions to access the length of a BSTR. In situations where you can be sure that a BSTR will not be translated from ANSI to Unicode or vice versa, you can use BSTRs to pass binary data. For example, if your code will run only on 16-bit systems and interact only with other 16-bit systems, you may use BSTRs. However, the preferred method of passing binary data is to use a SAFEARRAY of VT_UI1.

A NULL pointer is a valid value for a BSTR variable; by convention, it is always treated the same as a pointer to a BSTR that contains zero characters. Also, by convention, calls to functions that take a BSTR reference parameter must pass either a NULL pointer or a pointer to an allocated BSTR. If the implementation of a function that takes a BSTR reference parameter assigns a new BSTR to the parameter, it must free the previously referenced BSTR.

SysAllocString

BSTR SysAllocString(*sz***)**
OLECHAR FAR* *sz*

Allocates a new string and copies the passed string into it. Returns NULL if insufficient memory exists or if NULL is passed in.

Parameter

sz

A zero-terminated string to copy.

Return Value   If successful, points to a BSTR containing the string. If insufficient memory exists or *sz* was NULL, returns NULL.

Strings created with **SysAllocString** should be freed with **SysFreeString**.

Example

```
inline void CStatBar::SetText(OLECHAR FAR* sz)
{
    SysFreeString(m_bstrMsg);
    m_bstrMsg = SysAllocString(sz);
}
```

SysAllocStringByteLen

BSTR SysAllocStringByteLen(*psz, len*)
char FAR* *psz*
unsigned int *len*

Allocates a new string of *len* bytes, copies *len* bytes from the passed string into it, and then appends a null character. Valid for 32-bit systems only.

Parameter

psz
    A zero-terminated string to copy, or NULL to keep the string uninitialized.

len
    Number of bytes to copy from *psz*. A null character is placed afterwards, making a total of *len*+1 bytes allocated.

Return Value   Points to a copy of the string or NULL, if insufficient memory exists.

Comments   If *psz* is NULL, a string of the requested length is allocated, but not initialized. The string *psz* can contain embedded null characters and need not end with a null. The returned string should later be freed with **SysFreeString**.

SysAllocStringLen

BSTR SysAllocStringLen(*pch, cch*)
OLECHAR FAR* *pch*
unsigned int *cch*

Allocates a new string, copies *cch* characters from the passed string into it, and then appends a null character.

Parameter	*pch* A pointer to *cch* characters to copy, or NULL to keep the string uninitialized. *cch* Number of characters to copy from *pch**. A null character is placed afterwards, making a total of *cch*+1 characters allocated.
Return Value	Points to a copy of the string or NULL, if insufficient memory exists.
Comments	If *pch* is NULL, a string of the requested length is allocated, but not initialized. The string *pch* can contain embedded null characters and need not end with a null. The returned string should later be freed with **SysFreeString**.

SysFreeString

void SysFreeString(*bstr***)**
BSTR *bstr*

Frees a string previously allocated by **SysAllocString**, **SysAllocStringByteLen**, **SysReAllocString**, **SysAllocStringLen**, or **SysReAllocStringLen**.

Parameter	*bstr* A BSTR allocated earlier or NULL. If NULL, the function simply returns.
Return Value	None.
| **Example** | ```
CStatBar::~CStatBar()
{
    SysFreeString(m_bstrMsg);
}
``` |

SysReAllocString

BOOL SysReAllocString(*pbstr, sz***)**
BSTR FAR* *pbstr*
OLECHAR FAR* *sz*

Allocates a new BSTR and copies the passed string into it, then frees the BSTR currently referenced by *pbstr* and resets *pbstr* to point to the new BSTR. Returns False if insufficient memory exists.
```

Parameter

pbstr
Points to a variable containing a BSTR.

sz
A zero-terminated string to copy.

Return Value   Returns False if insufficient memory exists.

SysReAllocStringLen

BOOL SysReAllocStringLen(*pbstr, pch, cch*)
BSTR FAR* *pbstr*
OLECHAR FAR* *pch*
unsigned int *cch*

Creates a new BSTR containing a specified number of characters from an old BSTR and frees the old BSTR.

Parameter

pbstr
Pointer to a variable containing a BSTR.

pch
Pointer to *cch* characters to copy, or NULL to keep the string uninitialized.

cch
Number of characters to copy from *pch**. A null character is placed afterwards, making a total of *cch*+1 characters allocated.

Return Value   Returns True if the string is successfully reallocated, or False if insufficient memory exists.

Comments   Allocates a new string, copies *cch* characters from the passed string into it, and then appends a null character. Frees the BSTR currently referenced by *pbstr* and resets *pbstr* to point to the new BSTR. If *pch* is NULL, a string of length *cch* is allocated, but not initialized.

The string *pch* can contain embedded null characters and need not end with a null.

SysStringByteLen

unsigned int SysStringByteLen(*bstr*)
BSTR *bstr*

Returns the length in bytes of a BSTR. Valid for 32-bit systems only.

Parameter

bstr
  A BSTR previously allocated. It cannot be NULL.

Return Value

The number of bytes in *bstr*, not including a terminating null character.

Comments

The value returned may be different from **fstrlen**(*bstr*), if the BSTR was allocated with **Sys[Re]AllocStringLen** or **SysAllocStringByteLen**, and the passed-in characters included a null character in the first *len* characters. For a BSTR allocated with **Sys[Re]AllocStringLen** or **SysAllocStringByteLen**, this function always returns the number of bytes specified in the *len* parameter at allocation time.

Example

```
// Draw the status message
//
TextOut(
    hdc,
    rcMsg.left + (m_dxFont / 2),
    rcMsg.top + ((rcMsg.bottom - rcMsg.top - m_dyFont) / 2),
    m_bstrMsg, SysStringByteLen(m_bstrMsg));
```

SysStringLen

unsigned int SysStringLen(*bstr*)
BSTR *bstr*

Returns the length of a BSTR.

Parameter

bstr
  A BSTR previously allocated; can't be NULL.

Return Value

The number of characters in *bstr*, not including a terminating null character.

Comments   The value returned may be different from **_fstrlen**(*bstr*), if the BSTR was allocated with **Sys[Re]AllocStringLen** or **SysAllocStringByteLen**, and the passed-in characters included a null character in the first *cch* characters. For a BSTR allocated with **Sys[Re]AllocStringLen** or **SysAllocStringByteLen**, this function always returns the number of characters specified in the *cch* parameter at allocation time.

Example
```
// Draw the status message
//
TextOut(
    hdc,
    rcMsg.left + (m_dxFont / 2),
    rcMsg.top + ((rcMsg.bottom - rcMsg.top - m_dyFont) / 2),
    m_bstrMsg, SysStringLen(m_bstrMsg));
```

Variant Manipulation Functions

Implemented by	Used by	Header filename	Import library name
OLEAUT32.DLL (32-bit systems)	Applications that expose or access programmable objects.	OLEAUTO.H	OLEAUT32.LIB
OLE2DISP.DLL (16-bit systems)		DISPATCH.H	OLE2DISP.LIB

These functions are provided to allow applications to manipulate VARIANTARG variables. Applications that implement **IDispatch** should test each VARIANTARG for all permitted types by attempting to coerce the variant to each type (using **VariantChangeType** or **VariantChangeTypeEx**). If objects are allowed, the application should always test for object types before other types. If an object type is expected, the application must test (via **IUnknown::QueryInterface**) whether the object is of the type desired.

Although applications can access and interpret the VARIANTARGs without these functions, using them ensures uniform conversion and coercion rules for all implementors of **IDispatch**. (For example, these functions automatically coerce numeric arguments to strings and vice versa, when necessary.)

Because variants can contain strings, references to scalars and objects, and arrays, certain data ownership rules must be obeyed. All the variant manipulation functions conform to the following rules:

1. All VARIANTARGs must be initialized by **VariantInit** before use.

2. For the types VT_UI1, VT_I2, VT_I4, VT_R4, VT_R8, VT_BOOL, VT_ERROR, VT_CY, VT_DATE, data is stored within the VARIANT structure. Any pointers to the data become invalid when the type of the variant is changed.

3. For VT_BYREF | any type, the memory pointed to by the variant is owned and freed by the caller of the function.

4. For VT_BSTR, there is only one owner for the string. All strings in variants must be allocated with the **SysAllocString** function. When releasing or changing the type of a variant with the VT_BSTR type, **SysFreeString** is called on the contained string.

5. For VT_ARRAY | any type, the rule is analogous to the rule for VT_BSTR. All arrays in variants must be allocated with **SafeArrayCreate**. When releasing or changing the type of a variant with the VT_ARRAY flag set, **SafeArrayDestroy** is called.

6. For VT_DISPATCH and VT_UNKNOWN, the pointed-to objects have reference counts that are incremented when they are placed in a variant. When releasing or changing the type of the variant, **Release** is called on the pointed-to object.

VariantChangeType

HRESULT VariantChangeType(*pvargDest, pvargSrc, wFlags, vtNew***)**
VARIANTARG FAR* *pvargDest*
VARIANTARG FAR* *pvargSrc*
unsigned short *wFlags*
VARTYPE *vtNew*

This function converts a variant from one type to another.

Parameters   *pvargDest*
   Pointer to the VARIANTARG to receive the coerced type. If this is the same as *pvargSrc*, the variant will be converted in place.

pvargSrc
   Pointer to the source VARIANTARG to be coerced.

wFlags

Flags that control the coercion. The only defined flag is VARIANT_NOVALUEPROP, which prevents the function from attempting to coerce an object to a fundamental type by getting the Value property. Applications should set this flag only if necessary, because it makes their behavior inconsistent with other applications.

vtNew

The type to coerce to. If the return code is S_OK, the *vt* field of the **pvargDest* will always be the same as this value.

Return Value

The SCODE obtained from the returned HRESULT is one of the following:

SCODE	Meaning
S_OK	Success.
DISP_E_BADVARTYPE	The variant type *vtNew* is not a valid type of variant.
DISP_E_OVERFLOW	The data pointed to by *pvargSrc* does not fit in the destination type.
DISP_E_TYPEMISMATCH	The argument could not be coerced to the specified type.
E_INVALIDARG	One of the arguments is invalid.
E_OUTOFMEMORY	Memory could not be allocated for the conversion.

Comments

The **VariantChangeType** function handles coercions between the fundamental types (including numeric-to-string and string-to-numeric coercions). A variant that has VT_BYREF set is coerced to a value by fetching the referenced value. An object is coerced to a value by invoking the object's Value property (DISPID_VALUE).

Typically, the implementor of **IDispatch::Invoke** determines which member is being accessed, then calls **VariantChangeType** to get the value of one or more arguments. For example, if the **IDispatch** call specifies a SetTitle member that takes one string argument, the implementor would call **VariantChangeType** to attempt to coerce the argument to VT_BSTR. If **VariantChangeType** did not return an error, the argument could then be fetched directly from the *bstrVal* field of the VARIANTARG. If **VariantChangeType** returned DISP_E_TYPEMISMATCH, the implementor would set **puArgErr* to 0 (indicating the argument in error) and return DISP_E_TYPEMISMATCH from **IDispatch::Invoke**.

Note that you should not attempt to change the type of a VARIANTARG in the *rgvarg* array in place.

Arrays of one type can't be converted to arrays of another type with this function.

See Also

VariantChangeTypeEx

VariantChangeTypeEx

HRESULT VariantChangeTypeEx(*pvargDest, pvargSrc, lcid, wFlags, vtNew*)
VARIANTARG FAR* *pvargDest*
VARIANTARG FAR* *pvargSrc*
LCID *lcid*
unsigned short *wFlags*
VARTYPE *vtNew*

This function converts a variant from one type to another using a locale ID.

Parameters

pvargDest

Pointer to the VARIANTARG to receive the coerced type. If this is the same as *pvargSrc*, the variant will be converted in place.

pvargSrc

Pointer to the source VARIANTARG to be coerced.

lcid

The locale ID for the variant to coerce. The locale ID is useful when the type of the source or destination VARIANTARG is VT_BSTR, VT_DISPATCH, or VT_DATE.

wFlags

Flags that control the coercion. The only defined flag is VARIANT_NOVALUEPROP, which prevents the function from attempting to coerce an object to a fundamental type by getting its Value property. Applications should set this flag only if necessary, because it makes their behavior inconsistent with other applications.

vtNew

The type to coerce to. If the return code is S_OK, the *vt* field of the **pvargDest* is guaranteed to be equal to this value.

Return Value

The SCODE obtained from the returned HRESULT is one of the following:

SCODE	Meaning
S_OK	Success.
DISP_E_BADVARTYPE	The variant type *vtNew* is not a valid type of variant.
DISP_E_OVERFLOW	The data pointed to by *pvargSrc* does not fit in the destination type.
DISP_E_TYPEMISMATCH	The argument could not be coerced to the specified type.
E_INVALIDARG	One of the arguments is invalid.
E_OUTOFMEMORY	Memory could not be allocated for the conversion.

Comments

The **VariantChangeTypeEx** function handles coercions between the fundamental types (including numeric to string and string to numeric coercions). To change a type with the VT_BYREF flag set to one without VT_BYREF set, **VariantChangeTypeEx** fetches the referenced value. Objects are coerced to fundamental types by fetching the value of the Value property.

Typically, the implementor of **IDispatch::Invoke** determines which member is being accessed, then calls **VariantChangeType** to get the value of one or more arguments. For example, if the **IDispatch** call specifies a SetTitle member that takes one string argument, the implementor would call **VariantChangeTypeEx** to attempt to coerce the argument to VT_BSTR. If **VariantChangeTypeEx** did not return an error, the argument could then be fetched directly from the *bstrVal* field of the VARIANTARG. If **VariantChangeTypeEx** returned DISP_E_TYPEMISMATCH, the implementor would set **puArgErr* to 0 (indicating the argument in error) and return DISP_E_TYPEMISMATCH from **IDispatch::Invoke**.

Note that you should not attempt to change the type of a VARIANTARG in the *rgvarg* array in place.

Arrays of one type can't be converted to arrays of another type with this function.

See Also

VariantChangeType

VariantClear

HRESULT VariantClear(*pvarg*)
VARIANTARG FAR* *pvarg*

Clears a variant.

Parameter

pvarg
Pointer to the VARIANTARG to clear.

Return Value

The SCODE obtained from the returned HRESULT is one of the following:

SCODE	Meaning
S_OK	Success.
DISP_E_ARRAYISLOCKED	The variant contains an array that is locked.
DISP_E_BADVARTYPE	The variant type *pvarg* is not a valid type of variant.
E_INVALIDARG	One of the arguments is invalid.

Comments   This function should be used to clear variables of type VARIANTARG (or
VARIANT) before the memory containing the VARIANTARG is freed (as when
a local variable goes out of scope).

The function clears a VARIANTARG by setting the *vt* field to VT_EMPTY and
the *wReserved* field to 0. The current contents of the VARIANTARG are
released first. If the *vt* field is VT_BSTR, the string is freed; if the *vt* field is
VT_DISPATCH, the object is released. If the *vt* field has the VT_ARRAY bit set,
the array is freed.

In certain cases, you may prefer to clear a variant in your own code, without
calling **VariantClear**. For example, it is permissible to change the type of a
VT_I4 variant to some other type without calling this function. However, you
must call **VariantClear** if you receive a VT_type that you are not prepared to
handle. Using **VariantClear** in these cases ensures that your code will continue
to work if OLE Automation adds new variant types in the future.

Example
```
for(i = 0; i < celt; ++i)
    VariantClear(&rgvar[i]);
```

VariantCopy

HRESULT VariantCopy(*pvargDest, pvargSrc*)
VARIANTARG FAR* *pvargDest*
VARIANTARG FAR* *pvargSrc*

Frees the destination variant and makes a copy of the source variant.

Parameters   *pvargDest*
Pointer to the VARIANTARG to receive the copy.

pvargSrc
Pointer to the VARIANTARG to be copied.

Return Value   The SCODE obtained from the returned HRESULT is one of the following:

SCODE	Meaning
S_OK	Success.
DISP_E_ARRAYISLOCKED	The variant contains an array that is locked.
DISP_E_BADVARTYPE	The source and destination have an invalid variant type (usually uninitialized).
E_OUTOFMEMORY	Memory could not be allocated for the copy.
E_INVALIDARG	The argument *pvargSrc* was VT_BYREF.

Comments   First, any memory owned by *pvargDest* is freed as in **VariantClear** (note that *pvargDest* must point to a valid initialized variant, and not simply an uninitialized memory location). Then, *pvargDest* receives an exact copy of the contents of *pvargSrc*. If *pvargSrc* is a VT_BSTR, a copy of the string is made. If *pvargSrc* is a VT_ARRAY, the entire array is copied. If *pvargSrc* is a VT_DISPATCH or VT_UNKNOWN, **AddRef** is called to increment the object's reference count.

VariantCopyInd

HRESULT VariantCopyInd(*pvarDest, pvargSrc***)**
VARIANT FAR* *pvarDest*
VARIANTARG FAR* *pvargSrc*

Frees the destination variant and makes a copy of the source VARIANTARG, performing the necessary indirection if the source is specified to be VT_BYREF.

Parameters   *pvarDest*
    Pointer to the VARIANTARG to receive the copy.

pvargSrc
    Pointer to the VARIANTARG to be copied.

Return Value   The SCODE obtained from the returned HRESULT is one of the following:

SCODE	Meaning
S_OK	Success.
DISP_E_ARRAYISLOCKED	The variant contains an array that is locked.
DISP_E_BADVARTYPE	The source and destination have an invalid variant type (usually uninitialized).
E_OUTOFMEMORY	Memory could not be allocated for the copy.
E_INVALIDARG	The argument *pvargSrc* was VT_ARRAY.

Comments   This function is useful when you need to make a copy of a variant and guarantee that it is not VT_BYREF, such as when handling arguments in an implementation of **IDispatch::Invoke**.

For example, if the source is a (VT_BYREF | VT_I2), the destination will be a ByVal VT_I2. The same is true for all legal VT_BYREF combinations including VT_VARIANT.

If *pvargSrc* is (VT_BYREF | VT_VARIANT) and the contained variant is also VT_BYREF, the contained variant is also dereferenced.

This function frees any existing contents of *pvarDest*.

VariantInit

void VariantInit(*pvarg*)
VARIANTARG FAR* *pvarg*

Initializes a variant.

Parameter

pvarg
Pointer to the VARIANTARG to initialize.

Comments

The **VariantInit** function initializes the VARIANTARG by setting the *vt* field to VT_EMPTY and the *wReserved* field to 0. Unlike **VariantClear**, this function does not interpret the current contents of the VARIANTARG. **VariantInit** should be used to initialize new local variables of type VARIANTARG (or VARIANT).

Example

```
for(i = 0; i < celt; ++i)
    VariantInit(&rgvar[i]);
```

Low-Level Variant Conversion Functions

The following low-level functions for converting variant data types are provided by OLEAUT32.DLL (for 32-bit systems) and OLE2DISP.DLL (for 16-bit systems). These functions are used by the higher-level variant manipulation functions, such as **VariantChangeType**, but may be called directly as well.

Convert to type	From type	Function
unsigned char	**unsigned char**	None
	short	**VarUI1FromI2**(*sIn, pbOut*)
	long	**VarUI1FromI4**(*lIn, pbOut*)
	float	**VarUI1FromR4**(*fltIn, pbOut*)
	double	**VarUI1FromR8**(*dblIn, pbOut*)
	CURRENCY	**VarUI1FromCy**(*cyIn, pbOut*)
	DATE	**VarUI1FromDate**(*dateIn, pbOut*)
	OLECHAR FAR*	**VarUI1FromStr**(*strIn, lcid, dwFlags, pbOut*)
	IDispatch FAR*	**VarUI1FromDisp**(*pdispIn, lcid, dwFlags, pbOut*)
	BOOL	**VarUI1FromBool**(*boolIn, pbOut*)

Convert to type	From type	Function
short	unsigned char	**VarI2FromUI1**(*bIn*, *psOut*)
	short	None
	long	**VarI2FromI4**(*lIn*, *psOut*)
	float	**VarI2FromR4**(*fltIn*, *psOut*)
	double	**VarI2FromR8**(*dblIn*, *psOut*)
	CURRENCY	**VarI2FromCy**(*cyIn*, *psOut*)
	DATE	**VarI2FromDate**(*dateIn*, *psOut*)
	OLECHAR FAR*	**VarI2FromStr**(*strIn*, *lcid*, *dwFlags*, *psOut*)
	IDispatch FAR*	**VarI2FromDisp**(*pdispIn*, *lcid*, *dwFlags*, *psOut*)
	BOOL	**VarI2FromBool**(*boolIn*, *psOut*)
long	unsigned char	**VarI4FromUI1**(*bIn*, *plOut*)
	short	**VarI4FromI2**(*sIn*, *plOut*)
	long	None
	float	**VarI4FromR4**(*fltIn*, *plOut*)
	double	**VarI4FromR8**(*dblIn*, *plOut*)
	CURRENCY	**VarI4FromCy**(*cyIn*, *plOut*)
	DATE	**VarI4FromDate**(*dateIn*, *plOut*)
	OLECHAR FAR*	**VarI4FromStr**(*strIn*, *lcid*, *dwFlags*, *plOut*)
	IDispatch FAR*	**VarI4FromDisp**(*pdispIn*, *lcid*, *dwFlags*, *plOut*)
	BOOL	**VarI4FromBool**(*boolIn*, *plOut*)
float	unsigned char	**VarR4FromUI1**(*bIn*, *prOut*)
	short	**VarR4FromI2**(*sIn*, *prOut*)
	long	**VarR4FromI4**(*lIn*, *prOut*)
	float	None
	double	**VarR4FromR8**(*dblIn*, *prOut*)
	CURRENCY	**VarR4FromCy**(*cyIn*, *prOut*)
	DATE	**VarR4FromDate**(*dateIn*, *prOut*)
	OLECHAR FAR*	**VarR4FromStr**(*strIn*, *lcid*, *dwFlags*, *prOut*)
	IDispatch FAR*	**VarR4FromDisp**(*pdispIn*, *lcid*, *dwFlags*, *prOut*)
	BOOL	**VarR4FromBool**(*boolIn*, *prOut*)

Convert to type	From type	Function
double	unsigned char	**VarR8FromUI1**(*bIn, pdblOut*)
	short	**VarR8FromI2**(*sIn, pdblOut*)
	long	**VarR8FromI4**(*lIn, pdblOut*)
	float	**VarR8FromR4**(*fltIn, pdblOut*)
	double	None
	CURRENCY	**VarR8FromCy**(*cyIn, pdblOut*)
	DATE	**VarR8FromDate**(*dateIn, pdblOut*)
	OLECHAR FAR*	**VarR8FromStr**(*strIn, lcid, dwFlags, pdblOut*)
	IDispatch FAR*	**VarR8FromDisp**(*pdispIn, lcid, dwFlags, pdblOut*)
	BOOL	**VarR8FromBool**(*boolIn, pdblOut*)
DATE	unsigned char	**VarDateFromUI1**(*bIn, pdateOut*)
	short	**VarDateFromI2**(*sIn, pdateOut*)
	long	**VarDateFromI4**(*lIn, pdateOut*)
	float	**VarDateFromR4**(*fltIn, pdateOut*)
	double	**VarDateFromR8**(*dblIn, pdateOut*)
	CURRENCY	**VarDateFromCy**(*cyIn, pdateOut*)
	DATE	None
	OLECHAR FAR*	**VarDateFromStr**(*strIn, lcid, dwFlags, pdateOut*)
	IDispatch FAR*	**VarDateFromDisp**(*pdispIn, lcid, dwFlags, pdateOut*)
	BOOL	**VarDateFromBool**(*boolIn, pdateOut*)
CURRENCY	unsigned char	**VarCyFromUI1**(*bIn, pcyOut*)
	short	**VarCyFromI2**(*sIn, pcyOut*)
	long	**VarCyFromI4**(*lIn, pcyOut*)
	float	**VarCyFromR4**(*fltIn, pcyOut*)
	double	**VarCyFromR8**(*dblIn, pcyOut*)
	CURRENCY	None
	DATE	**VarCyFromDate**(*dateIn, pcyOut*)

Convert to type	From type	Function
CURRENCY (*continued*)	OLECHAR FAR*	**VarCyFromStr**(*strIn*, *lcid*, *dwFlags*, *pcyOut*)
	IDispatch FAR*	**VarCyFromDisp**(*pdispIn*, *lcid*, *dwFlags*, *pcyOut*)
	BOOL	**VarCyFromBool**(*boolIn*, *pcyOut*)
BSTR	unsigned char	**VarBstrFromUI1**(*bIn*, *lcid*, *dwFlags*, *pbstrOut*)
	short	**VarBstrFromI2**(*sIn*, *lcid*, *dwFlags*, *pbstrOut*)
	long	**VarBstrFromI4**(*lIn*, *lcid*, *dwFlags*, *pbstrOut*)
	float	**VarBstrFromR4**(*fltIn*, *lcid*, *dwFlags*, *pbstrOut*)
	double	**VarBstrFromR8**(*dblIn*, *lcid*, *dwFlags*, *pbstrOut*)
	CURRENCY	**VarBstrFromCy**(*cyIn*, *lcid*, *dwFlags*, *pbstrOut*)
	DATE	**VarBstrFromDate**(*dateIn*, *lcid*, *dwFlags*, *pbstrOut*)
	OLECHAR FAR*	None
	IDispatch FAR*	**VarBstrFromDisp**(*pdispIn*, *lcid*, *dwFlags*, *pbstrOut*)
	BOOL	**VarBstrFromBool**(*boolIn*, *lcid*, *dwFlags*, *pbstrOut*)
BOOL	unsigned char	**VarBoolFromUI1**(*bIn*, *pboolOut*)
	short	**VarBoolFromI2**(*sIn*, *pboolOut*)
	long	**VarBoolFromI4**(*lIn*, *pboolOut*)
	float	**VarBoolFromR4**(*fltIn*, *pboolOut*)
	double	**VarBoolFromR8**(*dblIn*, *pboolOut*)
	CURRENCY	**VarBoolFromCy**(*cyIn*, *pboolOut*)
	DATE	**VarBoolFromDate**(*dateIn*, *pboolOut*)
	OLECHAR FAR*	**VarBoolFromStr**(*strIn*, *lcid*, *dwFlags*, *pboolOut*)
	IDispatch FAR*	**VarBoolFromDisp**(*pdispIn*, *lcid*, *dwFlags*, *pboolOut*)
	BOOL	None

Parameters

bIn, sIn, lIn, fltIn, dblIn, cyIn, dateIn, strIn, pdispIn, boolIn
The value to coerce. These parameters have following data types:

Parameter	Data type
bIn	**unsigned char**
sIn	**short**
lIn	**long**
fltIn	**float**
dblIn	**double**
cyIn	CURRENCY
dateIn	DATE
strIn	OLECHAR FAR*
pdispIn	IDispatch FAR*
boolIn	BOOL

lcid
For conversions from string and VT_DISPATCH input, the locale ID to use for the conversion. For a list of locale IDs, see "Supporting Multiple National Languages" in Chapter 2.

dwFlags
One or more of the following flags:

Flag	Description
LOCALE_NOUSEROVERRIDE	Use the system default locale settings, rather than custom user locale settings.
VAR_TIMEVALUEONLY	Omit the date portion of a VT_DATE and return the time only. Applies to conversions to or from dates.
VAR_DATEVALUEONLY	Omit the time portion of a VT_DATE and return the time only. Applies to conversions to or from dates.

pbOut, psOut, plOut, pfltOut, pdblOut, pcyOut, pstrOut, pdispOut, pboolOut
A pointer to the coerced value. These parameters have following data types:

Parameter	Data type
pbOut	**unsigned char**
psOut	**short**
plOut	**long**
pfltOut	**float**
pdblOut	**double**
pcyOut	CURRENCY
pdateOut	DATE
pstrOut	OLECHAR FAR*
pdispOut	IDispatch FAR*
pboolOut	BOOL

Return Value   The SCODE obtained from the returned HRESULT is one of the following:

SCODE	Meaning
S_OK	Success.
DISP_E_BADVARTYPE	The input parameter is not a valid type of variant.
DISP_E_OVERFLOW	The data pointed to by the output parameter does not fit in the destination type.
DISP_E_TYPEMISMATCH	The argument could not be coerced to the specified type.
E_INVALIDARG	One of the arguments is invalid.
E_OUTOFMEMORY	Memory could not be allocated for the conversion.

Date and Time Conversion Functions

The following functions to convert between dates and times stored in MS-DOS format and the variant representation are provided by OLEAUT32.DLL (for 32-bit systems) and OLE2DISP.DLL (for 16-bit systems).

DosDateTimeToVariantTime

int DosDateTimeToVariantTime(*wDOSDate*, *wDOSTime*, *pvtime*)
unsigned short *wDOSDate*
unsigned short *wDOSTime*
double FAR* *pvtime*

Converts the MS-DOS representation of time to the date and time representation stored in variant.

Parameters

wDOSDate
    The MS-DOS date to convert.

wDOSTime
    The MS-DOS time to convert.

pvtime
    Pointer to the location to store the converted time.

Return Value

One of the following:

Result	Meaning
True	Success
False	Failure

Comments

MS-DOS records file dates and times as packed 16-bit values. An MS-DOS *date* has the following format:

Bits	Contents
0-4	Day of the month (1-31)
5-8	Month (1 = January, 2 = February, and so on)
9-15	Year offset from 1980 (add 1980 to get actual year)

An MS-DOS *time* has the following format:

Bits	Contents
0-4	Second divided by 2
5-10	Minute (0-59)
11-15	Hour (0-23 on a 24-hour clock)

VariantTimeToDosDateTime

int VariantTimeToDosDateTime(*vtime*, *pwDOSDate*, *pwDOSTime*)
double *vtime*
unsigned short FAR* *pwDOSDate*
unsigned short FAR* *pwDOSTime*

Converts the variant representation of a date and time to MS-DOS date and time values.

Parameters

vtime
    The variant time to convert.

pwDOSDate
    Pointer to location to store the converted MS-DOS date.

pwDOSTime
    Pointer to location to store the converted MS-DOS time.

Return Value

One of the following:

Result	Meaning
True	Success
False	Failure

Comments

A variant time is stored as an 8-byte real value (**double**), representing a date between January 1, 1753 and December 31, 2078, inclusive. The value 2.0 represents January 1, 1900; 3.0 represents January 2, 1900, and so on. Adding 1 to the value increments the date by a day. The fractional part of the value represents the time of day. Thus, 2.5 represents noon on January 1, 1900; 3.25 is 6:00 a.m. on January 2, 1900; and so on. Negative numbers represent the dates prior to December 30, 1899.

See the Comments section of "**DosDateTimeToVariantTime**" for a description of the MS-DOS date and time formats.

CHAPTER 7

MkTypLib and Object Description Language

When you expose OLE Automation objects, you permit interoperability with other vendors' programs. For others to use your objects, they must have access to the objects' characteristics (properties and methods). To make this information public, you can:

- Publish object and type definitions (for example, as printed documentation).
- Code objects into a compiled .C or .CPP file, so they can be accessed using **IDispatch::GetTypeInfo** or implementations of the **ITypeInfo** and **ITypeLib** interfaces.
- Use the MkTypLib tool to create a type library that contains the objects, then make the type library available to others.

MkTypLib compiles scripts that are written in the Object Description Language (ODL). This chapter provides a reference to the MkTypLib tool and ODL.

Contents of a Type Library

A *type library* is a file or component within another file that contains OLE Automation standard descriptions of exposed objects, properties, and methods. A type library may contain any of the following:

- Information about data types, such as aliases, enumerations, structures, or unions.
- Descriptions of one or more objects, such as a module, interface, **IDispatch** interface (dispinterface), or component object class (coclass). Each of these descriptions is commonly referred to as a *typeinfo*.
- References to type descriptions from other type libraries.

Including the type library with your product makes information about the objects it contains available to your customers' applications and programming tools. You can ship type libraries in any of the following forms:

- A resource in a dynamic-link library (DLL). This resource should have the type **typelib** and an integer ID. It must be declared in the resource (.RC) file as follows:

```
1 typelib mylib1.tlb
2 typelib mylib2.tlb
```

  There can be multiple type library resources in a DLL. Application developers use the resource compiler to add the .TLB file to their own DLL. A DLL with one or more type library resources typically has the extension .OLB (object library).

- A resource in an .EXE file. The file may contain multiple type libraries.
- A stand-alone binary file. The .TLB file output by MkTypLib is a binary file.

Object browsers, compilers, and similar tools access type libraries through the **ITypeLib**, **ITypeInfo**, and **ITypeComp** interfaces. Type library tools (such as MkTypLib) can be created using the **ICreateTypeLib** and **ICreateTypeInfo** interfaces.

MkTypLib: Type Library Creation Tool

MkTypLib processes scripts written in the Object Description Language (ODL), producing a type library (.TLB) and an optional C or C++ style header file.

MkTypLib uses the **ICreateTypeLib** and **ICreateTypeInfo** interfaces to create type libraries. Type libraries can, in turn, be accessed by tools such as type browsers and compilers that use the **ITypeLib** and **ITypeInfo** interfaces, as shown in the following figure.

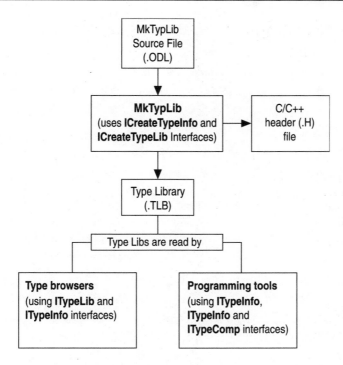

Invoking MkTypLib

To invoke MkTypLib, choose the Run command from either the Program Manager or the File Manager File menu, then enter the following command line in the dialog box:

MkTypLib [*options*] *ODLfile*

MkTypLib creates a type library (.TLB) file based on the object description script in the file specified by *ODLfile*. It can optionally produce a header file (extension .H), which is a stripped version of the input file suitable for inclusion in C or C++ programs that want to access the types defined in the input file. In the header file, MkTypLib inserts DEFINE_GUID macros for each element (interface, dispinterface, and so forth) defined in the type library.

The *options* can be a series of options prefixed with a hyphen (-) or a slash (/) as follows:

Option	Description
/? or **/help**	Displays command line Help. The *ODLfile* does not need to be specified in this case.
/align:*alignment*	Sets the default alignment for types in the library. An *alignment* value of 1 indicates natural alignment; *n* indicates alignment on byte *n*.
/cpp_cmd *cpppath*	Specifies *cpppath* as the command to run the C preprocessor. By default, MkTypLib invokes CL.
/cpp_opt *"options"*	Specifies options for the C preprocessor. Default is "**/C /E /D__MKTYPLIB__**."
/D *define*[*=value*]	Defines the name *define* for the C preprocessor. The *value* is its optional value. No space is allowed between the equal sign (=) and the value.
/h *filename*	Specifies *filename* as the name for a stripped version of the input file. This file can be used as a C or C++ header file.
/I *includedir*	Specifies *includedir* as the directory where include files are located for the C preprocessor.
/nocpp	Suppresses invocation of the C preprocessor.
/nologo	Disables display of the copyright banner.
/o *outputfile*	Redirects output (for example, error messages) to specified *outputfile*.
/tlb *filename*	Specifies *filename* as the name of the output .TLB file. If not specified, this is the same as the name of the *ODLfile* with the extension .TLB.
/win16 /win32 /mac /mips /alpha /ppc /ppc32	Specifies type of output type library to produce. Default is the current operating system.
/w0	Disables warnings.

Although MkTypLib offers minimal error reporting, error messages include accurate line and column number information that can be used with text editors to locate the source of errors.

MkTypLib spawns the C preprocessor. The symbol **__MKTYPLIB__** is predefined for the preprocessor.

ODL File Syntax

The general syntax for an ODL file is as follows:

[*attributes*] **library** *libname* {*definitions*};

The *attributes* associate characteristics with the library, such as its Help file and UUID. Attributes must be enclosed in square brackets.

The *definitions* consist of the descriptions of the imported libraries, data types, modules, interfaces, dispinterfaces, and coclasses that are part of the type library. Braces ({ }) must surround the definitions.

The following table summarizes the elements that may appear in *definitions*. Each element is described in detail in the section, "ODL Reference."

Purpose	Library element	Description
Allows references to other type libraries.	importlib (*lib1*)	Specifies an external type library that contains definitions referenced in this type library.
Declares data types used by the objects in this type library.	**typedef** [*attributes*] *aliasname*	An alias declared using C syntax. Must have at least one *attribute* to be included in the type library.
	typedef [*attributes*] **enum**	An enumeration declared using C **typedef** and **enum** keywords.
	typedef [*attributes*] **struct**	A structure declared using C **typedef** and **struct** keywords.
	typedef [*attributes*] **union**	A union declared using C **typedef** and **union** keywords.
Describes functions that enable querying the DLL.	[*attributes*] **module**	Constants and general data functions whose actions are not restricted to any specified class of objects.
Describes interfaces.	[*attributes*] **dispinterface**	An interface describing the methods and properties for an object that must be accessed through **IDispatch::Invoke**.
	[*attributes*] **interface**	An interface describing the methods and properties for an object that may be accessed through **IDispatch::Invoke** or through VTBL entries.
Describes OLE classes.	[*attributes*] **coclass**	Specifies a top-level object, with all its interfaces and dispinterfaces.

Within the library description, modules, interfaces, dispinterfaces, and coclasses follow the same general syntax:

[*attributes*] *elementname typename* {
   memberdescriptions
};

The *attributes* set characteristics for the element. The *elementname* is a keyword that indicates the kind of item (**module**, **interface**, **dispinterface**, or **coclass**), and the *typename* defines the name of the item. The *memberdescriptions* define the members (constants, functions, properties, and methods) of each element.

Aliases, enumerations, unions, and structures have the following syntax:

typedef [*typeattributes*] *typekind typename* {
   memberdescriptions
};

For these types, the attributes follow the **typedef** keyword, and the *typekind* indicates the data type (**enum**, **union**, or **struct**). See the keyword descriptions for details.

Note The square brackets ([])and braces ({ }) in these descriptions are part of the syntax, not descriptive symbols. The semicolon after the closing brace (}) that terminates the library definition (and all other type definitions) is optional.

ODL File Example

The following example shows the ODL file for the Lines sample, extracted from LINES.ODL:

```
[
    uuid(3C591B20-1F13-101B-B826-00DD01103DE1),        // LIBID_Lines
    helpstring("Lines 1.0 Type Library"),
    lcid(0x0409),
    version(1.0)
]
library Lines
{
    importlib("stdole.tlb");
    #define DISPID_NEWENUM -4

    [
        uuid(3C591B25-1F13-101B-B826-00DD01103DE1),   // IID_IPoint
        helpstring("Point object."),
        oleautomation,
        dual
    ]
```

```
interface IPoint : IDispatch
{
    [propget, helpstring("Returns and sets x coordinate.")]
    HRESULT x([out, retval] int* retval);
    [propput, helpstring("Returns and sets x coordinate.")]
    HRESULT x([in] int Value);

    [propget, helpstring("Returns and sets y coordinate.")]
    HRESULT y([out, retval] int* retval);
    [propput, helpstring("Returns and sets y coordinate.")]
    HRESULT y([in] int Value);
}

// Additional interfaces omitted for brevity

[
        uuid(3C591B27-1F13-101B-B826-00DD01103DE1),      // IID_IPoints
        helpstring("Points collection."),
        oleautomation,
        dual
]
interface IPoints : IDispatch
{
    [propget, helpstring("Returns number of points in collection.")]
    HRESULT Count([out, retval] long* retval);

    [propget, id(0),
    helpstring("Given an index, returns a point in the collection")]
    HRESULT Item([in] long Index, [out, retval] IPoint** retval);

    [propget, restricted, id(DISPID_NEWENUM)]    // Must be propget.
    HRESULT _NewEnum([out, retval] IUnknown** retval);
}

// Additional interface omitted for brevity

[
        uuid(3C591B22-1F13-101B-B826-00DD01103DE1),  // IID_IApplication
        helpstring("Application object."),
        oleautomation,
        dual
]
interface IApplication : IDispatch
{
    [propget, helpstring("Returns the application of the object.")]
    HRESULT Application([out, retval] IApplication** retval);

    [propget,
        helpstring("Returns the full name of the application.")]
    HRESULT FullName([out, retval] BSTR* retval);
```

```
        [propget, id(0),
        helpstring("Returns the name of the application.")]
        HRESULT Name([out, retval] BSTR* retval);

        [propget, helpstring("Returns the parent of the object.")]
        HRESULT Parent([out, retval] IApplication** retval);

        [propput]
        HRESULT Visible([in] boolean VisibleFlag);
        [propget, helpstring
        ("Sets or returns whether the main window is visible.")]
        HRESULT Visible([out, retval] boolean* retval);

        [helpstring("Exits the application.")]
        HRESULT Quit();

    // Additional methods omitted for brevity

        [helpstring("Creates new Point object initialized to (0,0).")]
        HRESULT CreatePoint([out, retval] IPoint** retval);
    }

    [
        uuid(3C591B21-1F13-101B-B826-00DD01103DE1),  // CLSID_Lines
        helpstring("Lines Class"),
        appobject
    ]
    coclass Lines
    {
        [default] interface IApplication;
            interface IDispatch;
    }
}
```

The example describes a library named Lines, which imports the standard OLE
library STDOLE.TLB. The #define directive defines the constant
DISPID_NEWENUM, which is needed for the _NewEnum property of the IPoints
collection.

The example shows declarations for three interfaces in the library: IPoint, IPoints,
and IApplication. Because all three are **dual** interfaces, their members may be
invoked through **IDispatch** or directly through VTBLs. In addition, all their
members return HRESULT values and pass their return values as **retval**
parameters. Therefore, they can support the **IErrorInfo** interface, through which
they can return detailed error information, no matter how they are invoked.

The IPoint interface has two properties, x and y, and two pairs of accessor functions to get and set the properties.

The IPoints interface is a collection of points. It supports three read-only properties, each of which has a single accessor function. The Count and Item properties return the number of points and the value of a single point, respectively. The _NewEnum property, required for collection objects, returns an enumerator object for the collection. This property has the **restricted** attribute, indicating that it should not be invoked from a macro language.

The IApplication interface describes the application object. It supports properties named Application, FullName, Name, Parent, Visible, and Pane; and methods named Quit, CreateLine, and CreatePoint.

Finally, the script defines a coclass named Lines. The **appobject** attribute makes the members of the coclass (IApplication and IDispatch) globally accessible in the type library. IApplication is defined as the **default** member, indicating that it is the programmability interface intended for use by macro languages.

Source File Contents

The following sections describe the proper format for comments, constants, identifiers, and other syntactic items within an ODL file.

Array Definitions

MkTypLib accepts both fixed-size arrays and arrays declared as SAFEARRAY.

Use C-style syntax for a fixed-size array:

type arrname[*size*];

To describe a SAFEARRAY, use the following syntax:

SAFEARRAY (*elementtype*) **arrayname*

A function returning a SAFEARRAY has the following syntax:

SAFEARRAY (*elementtype*) *myfunction*(*parameterlist*);

Comments

To include comments in an ODL file, use C-style syntax in either block form (/*...*/) or single-line form (//). MkTypLib ignores the comments, and does not preserve them in the header (.H) file.

Constants

A constant can be either numeric or a string, depending on the attribute.

Numerics

Numeric input is usually an integer (in either decimal or in hexadecimal using the standard **0x** format), but may also be a single character constant (for example, \0).

Strings

A string is delimited by double-quotation marks (") and may not span multiple lines. The backslash character (\) acts as an escape character. The backslash character followed by any character (even another backslash) prevents the second character from being interpreted with any special meaning; the backslash is not included in the text.

For example, to include a double-quotation mark (") in the text without causing it to be interpreted as the closing delimiter, precede it with a backslash (\"). Similarly, you can use a double backslash (\\) to put a backslash into the text. Some examples of valid strings are:

```
"commandName"
"This string contains a \"quote\"."
"Here's a pathname: c:\\bin\\binp"
```

A string can be up to 255 characters long.

Filenames

A filename is a string that represents either a full or partial path. OLE Automation expects to find files in directories referenced by the type library registration entries, so partial pathnames are typically used. See Chapter 2, "Exposing OLE Automation Objects," for more information about registration.

Forward Declarations

Forward declarations permit forward references to types. Forward references have the following form:

```
typedef struct mydata;
interface aninterface;
dispinterface fordispatch;
coclass pococlass;
```

The Globally Unique ID (GUID)

A UUID is a globally unique ID (GUID). This number is created by running the GUIDGEN.EXE command-line program. GUIDGEN will never produce the same number twice, no matter how many times it is run or how many different machines it runs on. Every entity (such as an interface) that needs to be uniquely identified has a GUID.

Identifiers

Identifiers can be up to 255 characters long, and must conform to C-style syntax. MkTypLib is case sensitive, but it generates type libraries that are case insensitive. Thus, it is possible to define a user-defined type whose name differs from that of a built-in type only by case. However, user-defined type names (and member names) that differ only in case refer to the same type or member. Except for property accessor functions, it is illegal for two members of a type to have the same name, regardless of case.

Intrinsic Data Types

The following data types are recognized by MkTypLib:

Type	Description
boolean	Data item that can have the values True or False. The size maps to VARIANT_BOOL.
char	8-bit signed data item.
double	64-bit IEEE floating-point number.
int	Signed integer, whose size is system-dependent.
float	32-bit IEEE floating-point number.
long	32-bit signed integer.
short	16-bit signed integer.
void	Allowed only as return type for a function, or in a function parameter list to indicate no arguments.
wchar_t	Unicode character accepted only for 32-bit type libraries.
BSTR	Length-prefixed string, as described in Chapter 5, "Dispatch Interfaces."
CURRENCY	8-byte fixed-point number.
DATE	64-bit floating-point fractional number of days since December 30, 1899.
HRESULT	Return type used for reporting error information in interfaces, as described in the *OLE Programmer's Guide and Reference*.

Type	Description
LPWSTR	Unicode string accepted only for 32-bit type libraries.
LPSTR	Zero-terminated string.
SCODE	Built-in error type that corresponds to VT_ERROR. An SCODE does not contain the additional error information provided by HRESULT.
VARIANT	One of the variant data types as described in Chapter 5, "Dispatch Interfaces."
IDispatch *	Pointer to **IDispatch** interface.
IUnknown *	Pointer to **IUnknown** interface. (Any OLE interface can be represented by its **IUnknown** interface.)

The keyword **unsigned** may be specified before **int**, **char**, **short**, and **long**.

String Definitions

Strings can be declared using the LPSTR type, which indicates a zero-terminated string, and with the BSTR type, which indicates a length-prefixed string (as defined in Chapter 5, "Dispatch Interfaces." In 32-bit type libraries, Unicode strings can be defined with the LPWSTR type.

ODL Reference

The remainder of this chapter provides reference material on the attributes, statements, and directives that are part of the Object Description Language (ODL).

Attribute Descriptions

The following sections describe the ODL attributes and list the types of objects to which they apply, and the equivalent flags set in the object's typeinfo.

appobject

Description	Identifies the Application object.
Allowed on	Coclass
Comments	Indicates that the members of the class may be accessed without qualification when accessing this type library.
Flags	TYPEFLAG_FAPPOBJECT

bindable

Description   Indicates that the property supports data binding.

Allowed on   Property

Comments   Refers to the property as a whole, so it must be specified wherever the property is defined. Therefore, you need to specify the attribute on both the property get description and on the property set description.

Flags   FUNCFLAG_FBINDABLE, VARFLAG_FBINDABLE

---

control

Description   Indicates that the item represents a control from which a container site will derive additional typelibs or coclasses.

Allowed on   Typelib, coclass

Comments   This attribute allows you to mark type libraries that describe controls so that they will not be displayed in type browsers intended for nonvisual objects.

Flags   TYPEFLAG_FCONTROL, LIBFLAG_FCONTROL

---

default

Description   Indicates that the interface or dispinterface represents the default programmability interface, intended for use by macro languages.

Allowed on   Coclass member

Comments   A coclass may have at most two **default** members. One represents the source interface or dispinterface, and the other represents the sink interface or dispinterface. If the **default** attribute is not specified for any member of the coclass or cotype, the first source and sink members that do not have the **restricted** attribute are treated as the defaults.

Flags   IMPLTYPEFLAG_FDEFAULT

defaultbind

Description   Indicates the single, bindable property that best represents the object.

Allowed on   Property

Comments   Properties that have the **defaultbind** attribute must also have the **bindable** attribute. You can't specify **defaultbind** on more than one property in a dispinterface.

This attribute is used by containers that have a user model involving binding to an object rather than binding to a property of an object. An object can support data binding but not have this attribute.

Flags   FUNCFLAG_FDEFAULTBIND, VARFLAG_FDEFAULTBIND

---

displaybind

Description   Indicates a property that should be displayed to the user as bindable.

Allowed on   Property

Comments   Properties that have the **displaybind** attribute must also have the **bindable** attribute. An object can support data binding but not have this attribute.

Flags   FUNCFLAG_FDISPLAYBIND, VARFLAG_FDISPLAYBIND

---

dllname (*str*)

Description   Defines the name of the DLL that contains the entry points for a module.

Allowed on   Module (required)

Comments   The *str* argument gives the filename of the DLL.

---

dual

Description   Identifies an interface that exposes properties and methods through **IDispatch** and directly through the VTBL.

Allowed on   Interface

Comments   The interface must be compatible with OLE Automation and derive from **IDispatch**. Not allowed on dispinterfaces.

The **dual** attribute creates an interface that is both a **Dispatch** interface and a Component Object Model (COM) interface. The first seven entries of the VTBL for a dual interface are the seven members of **IDispatch**, and the remaining entries are OLE COM entries for direct access to members of the dual interface. All the parameters and return types specified for members of a dual interface must be OLE Automation-compatible types.

All members of a dual interface must pass an HRESULT as the function return value. Members that need to return other values should specify the last parameter as [**retval**, **out**] indicating an output parameter that returns the value of the function. In addition, members that need to support multiple locales should pass an **lcid** parameter.

A dual interface provides for both the speed of direct VTBL binding and the flexibility of **IDispatch** binding. For this reason, dual interfaces are recommended whenever possible.

Note If your application accesses object data by casting the THIS pointer within the interface call, you should check the VTBL pointers in the object against your own VTBL pointers to ensure that you are connected to the appropriate proxy.

Specifying **dual** on an interface implies that the interface is compatible with OLE Automation, and therefore causes both the TYPEFLAG_FDUAL and TYPEFLAG_FOLEAUTOMATION flags to be set.

Flags   TYPEFLAG_FDUAL, TYPEFLAG_FOLEAUTOMATION

---

entry(*entryid*)

Description   Identifies the entry point in the DLL.

Allowed on   Functions in a module (required)

Comments   If *entryid* is a string, this is a named entry point. If *entryid* is a number, the entry point is defined by an ordinal. This attribute provides a way to obtain the address of a function in a module.

helpcontext(*numctxt*)

Description   Sets the context within the Help file.

Allowed on   Library, interface, dispinterface, struct, enum, union, module, typedef, method, struct member, enum value, property, coclass, const

Comments   Retrieved via the **GetDocumentation** functions in the **ITypeLib** and **ITypeInfo** interfaces. The *numctxt* is a 32-bit Help context within the Help file.

---

helpfile(*filename*)

Description   Sets the name of the Help file.

Allowed on   Library

Comments   Retrieved via the **GetDocumentation** functions in the **ITypeLib** and **ITypeInfo** interfaces.

All types in a library share the same Help file.

---

helpstring(*string*)

Description   Sets the Help string.

Allowed on   Library, interface, dispinterface, struct, enum, union, module, typedef, method, struct member, enum value, property, coclass, const

Comments   Retrieved via the **GetDocumentation** functions in the **ITypeLib** and **ITypeInfo** interfaces.

---

hidden

Description   Indicates that the item exists but should not be displayed in a user-oriented browser.

Allowed on   Property, method, coclass, dispinterface, interface, library

Comments

This attribute allows you to remove members from your interface (by shielding them from further use) while maintaining compatibility with existing code.

When specified for a library, the attribute prevents the entire library from being displayed. It is intended for use by controls. Hosts need to create a new type library that wraps the control with extended properties.

Flags

VARFLAG_FHIDDEN, FUNCFLAG_FHIDDEN, TYPEFLAG_FHIDDEN

id(*num*)

Description

Identifies the DISPID of the member.

Allowed on

Method or property in an interface or dispinterface

Comments

The *num* is a 32-bit integral value in the following format:

Bits	Value
0–15	Offset. Any value is permissible.
16–21	The nesting level of this typeinfo in the inheritance hierarchy. For example: `interface mydisp : IDispatch` The nesting level of **IUnknown** is 0, **IDispatch** is 1, and mydisp is 2.
22–25	Reserved; must be zero
26–28	DISPID value.
29	True if this is the member ID for a FuncDesc; otherwise False.
30–31	Must be 01.

Negative IDs are reserved for use by OLE Automation.

in

Description

Specifies an input parameter.

Allowed on

Parameter

Comments

The parameter may be a pointer (such as **char** *) but the value it refers to is not returned.

lcid

Description	Indicates that the parameter is a locale ID.
Allowed on	Parameter in a member of an interface
Comments	At most one parameter may have this attribute. The parameter must have the **in** attribute and can't have the **out** attribute, and its type must be **long**. The **lcid** attribute is not allowed on dispinterfaces.

The **lcid** attribute allows members in the VTBL to receive an LCID at invocation. By convention, the **lcid** parameter is the last parameter that does not have the **retval** attribute. If the member specifies **propertyput** or **propertyputref**, the **lcid** parameter must precede the parameter that represents the right side of the property assignment.

ITypeInfo::Invoke passes the LCID of the typeinfo into the **lcid** parameter. Parameters with this attibute are not displayed in user-oriented browsers.

lcid(*numid*)

Description	Identifies the locale for a type library.
Allowed on	Library
Comments	The *numid* is a 32-bit locale ID as used in Win32 National Language Support. The locale ID is typically entered in hexadecimal.

licensed

Description	Indicates that the class is licensed.
Allowed on	Coclass
Flags	TYPEFLAG_FLICENSED

nonextensible

Description	Indicates that the **IDispatch** implementation includes only the properties and methods listed in the interface description.
Allowed on	Dispinterface, interface
Comments	The interface must have the **dual** attribute.
	By default, OLE Automation assumes that interfaces may add members at run time; that is, it assumes they are extensible.
Flags	TYPEFLAG_FNONEXTENSIBLE

odl

Description	Identifies an interface as an ODL interface.
Allowed on	Interface (required)
Comments	This attribute must appear on all interfaces.

oleautomation

Description	Indicates that an interface is compatible with OLE Automation.
Allowed on	Interface
Comments	Not allowed on dispinterfaces.

The **oleautomation** attribute indicates that an interface is compatible with OLE Automation. The parameters and return types specified for its members must be OLE Automation-compatible, as listed in the following table.

Type	Description
boolean	Data item that can have the value True or False. The size corresponds to VARIANT_BOOL.
unsigned char	8-bit unsigned data item.
double	64-bit IEEE floating-point number.
float	32-bit IEEE floating-point number.

Type	Description
int	Signed integer, whose size is system-dependent.
long	32-bit signed integer.
short	16-bit signed integer.
BSTR	Length-prefixed string, as described in Chapter 5, "Dispatch Interfaces."
CURRENCY	8-byte fixed-point number.
DATE	64-bit floating-point fractional number of days since December 30, 1899.
SCODE	Built-in error type that corresponds to VT_ERROR.
typedef enum *myenum*	Signed integer, whose size is system-dependent.
interface IDispatch *	Pointer to **IDispatch** interface (VT_DISPATCH).
interface IUnknown *	Pointer to interface that does not derive from **IDispatch** (VT_UNKNOWN). (Any OLE interface can be represented by its **IUnknown** interface.)
dispinterface *Typename* *	Pointer to **IDispatch**-derived interface (VT_DISPATCH).
coclass *Typename* *	Pointer to a coclass name (VT_UNKNOWN).
[oleautomation] interface *Typename* *	Pointer to an interface that derives from **IDispatch**.

A parameter is compatible with OLE Automation if its type is an OLE Automation-compatible type, a pointer to an OLE Automation-compatible type, or a SAFEARRAY of an OLE Automation-compatible type.

A return type is compatible with OLE Automation if its type is an HRESULT or is **void**. Methods in OLE Automation must return either HRESULT or **void**.

A member is compatible with OLE Automation if its return type and all of its parameters are OLE-Automation compatible.

An interface is compatible with OLE Automation if it derives from **IDispatch** or IUnknown, if it has the **oleautomation** attribute, and if all of its VTBL entries are OLE-Automation compatible. For 32-bit systems, the calling convention for all methods in the interface must be STDCALL. For 16-bit systems, all methods must have the CDECL calling convention. Every dispinterface is OLE Automation-compatible.

Flags   TYPEFLAG_FOLEAUTOMATION

optional

Description	Specifies an optional parameter.
Allowed on	Parameter
Comments	Valid only if the parameter is of type VARIANT or VARIANT*. All subsequent parameters of the function must also be **optional**.

out

Description	Specifies an output parameter.
Allowed on	Parameter
Comments	The parameter must be a pointer to memory that will receive a result.

propget

Description	Specifies a property accessor function.
Allowed on	Functions; methods in interfaces and dispinterfaces
Comments	The property must have the same name as the function. At most, one of **propget**, **propput**, and **propputref** can be specified for a function.
Flags	INVOKE_PROPERTYGET

propput

Description	Specifies a property-setting function.
Allowed on	Functions; methods in interfaces and dispinterfaces
Comments	The property must have the same name as the function. At most, one of **propget**, **propput** and **propputref** can be specified.
Flags	INVOKE_PROPERTYPUT

propputref

Description	Specifies a property-setting function that uses a reference instead of a value.
Allowed on	Functions; methods in interfaces and dispinterfaces
Comments	The property must have the same name as the function. At most, one of **propget**, **propput** and **propputref** can be specified.
Flags	INVOKE_PROPERTYPUTREF

public

Description	Includes an alias declared with the **typedef** keyword in the type library.
Allowed on	Aliases declared with **typedef**
Comments	By default, an alias that is declared with **typedef** and has no other attributes is treated as a **#define** and is not included in the type library. Using the **public** attribute ensures that the alias becomes part of the type library.

readonly

Description	Prohibits assignment to a variable.
Allowed on	Variable
Flags	VARFLAG_FREADONLY

requestedit

Description	Indicates that the property supports the OnRequestEdit notification.
Allowed on	Property
Comments	The property supports the OnRequestEdit notification, raised by a property before it is edited. An object can support data binding but not have this attribute.
Flags	FUNCFLAG_FREQUESTEDIT, VARFLAG_FREQUESTEDIT

restricted

Description Prevents the item from being used by a macro programmer.

Allowed on Type library, coclass member, member of a module or interface

Comments Allowed on a member of a coclass, independent of whether the member is a dispinterface or interface, and independent of whether the member is a sink or source. A member of a coclass can't have both the **restricted** and **default** attributes.

Flags IMPLTYPEFLAG_FRESTRICTED, FUNCFLAG_FRESTRICTED

---

retval

Description Designates the parameter that receives the return value of the member.

Allowed on Parameters of interface members that describe methods or get properties

Comments This attribute may be used only on the last parameter of the member. The parameter must have the **out** attribute and must be a pointer type.

Parameters with this attibute are not displayed in user-oriented browsers.

Flags IDLFLAG_FRETVAL

---

source

Description Indicates that a member is a source of events.

Allowed on Member of a coclass; property or method.

Comments For a member of a coclass, this attribute means that the member is called rather than implemented.

On a property or method, indicates that the member returns an object or VARIANT that is a source of events. The object implements **IConnectionPointContainer**.

Flags IMPLTYPEFLAG_FSOURCE, VARFLAG_SOURCE, FUNCFLAG_SOURCE

string

Description	Specifies a string.
Allowed on	Struct, member, parameter, property
Comments	Included only for compatibility with IDL; use LPSTR for a zero-terminated string.

uuid(*uuidval*)

Description	Specifies the UUID of the item.
Allowed on	Required for library, dispinterface, interface, and coclass; optional on struct, enum, union, module, and typedef
Comments	The *uuidval* is a 16-byte value formatted as hexadecimal digits in the following format: `12345678-1234-1234-1234-123456789ABC`. This value is returned in the TypeAttr structure retrieved by **TypeInfo::GetTypeAttr.**

vararg

Description	Indicates a variable number of arguments.
Allowed on	Function
Comments	Indicates that the last parameter is a safe array of VARIANT type, which contains all the remaining parameters.

version(*versionval*)

Description	Specifies a version number.
Allowed on	Library, struct, module, dispinterface, interface, coclass, enum, union.
Comments	The argument *versionval* is a real number in the format *n.m*, where *n* is a major version number and *m* is a minor version number.

ODL Statements and Directives

The following sections describe the statements and directives that make up the Object Description Language.

The coclass Statement

Describes the GUID and supported interfaces for a component object.

Syntax

[*attributes*]
coclass classname {
    [attributes2] [interface | dispinterface] interfacename;
    . . .
};

Syntax Elements

attributes
The **uuid** attribute is required on a coclass. This is the same **uuid** that is registered as a CLSID in the system registration database. The **helpstring, helpcontext, licensed, version, control, hidden,** and **appobject** attributes are accepted, but not required, before a **coclass** definition. See "Attribute Descriptions" for more information on the attributes accepted before a coclass definition. The **appobject** attribute makes the functions and properties of the coclass globally available in the type library.

classname
Name by which the common object is known in the type library.

attributes2
Optional attributes for the interface or dispinterface. The **source, default,** and **restricted** attributes are accepted on an interface or dispinterface within a coclass.

interfacename
Either an interface declared with the **interface** keyword, or a dispinterface declared with the **dispinterface** keyword.

Comments

The Microsoft Component Object Model defines a class as an implementation that allows **QueryInterface** between a set of interfaces.

Examples

```
[ uuid(BFB73347-822A-1068-8849-00DD011087E8), version(1.0),
helpstring("A class"), helpcontext(2481), appobject]
coclass myapp {
    [source] interface IMydocfuncs;
    dispinterface DMydocfuncs;
};
```

```
[uuid 00000000-0000-0000-0000-123456789019]
coclass foo
{
    [restricted] interface bar;
    interface baz;
}
```

The dispinterface Statement

Defines a set of properties and methods on which you can call **IDispatch::Invoke**. A dispinterface may be defined by explicitly listing the set of supported methods and properties (Syntax 1) or by listing a single interface (Syntax 2).

Syntax 1

[*attributes*]
dispinterface *intfname* {
    properties:
       proplist
    methods:
       methlist
};

Syntax 2

[*attributes*]
dispinterface *intfname* {
    interface *interfacename*
};

Syntax Elements

attributes
> The **helpstring**, **helpcontext**, **hidden**, **uuid**, and **version** attributes are accepted before **dispinterface**. See "Attribute Descriptions" for more information on the attributes accepted before a **dispinterface** definition. Attributes (including the brackets) may be omitted. The **uuid** attribute is required.

intfname
> The name by which the **dispinterface** is known in the type library. This name must be unique within the type library.

interfacename
> (Syntax 2) The name of the interface to declare as an **IDispatch** interface.

proplist

(Syntax 1) An optional list of properties supported by the object, declared in the form of variables. This is the short form for declaring the property functions in the methods list. See the comments section for details. ·

methlist

(Syntax 1) A list comprising a function prototype for each method and property in the **dispinterface**. Any number of function definitions can appear in *methlist*. A function in *methlist* has the following form:

[*attributes*] *returntype methname(params)*;

The following attributes are accepted on a method in a **dispinterface**: **helpstring**, **helpcontext**, **string** (for compatibility with IDL), **bindable**, **defaultbind**, **displaybind**, **propget**, **propput**, **propputref**, and **vararg.** If **vararg** is specified, the last parameter must be a safe array of VARIANT type.

The parameter list is a comma-delimited list, each element of which has the following form:

[*attributes*] *type paramname*

The *type* can be any declared or built-in type, or a pointer to any type. Attributes on parameters are:

in, **out**, **optional**, **string**

If **optional** appears, it must only be specified on the rightmost parameters, and the types of those parameters must be VARIANT.

Comments

Method functions are specified exactly as described in "The module Statement," except that the **entry** attribute is not allowed. Note that STDOLE32.TLB (STDOLE.TLB on 16-bit systems) must be imported, because a **dispinterface** inherits from **IDispatch**.

You can declare properties in either the properties or methods lists. Declaring properties in the properties list does not indicate the type of access the property supports (that is, get, put, or putref). Specify the **readonly** attribute for properties that don't support put or putref. If you declare the property functions in the methods list, functions for one property all have the same ID.

Using Syntax 1, the **properties:** and **methods:** tags are required. The **id** attribute is also required on each member. For example:

```
properties:
    [id(0)] int Value;   // Default property.
methods:
    [id(1)] void Show();
```

Unlike **interface** members, **dispinterface** members cannot use the **retval** attribute to return a value in addition to an HRESULT error code. The **lcid** attribute is likewise invalid for dispinterfaces, because **IDispatch::Invoke** passes an LCID. However, it is possible to redeclare an interface that uses these attributes.

Using Syntax 2, interfaces that support **IDispatch** and are declared earlier in an ODL script can be redeclared as **IDispatch** interfaces as follows:

```
dispinterface helloPro {
    interface hello;
};
```

The preceding example declares all of the members of hello and all of the members that hello inherits as supporting **IDispatch**. In this case, if hello were declared earlier with **lcid** and **retval** members that returned HRESULTs, MkTypLib would remove each **lcid** parameter and HRESULT return type, and instead mark the return type as that of the **retval** parameter.

The properties and methods of a dispinterface are not part of the VTBL of the dispinterface. Consequently, **CreateStdDispatch** and **DispInvoke** can't be used to implement **IDispatch::Invoke**. The dispinterface is used when an application needs to expose existing non-VTBL functions through OLE Automation. These applications can implement **IDispatch::Invoke** by examining the *dispidMember* parameter and directly calling the corresponding function.

Example

```
[ uuid(BFB73347-822A-1068-8849-00DD011087E8), version(1.0),
helpstring("Useful help string."), helpcontext(2480)]
dispinterface MyDispatchObject {
    properties:
        [id(1)] int x;   //An integer property named x
        [id(2)] BSTR y; //A string property named y
    methods:
        [id(3)] void show(); //No arguments, no result
        [id(11)] int computeit(int inarg, double *outarg);
};

[uuid 00000000-0000-0000-0000-123456789012]
dispinterface MyObject
{
    properties:
    methods:
        [id(1), propget, bindable, defaultbind, displaybind]
        long x();

        [id(1), propput, bindable, defaultbind, displaybind]
        void x(long rhs);
}
```

The enum Statement

Defines a C-style enumerated type.

Syntax

typedef [*attributes*] **enum** [*tag*] {
   enumlist
} *enumname*;

Syntax Elements

attributes

The **helpstring, helpcontext, hidden**, and **uuid** attributes are accepted before an **enum**. The **helpstring** and **helpcontext** attributes are accepted on an enumeration element. See "Attribute Descriptions" for more information on the attributes accepted before an enumeration definition. Attributes (including the brackets) may be omitted. If **uuid** is omitted, the enumeration is not uniquely specified in the system.

tag

An optional tag, as with a C **enum**.

enumlist

List of enumerated elements.

enumname

Name by which the enumeration is known in the type library.

Comments

The **enum** keyword must be preceded by **typedef**. The enumeration description must precede other references to the enumeration in the library. If = *value* is not specified for enumerators, the numbering progresses as with enumerations in C. The type of the **enum** elements is **int**, the system default integer, which depends on the target type library specification.

Examples

```
typedef [uuid(DEADF00D-C0DE-B1FF-F001-A100FF001ED),
        helpstring("Farm Animals are friendly"), helpcontext(234)]
enum {
    [helpstring("Moo")] cows = 1,
    pigs = 2
} ANIMALS;
```

The importlib Directive

Makes types that have already been compiled into another type library available to the library currently being created. All **importlib** directives must precede the other type descriptions in the library.

Syntax

importlib(*filename*);

Syntax Elements   filename
        The location of the type library file when MkTypLib is executed.

Comments   The **importlib** directive makes any type defined in the imported library accessible from within the library being compiled. Ambiguity is resolved as follows. The current library is searched for the type. If the type can't be found, MkTypLib searches the imported library that is lexically first, then the next, and so on. To import a type name in code, you must enter the name as *libname.typename,* where *libname* is the library name as it appeared in the **library** statement when the library was compiled.

The imported type library should be distributed with the library being compiled.

Example   The following example imports the libraries STDOLE.TLB and MYDISP.TLB:

```
library BrowseHelper
{
    importlib("stdole.tlb");
    importlib("mydisp.tlb");
//Additional text omitted
}
```

The interface Statement

Defines an interface, which is a set of function definitions. An interface can inherit from any base interface.

Syntax   [*attributes*]
interface *interfacename* [*:baseinterface*] {
    functionlist
};

Syntax Elements   *attributes*
        The **dual, helpstring, helpcontext, hidden, odl, oleautomation, uuid,** and **version** attributes are accepted before **interface**. If the interface is a member of a coclass, the **source, default,** and **restricted** attributes are also accepted. See "Attribute Descriptions" for more information on the attributes accepted before an interface definition.

        The **odl** and **uuid** attributes are required on all interface declarations.

interfacename
        The name by which the interface is known in the type library.

baseinterface

> The name of the interface that is the base class for this interface.

functionlist

> List of function prototypes for each function in the interface. Any number of function definitions can appear in the function list. A function in the function list has the following form:
>
> [*attributes*] *returntype* [*calling convention*] *funcname*(*params*);
>
> The following attributes are accepted on a function in an interface: **helpstring, helpcontext, string, propget, propput, propputref, bindable, defaultbind, displaybind**, and **vararg**. If **vararg** is specified, the last parameter must be a safe array of VARIANT type. The optional *calling convention* can be any one of **__pascal/_pascal/pascal** or **__cdecl/_cdecl/cdecl, __stdcall/_stdcall/stdcall**. In other words, the calling convention specification can include up to two leading underscores.
>
> The parameter list is a comma-delimited list as follows:
>
> [*attributes*] *type paramname*
>
> The *type* can be any previously declared type, built-in type, a pointer to any type, or a pointer to a built-in type. Attributes on parameters are:
>
> **in, out, optional, string**
>
> If **optional** appears, it must only be specified on the rightmost parameters, and the types of those parameters must be VARIANT.

Comments

Because the functions described by the **interface** statement are in the VTBL, you can use **DispInvoke** and **CreateStdDispatch** to provide an implementation of **IDispatch::Invoke**. For this reason, **interface** is more commonly used than **dispinterface** to describe the properties and methods of an object.

Functions in interfaces are the same as described in "The **module** Statement," except that the **entry** attribute is not allowed.

Members of interfaces that need to raise exceptions should return an HRESULT and specify a **retval** parameter for the actual return value. The **retval** parameter is always the last parameter in the list.

Examples

The following example defines an interface named Hello with two member functions, HelloProc and Shutdown:

```
[uuid(BFB73347-822A-1068-8849-00DD011087E8), version(1.0)]
interface hello : IUnknown
{
void HelloProc([in, string] unsigned char * pszString);
void Shutdown(void);
};
```

The next example defines a **dual** interface named IMyInt, which has a pair of accessor functions for the MyMessage property and a method that returns a string.

```
[dual]
interface IMyInt : IDispatch
{
    //A property that is a string
    [propget] HRESULT MyMessage([in, lcid] LCID lcid,
                                [out, retval] BSTR *pbstrRetVal);
    [propput] HRESULT MyMessage([in] BSTR rhs, [in, lcid] DWORD lcid);

    //A method returning a string
    HRESULT SayMessage([in] long NumTimes,
                       [in, lcid] DWORD lcid,
                       [out, retval] BSTR *pbstrRetVal);
}
```

The members of this interface return error information and function return values through the HRESULT values and **retval** parameters, respectively. Tools that access the members can return the HRESULT to their users, or can simply expose the **retval** parameter as the return value and handle the HRESULT transparently.

Note that a **dual** interface must derive from **IDispatch**.

The library Statement

Describes a type library. This description contains all the other information in a MkTypLib input file.

Syntax

[attributes] **library** libname {
    definitions
};

Syntax Elements

attributes
The **helpstring**, **helpcontext**, **lcid, restricted, hidden, control**, and **uuid** attributes are accepted before a **library** statement. See "Attribute Descriptions" for more information on the attributes accepted before a library definition. The **uuid** attribute is required.

libname
The name by which the type library is known.

definitions
Descriptions of any imported libraries, data types, modules, interfaces, dispinterfaces, and coclasses relevant to the object being exposed.

Comments   The **library** statement must precede any other type definitions.

Example

```
[
    uuid(F37C8060-4AD5-101B-B826-00DD01103DE1), // LIBID_Hello
    helpstring("Hello 2.0 Type Library"),
    lcid(0x0409),
    version(2.0)
]
library Hello
{
    importlib("stdole.tlb");
    [
        uuid(F37C8062-4AD5-101B-B826-00DD01103DE1), // IID_IHello
        helpstring("Application object for the Hello application."),
        oleautomation,
        dual
    ]
    interface IHello : IDispatch
    {
        [propget, helpstring("Returns the application of the object.")]
        HRESULT Application([in, lcid] long localeID,
            [out, retval] IHello** retval)
    }
}
```

The module Statement

Defines a group of functions, typically a set of DLL entry points.

Syntax

[attributes]
module modulename {
    elementlist
};

Syntax Elements   attributes

The **uuid**, **version**, **helpstring**, **helpcontext**, **hidden**, and **dllname** attributes are accepted before a **module** statement. See "Attribute Descriptions" for more information on the attributes accepted before a module definition. The **dllname** attribute is required. If **uuid** is omitted, the module is not uniquely specified in the system.

modulename

The name of the module.

elementlist

List of constant definitions and function prototypes for each function in the DLL. Any number of function definitions can appear in the function list. A function in the function list has the following form:

[*attributes*] *returntype* [*calling convention*] *funcname*(*params*);
[*attributes*] **const** *constname* = *constval*;

Only the **helpstring** and **helpcontext** attributes are accepted for a **const**.

The following attributes are accepted on a function in a module: **helpstring**, **helpcontext**, **string**, **entry**, **propget**, **propput**, **propputref**, **vararg**. If **vararg** is specified, the last parameter must be a safe array of VARIANT type.

The optional *calling convention* can be one of **__pascal/_pascal/pascal**, **__cdecl/_cdecl/cdecl**, or **__stdcall/_stdcall/stdcall**. The *calling convention* can include up to two leading underscores.

The parameter list is a comma-delimited list of:

[*attributes*] *type paramname*

The *type* can be any previously declared type or built-in type, a pointer to any type, or a pointer to a built-in type. Attributes on parameters are:

in, **out**, **optional**

If **optional** appears, it must only be specified on the rightmost parameters, and the types of those parameters must be VARIANT.

Comments

The header file (.H) output for modules is a series of function prototypes. The **module** keyword and surrounding brackets are stripped from the header (.H) file output, but a comment (\\ **module** *modulename*) is inserted before the prototypes. The keyword **extern** is inserted before the declarations.

Example

```
[uuid(D00BED00-CEDE-B1FF-F001-A100FF001ED),
    helpstring("This is not GDI.EXE"), helpcontext(190),
    dllname("MATH.DLL")]
module somemodule{
    [helpstring("Color for the frame")] unsigned long const COLOR_FRAME
        = 0xH80000006;
    [helpstring("Not a rectangle but a square"), entry(1)] pascal double
square([in] double x);
    };
```

The struct Statement

Defines a C-style structure.

Syntax

typedef [*attributes*]
struct [*tag*] {
   memberlist
} *structname*;

Syntax Elements

attributes

The **helpstring**, **helpcontext**, **uuid**, **hidden**, and **version** attributes are accepted before a **struct** statement. The **helpstring**, **helpcontext**, **string** attributes are accepted on a structure member. See "Attribute Descriptions" for more information on the attributes accepted before a structure definition. Attributes (including the brackets) may be omitted. If **uuid** is omitted, the structure is not uniquely specified in the system.

tag

An optional tag, as with a C **struct**.

memberlist

List of structure members defined with C syntax.

structname

Name by which the structure is known in the type library.

Comments

The **struct** keyword must be preceded with **typedef**. The structure description must precede other references to the structure in the library. Members of a **struct** can be of any built-in type, or any type defined lexically as a **typedef** before the **struct**. See the sections "String Definitions" and "Array Definitions" for a description of how strings and arrays can be entered.

Example

```
typedef [uuid(BFB7334B-822A-1068-8849-00DD011087E8),
    helpstring("A task"), helpcontext(1019)]
struct {
    DATE startdate;
    DATE enddate;
    BSTR ownername;
    SAFEARRAY (int) subtasks;
    int A_C_array[10];
} TASKS;
```

The typedef Statement

Creates an alias for a type.

Syntax

typedef [*attributes*] *basetype aliasname*;

Syntax Elements

attributes
Any attribute specifications must follow the **typedef** keyword. If no attributes and no other type (for example **enum**, **struct**, or **union**) are specified, the alias is treated as a **#define** and does not appear in the type library. If no other attribute is desired, **public** can be used to explicitly include the alias in the type library. The **helpstring**, **helpcontext**, and **uuid** attributes are accepted before a **typedef**. See "Attribute Descriptions" for more information. If **uuid** is omitted, the typedef is not uniquely specified in the system.

aliasname
Name by which the type will be known in the type library.

basetype
The type for which the alias is defined.

Comments

The **typedef** keyword must also be used whenever a **struct** or **enum** is defined. The name recorded for the **enum** or **struct** is the typedef name, not the tag for the enumeration. No attributes are required to make sure the alias appears in the type library.

Enumerations, structures, and unions must be defined with the **typedef** keyword. The *attributes* for a type defined with **typedef** are enclosed in brackets following the **typedef** keyword. If a simple alias **typedef** has no attributes, it is treated like a #define and the *aliasname* does not appear in the library. Any attribute (use **public** if no others are desired) specified between the **typedef** keyword and the rest of a simple alias definition causes the alias to appear explicitly in the type library. The *attributes* typically include such items as a Help string and Help context.

Examples

```
typedef [public]  long DWORD;
```

The preceding example creates a type description for an alias type with the name DWORD.

```
typedef enum {
        TYPE_FUNCTION = 0,
        TYPE_PROPERTY = 1,
        TYPE_CONSTANT = 2,
        TYPE_PARAMETER = 3
    } OBJTYPE;
```

The second example creates a type description for an enumeration named OBJTYPE, which has four enumerator values.

The union Statement

Defines a C-style union.

Syntax

typedef [*attributes*] **union** [*tag*] {
   memberlist
} *unionname*;

Syntax Elements

attributes

The **helpstring, helpcontext, uuid, hidden**, and **version** attributes are accepted before a **union**. The **helpstring, helpcontext**, and **string** attributes are accepted on a union member. See "Attribute Descriptions" for more information on the attributes accepted before a union definition. Attributes (including the square brackets) may be omitted. If **uuid** is omitted, the union is not uniquely specified in the system.

tag

An optional tag, as with a C **union**.

memberlist

List of union members defined with C syntax.

unionname

Name by which the union is known in the type library.

Comments

The **union** keyword must be preceded with **typedef**. The union description must precede other references to the structure in the library. Members of a **union** can be of any built-in type, or any type defined lexically as a **typedef** before the **union**. See the sections "String Definitions" and "Array Definitions" for a description of how strings and arrays can be entered.

Example

```
[uuid(BFB7334C-822A-1068-8849-00DD011087E8), helpstring("A task"),
helpcontext(1019)]
typedef union {
    COLOR polycolor;
    int cVertices;
    boolean filled;
    SAFEARRAY (int) subtasks;
} UNIONSHOP;
```

C H A P T E R   8

Type Description Interfaces

The type description interfaces provide a way to read and bind to the descriptions of objects in a type library. The descriptions are used by OLE Automation controllers when they browse, create, and manipulate OLE Automation objects.

The type description interfaces include:

- **ITypeLib**—Used to retrieve information about a type library.
- **ITypeInfo**—Used to read the type information within the type library.
- **ITypeComp**—Used when creating compilers that use type information.

Overview of Interfaces

A type library is a container for type descriptions. **ITypeLib** provides access to information about a type description's containing library. **ITypeInfo** lets you access the type descriptions in a type library. The following table describes the member functions of each of the type description interfaces:

Category	Member name	Purpose
ITypeLib	FindName	Finds occurrences of a type description in a type library.
	GetDocumentation	Retrieves the library's documentation string, name of the complete Help file path and name, and the context ID for the library Help topic in the Help file.
	GetLibAttr	Retrieves the structure containing the library's attributes.
	GetTypeComp	Retrieves a pointer to the **ITypeComp** for a type library. This enables a client compiler to bind to the library's types, variables, constants and global functions.

Category	Member name	Purpose
ITypeLib (*continued*)	**GetTypeInfo**	Retrieves the specified type description in the library.
	GetTypeInfoCount	Retrieves the number of type descriptions in the library.
	GetTypeInfoType	Retrieves the type of a type description.
	GetTypeInfoOfGuid	Retrieves the type description corresponding to the specified GUID.
	IsName	Indicates whether a passed-in string contains the name of a type or member described in the library.
	ReleaseTLibAttr	Releases TLIBATTR originally obtained from **ITypeLib::GetLibAttr**.
ITypeInfo	**AddressOfMember**	Retrieves the addresses of static functions or variables, such as those defined in a DLL.
	CreateInstance	Creates a new instance of a type that describes a component object class (coclass).
	GetContainingTypeLib	Retrieves both the type library that contains a specific type description and the index of the type description within the type library.
	GetDllEntry	Retrieves a description or specification of an entry point for a function in a DLL.
	GetDocumentation	Retrieves the documentation string, name of the complete Help file path and name, and the context ID for the Help topic for a specified type description.
	GetFuncDesc	Retrieves the FUNCDESC structure containing information about a specified function.
	GetIDsOfNames	Maps between member names and member IDs and parameter names and parameter IDs.

Category	Member name	Purpose
ITypeInfo (*continued*)	**GetImplTypeFlags**	Retrieves the IMPLTYPE flags for an interface.
	GetMops	Retrieves marshaling information.
	GetNames	Retrieves the variable with the specified member ID, or the name of the function and parameter names corresponding to the specified function ID.
	GetRefTypeInfo	Retrieves the type descriptions referenced by a given type description.
	GetRefTypeOfImplType	Retrieves the type description of the specified implemented interface types for a coclass, or an inherited interface.
	GetTypeAttr	Retrieves a TYPEATTR structure containing the attributes of the type description.
	GetTypeComp	Retrieves the **ITypeComp** interface for the type description, which enables a client compiler to bind to the type description's members.
	GetVarDesc	Retrieves a VARDESC structure describing the specified variable.
	Invoke	Invokes a method or accesses a property of an object that implements the interface described by the type description.
	ReleaseFuncDesc	Releases a FUNCDESC previously returned by **GetFuncDesc**.
	ReleaseTypeAttr	Releases a TYPEATTR previously returned by **GetTypeAttr**.
	ReleaseVarDesc	Releases a VARDESC previously returned by **GetVarDesc**.
ITypeComp	**Bind**	Maps a name to a member of a type, or binds global variables and functions contained in a type library.
	BindType	Binds to the type descriptions contained within a type library.

Overview of Functions

The functions for loading, registering, and querying type libraries are provided by OLEAUT32.DLL (for 32-bit systems) and TYPELIB.DLL (for 16-bit systems).

Category	Function name	Purpose
Library loading	**LoadTypeLib**	Loads and registers a type library.
	LoadRegTypeLib	Uses registry information to load a type library.
Library registration	**RegisterTypeLib**	Adds information about a type library to the system registry.
	QueryPathOfRegType Lib	Retrieves the path of a registered type library.
Type compilation	**LHashValOfNameSys** **LHashValOfName**	Computes a hash value for a name that can then be passed to **ITypeComp::Bind**, **ITypeComp::BindType**, **ITypeLib::IsName**, or **ITypeLib::FindName**.

ITypeLib Interface

Implemented by	Used by	Header filename
OLEAUT32.DLL (32-bit systems) **TYPELIB.DLL** (16-bit systems)	Tools that need to access the descriptions of objects contained in type libraries.	**OLEAUTO.H** **DISPATCH.H**

Data describing a set of objects is stored in a type library. A type library may be a stand-alone binary file (.TLB), a resource in a DLL or .EXE file, or part of a compound document file.

A type library contains descriptions of one or more objects, and is accessed through the **ITypeLib** interface. The descriptions of individual objects are accessed through the **ITypeInfo** interface. The system registry contains a list of all the installed type libraries. Type library organization is illustrated in the following figure:

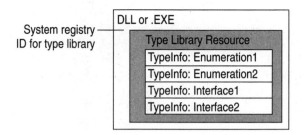

The **ITypeLib** interface provides methods for accessing a library of type descriptions. This interface supports the following:

- Generalized containment for type information. **ITypeLib** allows iteration over the type descriptions contained in the library.

- Global functions and data. A type library can contain descriptions of a set of modules, each of which is the equivalent of a C or C++ source file that exports data and functions. The type library supports compiling references to the exported data and functions.

- General information, including a user-readable name for the library and Help for the library as a whole.

Structures and Enumerations

The **ITypeLib** interface uses the following structures and enumerations:

LIBFLAGS

The LIBFLAGS enumeration defines flags that apply to type libraries. LIBFLAGS is defined as follows:

```
typedef enum tagLIBFLAGS {
    LIBFLAG_FRESTRICTED = 0x01
    , LIBFLAG_FCONTROL = 0x02
    , LIBFLAG_FHIDDEN = 0x04
} LIBFLAGS;
```

Value	Description
LIBFLAG_FCONTROL	The type library describes controls and should not be displayed in type browsers intended for nonvisual objects.
LIBFLAG_FRESTRICTED	The type library is restricted and should not be displayed to users.
LIBFLAG_FHIDDEN	The type library should not be displayed to users, though its use is not restricted. It is intended for use by controls. Hosts need to create a new typelib that wraps the control with extended properties.

SYSKIND

The SYSKIND identifies the target operating system platform.

```
typedef enum tagSYSKIND[
    SYS_WIN16,
    SYS_WIN32,
    SYS_MAC
] SYSKIND;
```

Value	Description
SYS_WIN16	The target operating system for the type library is 16-bit Windows systems. Data members are packed.
SYS_WIN32	The target operating system for the type library is 32-bit Windows systems. Data members are naturally aligned (for example, 2-byte integers are aligned on even-byte boundaries; 4-byte integers are aligned on quad-word boundaries, and so forth).
SYS_MAC	The target operating system for the type library is Macintosh. All data members are aligned on even-byte boundaries.

TLIBATTR

The TLIBATTR structure contains information about a type library. Information from this structure is used to identify the type library and to provide national language support for member names.

```
typedef struct FARSTRUCT tagTLIBATTR {
    GUID guid;                       // Unique ID of the library
    LCID lcid;                       // Language/locale of the library
    SYSKIND syskind;                 // Target hardware platform
    unsigned short wMajorVerNum;     // Major version number
    unsigned short wMinorVerNum;     // Minor version number
    unsigned short wLibFlags;        // Library flags
} TLIBATTR, FAR * LPTLIBATTR;
```

For more information on national language support, see "Supporting Multiple National Languages" in Chapter 2, and refer to the NLS API reference material in the Windows NT documentation.

ITypeLib::FindName

HRESULT ITypeLib::FindName(*szNameBuf*, *lHashVal*, *rgptinfo*, *rgmemid*, *pcFound*)
OLECHAR FAR* *szNameBuf*
unsigned long *lHashVal*
ITypeInfo FAR* FAR* *rgptinfo*
MEMBERID FAR* *rgmemid*
unsigned int FAR* *pcFound*

Finds occurrences of a type description in a type library. This may be used to quickly verify that a name exists in a type library.

Parameter

szNameBuf
> The name to search for.

lHashVal
> A hash value to speed up the search, computed by **LHashValOfNameSys**. If *lHashVal* = 0, a value will be computed for you.

rgptinfo
> On return, an array of pointers to the type descriptions that contain the name specified in *szNameBuf*. May not be NULL.

rgmemid
> An array of the MEMBERIDs of the found items; *rgmemid*[*i*] is the MEMBERID which indexes into the type description specified by *rgptinfo*[*i*]. May not be NULL.

pcFound
> On entry, indicates how many instances to look for. For example, you may call with *pcFound = 1 in order to find the first occurrence. In this case, the search stops when one is found.
>
> On exit, indicates the number of instances that were found. If the in and out values of *pcFound are identical, there may be more type descriptions that contain the name.

Return Value   The SCODE obtained from the returned HRESULT is one of the following:

SCODE	Meaning
S_OK	Success.
E_OUTOFMEMORY	Out of memory.
E_INVALIDARG	One or more of the arguments is invalid.
TYPE_E_IOERROR	The function could not write to the file.
TYPE_E_INVDATAREAD	The function could not read from the file.
TYPE_E_UNSUPFORMAT	The type library has an old format.
TYPE_E_INVALIDSTATE	The type library could not be opened.
TYPE_E_CANTLOADLIBRARY	The library or DLL could not be loaded.
TYPE_E_ELEMENTNOTFOUND	The element was not found.

Comments   Passing *pcFound* = *n* indicates that there is enough room in the *rgptinfo* and *rgmemid* arrays for *n* (*ptinfo*, *memid*) pairs. The function returns MEMID_NIL in *rgmemid*[*i*] if the name in *szNameBuf* is the name of the typeinfo in *rgptinfo*[*i*].

ITypeLib::GetDocumentation

HRESULT ITypeLib::GetDocumentation(*index, lpbstrName, lpbstrDocString, lpdwHelpContext, lpbstrHelpFile*)
int *index*
BSTR FAR* *lpbstrName*
BSTR FAR* *lpbstrDocString*
unsigned long FAR* *lpdwHelpContext*
BSTR FAR* *lpbstrHelpFile*

Retrieves the library's documentation string, name of the complete Help file path and name, and the context ID for the library Help topic in the Help file.

Parameter   *index*
Index of the type description whose documentation is to be returned; if index is −1, then the documentation for the library itself is returned.

lpbstrName
Returns a BSTR that contains the name of the specified item. If the caller does not need the item name, then *lpbstrName* can be NULL.

lpbstrDocString
Returns a BSTR that contains the documentation string for the specified item. If the caller does not need the documentation string, then *lpbstrDocString* can be NULL.

lpdwHelpContext
> Returns the Help context ID associated with the specified item. If the caller does not need the Help context ID, then *lpdwHelpContext* can be NULL.

lpbstrHelpFile
> Returns a BSTR that contains the fully qualified name of the Help file. If the caller does not need the Help filename, then *lpbstrHelpFile* can be NULL.

Return Value

The SCODE obtained from the returned HRESULT is one of the following:

SCODE	Meaning
S_OK	Success.
STG_E_INSUFFICIENTMEMORY	Out of memory.
E_INVALIDARG	One or more of the arguments is invalid.
TYPE_E_IOERROR	The function could not write to the file.
TYPE_E_INVDATAREAD	The function could not read from the file.
TYPE_E_UNSUPFORMAT	The type library has an old format.
TYPE_E_INVALIDSTATE	The type library could not be opened.
TYPE_E_ELEMENTNOTFOUND	The element was not found.

Comments

The caller should free the BSTR parameters *lpbstrName*, *lpbstrDocString*, and *lpbstrHelpFile*.

Example

```
for (i = 0; i < utypeinfoCount; i++)
{
    CHECKRESULT(ptlib->GetDocumentation(i, &bstrName,
                                          NULL, NULL, NULL));
    .
    .
    .
    SysFreeString(bstrName);
}
```

ITypeLib::GetLibAttr

HRESULT ITypeLib::GetLibAttr(*lplptlibattr***)**
TLIBATTR FAR* FAR* *lplptlibattr*

Retrieves the structure containing the library's attributes.

Parameter

lplptlibattr
> Pointer to a structure containing the library's attributes.

Return Value	The SCODE obtained from the returned HRESULT is one of the following:

SCODE	Meaning
S_OK	Success.
E_OUTOFMEMORY	Out of memory.
E_INVALIDARG	One or more of the arguments is invalid.
TYPE_E_IOERROR	The function could not write to the file.
TYPE_E_INVDATAREAD	The function could not read from the file.
TYPE_E_UNSUPFORMAT	The type library has an unsupported format.
TYPE_E_INVALIDSTATE	The type library could not be opened.

Comments   Use **ITypeLib::ReleaseTLibAttr** to free the memory occupied by the TLIBATTR structure.

ITypeLib::GetTypeComp

HRESULT ITypeLib::GetTypeComp(*lplptcomp*)
ITypeComp FAR* FAR* *lplptcomp*

Enables a client compiler to bind to the library's types, variables, constants and global functions.

Parameter   *lplptcomp*
Points to a pointer to the **ITypeComp** instance for this **ITypeLib** that a client compiler can use to bind to types in the **ITypeLib** and to the global functions, variables, and constants defined in the **ITypeLib**.

Return Value   The SCODE obtained from the returned HRESULT is one of the following:

SCODE	Meaning
S_OK	Success.
E_OUTOFMEMORY	Out of memory.
E_INVALIDARG	One or more of the arguments is invalid.
TYPE_E_IOERROR	The function could not read from the file.
TYPE_E_INVDATAREAD	The function could not read from the file.
TYPE_E_UNSUPFORMAT	The type library has an old format.
TYPE_E_INVALIDSTATE	The type library could not be opened.
TYPE_E_WRONGTYPEKIND	Type mismatch.

Comments

The **Bind** function of the returned **TypeComp** binds to global functions, variables, constants, enumerated values, and coclass members. The **Bind** function also binds the names of the TYPEKINDs of TKIND_MODULE, TKIND_ENUM, and TKIND_COCLASS. These names shadow any global names defined within the type information. The members of TKIND_ENUM, TKIND_MODULE, and TKIND_COCLASS types marked as Application objects can be directly bound to from **ITypeComp**, without specifying the name of the module.

ITypeComp::Bind and **ITypeComp::BindType** accept only unqualified names. **ITypeLib::GetTypeComp** returns a pointer to the **ITypeComp** interface, which is then used to bind to global elements in the library. The names of some types (TKIND_ENUM, TKIND_MODULE, and TKIND_COCLASS) share the name space with variables, functions, constants, and enumerators. If a member requires qualification to differentiate it from other items in the name space, **GetTypeComp** can be called successively for each qualifier in order to bind to the desired member. This allows programming language compilers to access members of modules, enumerations, and coclasses, even though the member can't be bound to with a qualified name.

ITypeLib::GetTypeInfo

HRESULT ITypeLib::GetTypeInfo(*index***,** *lplpitinfo***)**
unsigned int *index*
ITypeInfo FAR* FAR* *lplpitinfo*

Retrieves the specified type description in the library.

Parameters

index
Index of the **ITypeInfo** to be returned.

lplpitinfo
If successful, returns a pointer to the **ITypeInfo**.

Return Value

The SCODE obtained from the returned HRESULT is one of the following:

SCODE	Meaning
S_OK	Success.
TYPE_E_ELEMENTNOTFOUND	*Index* is outside the range of 0 to **GetTypeInfoCount**() –1.
E_OUTOFMEMORY	Out of memory.
E_INVALIDARG	One or more of the arguments is invalid.
TYPE_E_IOERROR	The function could not read from the file.

SCODE	Meaning
TYPE_E_INVDATAREAD	The function could not read from the file.
TYPE_E_UNSUPFORMAT	The type library has an old format.
TYPE_E_REGISTRYACCESS	There was an error accessing the system registration database.
TYPE_E_INVALIDSTATE	The type library could not be opened.

Comments   For dual interfaces, **ITypeLib::GetTypeInfo** returns only the TKIND_DISPATCH typeinfo. To get the TKIND_INTERFACE typeinfo, call **ITypeInfo::GetRefTypeOfImplType** on the TKIND_DISPATCH typeinfo, passing an index of –1. Then pass the returned typeinfo handle to **ITypeInfo::GetRefTypeInfo**.

Example   The following example gets the TKIND_INTERFACE typeinfo for a dual interface.

```
ptlib->GetTypeInfo((unsigned int) dwIndex, &ptypeinfoDisp);
ptypeinfoDisp->GetRefTypeOfImplType(-1, &phreftype);
ptypeinfoDisp->GetRefTypeInfo(phreftype, &ptypeinfoInt);
```

ITypeLib::GetTypeInfoCount

unsigned int ITypeLib::GetTypeInfoCount( )

Comments   Returns the number of type descriptions in the type library.

ITypeLib::GetTypeInfoOfGuid

HRESULT ITypeLib::GetTypeInfoOfGuid(*lpguid*, *lplpitinfo*)
REFGUID *lpguid*
ITypeInfo FAR* FAR* *lplpitinfo*

Retrieves the type description corresponding to the specified GUID.

Parameters   *lpguid*
    Pointer to the globally unique ID of the type description.

lplpitinfo
    Pointer to a pointer to the **ITypeInfo**.

Return Value   The SCODE obtained from the returned HRESULT is one of the following:

SCODE	Meaning
S_OK	Success.
TYPE_E_ELEMENTNOTFOUND	No type description was found in the library with the specified *guid*.
E_OUTOFMEMORY	Out of memory.
E_INVALIDARG	One or more of the arguments is invalid.
TYPE_E_IOERROR	The function could not write to the file.
TYPE_E_INVDATAREAD	The function could not read from the file.
TYPE_E_UNSUPFORMAT	The type library has an old format.
TYPE_E_REGISTRYACCESS	There was an error accessing the system registration database.
TYPE_E_INVALIDSTATE	The type library could not be opened.

ITypeLib::GetTypeInfoType

HRESULT ITypeLib::GetTypeInfoType(*index*, *ptypekind*)
unsigned int *index*
TYPEKIND FAR* *ptypekind*

Retrieves the type of a type description.

Parameters   *index*
    The index of the type description within the type library.

ptypekind
    A pointer to the TYPEKIND for the type description.

Return Value   The SCODE obtained from the returned HRESULT is one of the following:

SCODE	Meaning
S_OK	Success.
TYPE_E_ELEMENTNOTFOUND	*Index* is outside the range of 0 to **GetTypeInfoCount**() -1.

ITypeLib::IsName

HResult ITypeLib::IsName(*szNameBuf*, *lHashVal*, *lpfName*)
OLECHAR FAR* *szNameBuf*
unsigned long *lHashVal*
BOOL *lpfName*

Indicates whether a passed-in string contains the name of a type or member described in the library.

Parameter

szNameBuf
 The string to test. If **IsName** is successful, *szNameBuf* is modified to match the case (capitalization) found in the type library.

lHashVal
 The hash value of *szNameBuf*.

lpfName
 Upon return, set to True if *szNameBuf* was found in the type library; otherwise False.

Return Value

The SCODE obtained from the returned HRESULT is one of the following:

SCODE	Meaning
S_OK	Success.
E_OUTOFMEMORY	Out of memory.
E_INVALIDARG	One or more of the arguments is invalid.
TYPE_E_IOERROR	The function could not read from the file.
TYPE_E_INVDATAREAD	The function could not read from the file.
TYPE_E_UNSUPFORMAT	The type library has an old format.
TYPE_E_INVALIDSTATE	The type library could not be opened.

ITypeLib::ReleaseTLibAttr

void ITypeLib::ReleaseTLibAttr(*lptlibattr*)
TLIBATTR FAR* *lptlibattr*

Releases TLIBATTR originally obtained from **ITypeLib::GetLibAttr**.

Parameter

lptlibattr
 Pointer to the TLIBATTR to be freed.

Comments   Releases the specified TLIBATTR. This TLIBATTR was previously obtained with a call to **GetTypeLib::GetLibAttr**.

ITypeInfo Interface

Implemented by	Used by	Header filename
OLEAUT32.DLL (32-bit systems) TYPELIB.DLL (16-bit systems)	Tools that need to access the descriptions of objects contained in type libraries.	OLEAUTO.H DLL (32-bit systems) DISPATCH.H (16-bit systems)

This section describes **ITypeInfo**, an interface usually used for reading information about objects. For example, an object browser tool could use **ITypeInfo** to extract information about the characteristics and capabilities of objects from type libraries.

Type information interfaces are intended to describe the parts of the application that can be called by outside clients, rather than those that might be used internally to build an application.

The **ITypeInfo** interface provides access to the following:

- The set of function descriptions associated with the type; for interfaces, this contains the set of member functions in the interface.
- The set of data member descriptions associated with the type; for structures, this contains the set of fields of the type.
- The general attributes of the type such as whether it describes a structure, an interface, and so forth.

You can use the type description of an **IDispatch** interface to implement the **IDispatch** interface. See the description of **CreateStdDispatch** in Chapter 5, "Dispatch Interfaces," for more information.

An **ITypeInfo** instance provides various information about a type, and is used in different ways. A compiler could use an **ITypeInfo** to compile references to members of the type. A type interface browser could use it to find information about each member of the type. An **IDispatch** implementor could use it to provide automatic delegation of **IDispatch** calls to an interface.

Type Descriptions

The information associated with an object described by **ITypeInfo** can include a set of functions, a set of data members, and various type attributes. It is essentially the same as the information described by a C++ class declaration. A C++ class declaration can be used to define both interfaces and structures, as well as any combination of functions and data members. In addition to interfaces and structure definitions, the **ITypeInfo** interface is used to describe other types, including enumerations and aliases. Because the interface to a C file or library is simply a set of functions and variable declarations, **ITypeInfo** is used to describe these as well.

Type information comprises individual type descriptions. Each type description must have one of the following forms:

Category	ODL keyword	Description
alias	**typedef**	An alias for another type.
enumeration	**enum**	An enumeration.
structure	**struct**	A structure.
union	**union**	A single data item that can have one of a specified group of types.
module	**module**	Data and functions not accessed through VTBL entries.
IDispatch interface	**dispinterface**	**IDispatch** properties and methods accessed through **IDispatch::Invoke**.
OLE interface	**interface**	OLE member functions accessed through VTBL entries.
Component object class	**coclass**	A component object class. Specifies an implementation of one or more OLE interfaces and one or more **IDispatch** interfaces.

Note that all bit flags that are not specifically used should be set to zero for future compatibility.

Alias

An alias has TypeKind = TKIND_ALIAS. An alias is an empty set of functions, an empty set of data members, and a type description (located in the TYPEATTR) which gives the actual type of the alias.

Enumeration

An enumeration has TypeKind = TKIND_ENUM. An enumeration is an empty set of functions and a set of constant data members.

Structure

A structure description has TypeKind = TKIND_RECORD. A structure is an empty set of functions and a set of per-instance data members.

Union

A union description has TypeKind = TKIND_UNION. A union is an empty set of functions and a set of per-instance data members, each of which has an instance offset of zero.

Module

A module has TypeKind = TKIND_MODULE. A module is a set of static functions and a set of static data members.

OLE-compatible Interfaces

An interface definition has TypeKind = TKIND_INTERFACE. An interface is a set of pure virtual functions and an empty set of data members. If a type description contains any virtual functions, then the pointer to the VTBL is the first 4 bytes of the instance.

The type information fully describes the member functions in the vtable, including parameter names and types and function return types. It may inherit from no more than one other interface.

Note that with interfaces and dispinterfaces, all members should have different names, except the accessor functions of properties. For property functions having the same name, the documentation string and Help context should be set for only one of the functions (because they conceptually define the same property).

Dispatch Interfaces

These include objects (TypeKind = TKIND_DISPATCH) that support the **IDispatch** interface with a specification of the dispatch data members (for example, properties) and methods supported through the object's **Invoke** implementation. All members of the dispinterface should have different IDs, except for the accessor functions of properties.

Dual Interfaces

Dual interfaces have two different typeinfos for the same interface. The TKIND_INTERFACE typeInfo describes the interface as a standard OLE COM interface. The TKIND_DISPATCH typeinfo describes the interface as a standard Dispatch interface. The **lcid** and **retval** parameters and HRESULT return types are removed, and the return type of the member is specified to be the same type as the **retval** parameter.

By default, the TypeKind for a dual interface is TKIND_DISPATCH. Tools that bind to interfaces should check the type flags for TYPEFLAG_FDUAL. If this flag is set, the TKIND_INTERFACE typeinfo is available through a call to **ITypeInfo::GetRefTypeOfImplType** with an index of −1, followed by a call to **ITypeInfo::GetRefTypeInfo**.

Component Object Classes (coclasses)

These include objects (TypeKind = TKIND_COCLASS) that support a set of implemented interfaces, which can be of either TKIND_INTERFACE or TKIND_DISPATCH.

Structures and Enumerations

Structures and enumerations used by **ITypeInfo** include the following:

ARRAYDESC

A pointer to an ARRAYDESC is contained within the TYPEDESC, which describes a C-style array. The TYPEDESC describes the type of the array's elements and information describing the array's dimensions. It is defined as follows:

```
typedef struct tagARRAYDESC{
    TYPEDESC tdescElem;          // Element type.
    unsigned short cDims;        // Dimension count.
    SAFEARRAYBOUND rgbounds[1];  // Variable length array containing one
                                 // element for each dimension.
} ARRAYDESC;
```

ELEMDESC

An ELEMDESC structure includes the type description and process-transfer information for a variable, a function, or a function parameter. It is defined as follows:

```
typedef struct tagELEMDESC{
    TYPEDESC tdesc;      // Type of the element.
    IDLDESC idldesc;     // Information needed for transferring the
                         // element between processes.
    } ELEMDESC;
```

FUNCDESC

A FUNCDESC describes a function, and is defined as follows:

```
typedef struct tagFUNCDESC {
    MEMBERID memid;            // Function member ID
    SCODE FAR* lprgscode;      // Legal SCODES for the function.
    ELEMDESC FAR* lprgelemdescParam;  // Array of parameter types
    FUNCKIND funckind;         // specifies whether the function is
                               // virtual, static, or dispatch-only.
    INVOKEKIND invkind;        // Invocation kind; indicates if this is a
                               //property function and if so, what kind.
    CALLCONV callconv;         // Specifies the function's calling
                               // convention.
    short cParams;             // Count of total number of parameters.
    short cParamsOpt;          // Count of optional parameters (detailed
                               // description below).
    short oVft;                // For FUNC_VIRTUAL, specifies the offset in
                               // the virtual function table.
    short cScodes;             // Count of permitted Scodes.
    ELEMDESC elemdescFunc;     // Contains the return type of the function.
    unsigned short wFuncFlags; // See below for definition of flags.
}   FUNCDESC;
```

The field *cParams* specifies the total number of required and optional parameters.

The *cParamsOpt* field specifies the form of optional parameters accepted by the function, as follows:

- A value of 0 specifies that no optional arguments are supported.

- A value of −1 specifies that the method's last parameter is a pointer to a safe array of variants. Any number of variant arguments greater than *cParams* −1 must be packaged by the caller into a safe array and passed as the final parameter. This array of optional parameters must be freed by the caller after control is returned from the call.

- Any other number indicates that the last *n* parameters of the function are variants and need not be specified explicitly by the caller. The parameters left unspecified should be filled in by the compiler or interpreter as variants of type VT_ERROR with the value DISP_E_PARAMNOTFOUND.

The fields *cScodes* and *lprgscode* store the count and the set of errors that a function can return. If *cScodes* = −1 then the set of errors is unknown. If *cScodes* = −1 or *cScodes* = 0, then *lprgscode* is undefined.

FUNCFLAGS

The FUNCFLAGS enumeration is defined as follows:

```
typedef enum tagFUNCFLAGS {
    FUNCFLAG_FRESTRICTED= 1
        , FUNCFLAG_FSOURCE= 0x2
        , FUNCFLAG_FBINDABLE= 0x4
        , FUNCFLAG_FREQUESTEDIT= 0x8
        , FUNCFLAG_FDISPLAYBIND= 0x10
        , FUNCFLAG_FDEFAULTBIND= 0x20
        , FUNCFLAG_FHIDDEN= 0x40
} FUNCFLAGS;
```

Value	Description
FUNCFLAG_FRESTRICTED	The function should not be accessible from macro languages. This flag is intended for system-level functions or functions that you do not want type browsers to display.
FUNCFLAG_FSOURCE	The function returns an object that is a source of events.
FUNCFLAG_FBINDABLE	The function that supports data binding.
FUNCFLAG_FDISPLAYBIND	The function that is displayed to the user as bindable; that is, FUNC_FBINDABLE must also be set.
FUNCFLAG_FDEFAULTBIND	The function that best represents the object. Only one function in a typeinfo may have this attribute.
FUNCFLAG_FHIDDEN	The function should not be displayed to the user, though it exists and is bindable.

FUNCKIND

The FUNCKIND enumeration is defined as follows:

```
typedef enum tagFUNCKIND {
    FUNC_VIRTUAL,
    FUNC_PUREVIRTUAL,
    FUNC_NONVIRTUAL,
    FUNC_STATIC,
    FUNC_DISPATCH,
} FUNCKIND;
```

Value	Description
FUNC_PUREVIRTUAL	The function is accessed through the virtual function table and takes an implicit *this* pointer.
FUNC_VIRTUAL	The function is accessed the same as PUREVIRTUAL, except the function has an implementation.
FUNC_NONVIRTUAL	The function is accessed by static address and takes an implicit *this* pointer.
FUNC_STATIC	The function is accessed by static address and does not take an implicit *this* pointer.
FUNC_DISPATCH	The function can be accessed only through **IDispatch**.

HREFTYPE

HREFTYPE is a handle that identifies a type description.

```
typedef unsigned long HREFTYPE;
```

IDLDESC

An IDLDESC contains information needed for transferring a structure element, parameter, or function return value between processes, and is defined as follows:

```
typedef struct FARSTRUCT tagIDLDESC {
    unsigned long dwReserved;
    unsigned short wIDLFlags;    /* IN, OUT, and so on */
} IDLDESCtypedef struct tagIDLDESC{
```

Note that *dwReserved* is reserved for future use and should be set to NULL.

IDLFLAGS

The IDLFLAGS are defined as follows:

```
#define IDLFLAG_NONE     0
#define IDLFLAG_FIN      0x1
#define IDLFLAG_FOUT     0x2
#define IDLFLAG_FLCID    0x4
#define IDLFLAG_FRETVAL  0x8
```

Value	Description
IDLFLAG_NONE	Whether the parameter passes or receives information is unspecified. **IDispatch** interfaces can use this flag.
IDLFLAG_FIN	Parameter passes information from the caller to the callee.
IDLFLAG_FOUT	Parameter returns information from the callee to the caller.
IDLFLAG_FIN I IDLFLAG_FOUT	Parameter passes and returns information.
IDLFLAG_FLCID	Parameter is the LCID of a client application.
IDLFLAG_FRETVAL	Parameter is the return value of the member.

IMPLTYPEFLAGS

The IMPLTYPEFLAGS are defined as follows:

```
/* IMPLTYPE Flags */
#define IMPLTYPEFLAG_FDEFAULT     0x1
#define IMPLTYPEFLAG_FSOURCE      0x2
#define IMPLTYPEFLAG_FRESTRICTED 0x4
```

Value	Description
IMPLTYPEFLAG_FDEFAULT	The interface or dispinterface represents the default for the source or sink.
IMPLTYPEFLAG_FSOURCE	This member of a coclass is called rather than implemented.
IMPLTYPEFLAG_FRESTRICTED	The member should not be displayed or programmable by users.

INVOKEKIND

The INVOKEKIND enumeration is defined as follows:

```
typedef enum tagINVOKEKIND {
    INVOKE_FUNC = DISPATCH_METHOD,
    INVOKE_PROPERTYGET = DISPATCH_PROPERTYGET,
    INVOKE_PROPERTYPUT = DISPATCH_PROPERTYPUT,
    INVOKE_PROPERTYPUTREF = DISPATCH_PROPERTYPUTREF
} INVOKEKIND;
```

Value	Description
INVOKE_FUNC	The member is called using normal function invocation syntax.
INVOKE_PROPERTYGET	The function is invoked by using normal property access syntax.
INVOKE_PROPERTYPUT	The function is invoked by using property value assignment syntax. Syntactically, a typical programming language might represent changing a property in the same way as assignment; for example: `object.property := value`.
INVOKE_PROPERTYPUTREF	The function is invoked by using property reference assignment syntax.

Note that in C, value assignment is written as `*pobj1 = *pobj2`, while reference assignment is written as `pobj1 = pobj2`. Other languages have other syntactic conventions. A property or data member may support value assignment only, reference assignment only, or both. For a more detailed description of property functions, see Chapter 5, "Dispatch Interfaces." These enumeration constants are the same constants that are passed to **IDispatch::Invoke** to specify the way in which a function is invoked.

MEMBERID

MEMBERID identifies the member in a type description. For **IDispatch** interfaces, this is the same as DISPID.

```
typedef DISPID MEMBERID;
```

This is a 32-bit integral value in the following format:

Bits	Value
0–15	Offset. Any value is permissible.
16–21	The nesting level of this typeinfo in the inheritance hierarchy. For example: `interface mydisp : IDispatch` The nesting level of **IUnknown** is 0, **IDispatch** is 1, and mydisp is 2.
22–25	Reserved; must be zero
26–28	DISPID value.
29	True if this is the member ID for a FuncDesc; otherwise False.
30–31	Must be 01.

Negative IDs are reserved for use by OLE Automation.

TYPEATTR

The TYPEATTR structure contains attributes of an **ITypeInfo**, and is defined as follows:

```
typedef struct FARSTRUCT tagTYPEATTR {
    GUID guid;                      // The GUID of the TypeInfo
    LCID lcid;                      // Locale of member names and doc
                                    // strings
    unsigned long dwReserved;
    MEMBERID memidConstructor;      // ID of constructor,MEMBERID_NIL if
                                    // None
    MEMBERID memidDestructor;       // ID of destructor, MEMBERID_NIL if
                                    // None
    OLECHAR FAR* lpstrSchema;       // Reserved for future use
    unsigned long cbSizeInstance;// The size of an instance of
                                    // this type.
    TYPEKIND typekind;              // The kind of type this typeinfo
                                    // describes.
    unsigned short cFuncs;          // Number of functions
    unsigned short cVars;           // Number of variables/data members
    unsigned short cImplTypes;      // Number of implemented interfaces
    unsigned short cbSizeVft;       // The size of this type's virtual
                                    // func table
    unsigned short cbAlignment;     // Byte alignment for an instance
                                    // of this type
    unsigned short wTypeFlags;
    unsigned short wMajorVerNum; // Major version number
    unsigned short wMinorVerNum; // Minor version number
    TYPEDESC tdescAlias;            // If TypeKind == TKIND_ALIAS,
                                    // specifies the type for which
                                    // this type is an alias
    IDLDESC idldescType;            // IDL attributes of the
                                    // described type
} TYPEATTR, FAR* LPTYPEATTR;
```

The *cbAlignment* field indicates how addresses are aligned. A value of 0 indicates alignment on the 64K boundary; 1 indicates no special alignment. For other values, *n* indicates aligned on byte *n*.

TYPEDESC

A TYPEDESC, which describes the type of a variable, the return type of a function, or the type of a function parameter, is defined as follows:

```
typedef struct FARSTRUCT tagTYPEDESC {
    union {
        /* VT_PTR|VT_SAFEAEEAY - the pointed-at type */
    struct FARSTRUCT tagTYPEDESC FAR* lptdesc;

        /* VT_CARRAY */
    struct FARSTRUCT tagARRAYDESC FAR* lpadesc;

        /* VT_USERDEFINED - this is used to get a TypeInfo for a user-
            defined type */
    HREFTYPE hreftype;

    }UNION_NAME(u);
    VARTYPE vt;
} TYPEDESC;
```

If the variable is VT_SAFEARRAY or VT_PTR, the union portion of the TYPEDESC contains a pointer to a TYPEDESC that specifies the element type.

TYPEFLAGS

The TYPEFLAGS enumeration is defined as follows:

```
typedef enum tagTYPEFLAGS {
    TYPEFLAG_FAPPOBJECT = 0x01
    , TYPEFLAG_FCANCREATE = 0x02
    , TYPEFLAG_FLICENSED = 0x04
    , TYPEFLAG_FPREDECLID = 0x08
    , TYPEFLAG_FHIDDEN = 0x10
    , TYPEFLAG_FCONTROL = 0x20
    , TYPEFLAG_FDUAL = 0x40
    , TYPEFLAG_FNONEXTENSIBLE = 0x80
    , TYPEFLAG_FOLEAUTOMATION = 0x100
} TYPEFLAGS;
```

Value	Description
TYPEFLAG_FAPPOBJECT	A type description that describes an Application object.
TYPEFLAG_FCANCREATE	Instances of the type can be created by **ITypeInfo::CreateInstance.**
TYPEFLAG_FLICENSED	The type is licensed.
TYPEFLAG_FPREDECLID	The type is predefined. The client application shoul automatically create a single instance of the object that has this attribute. The name of the variable tha points to the object is the same as the class name of the object.
TYPEFLAG_FHIDDEN	The type should not be displayed to browsers.
TYPEFLAG_FCONTROL	The type is a control from which other types will be derived, and should not be displayed to users.
TYPEFLAG_FDUAL	The types in the interface derive from **IDispatch** an are fully compatible with OLE Automation. Not allowed on **Dispatch** interfaces.
TYPEFLAG_FNONEXTENSIBLE	The interface can't add members at run time.
TYPEFLAG_FOLEAUTOMATION	The types used in the interface are fully compatible with OLE, and may be displayed in an object browser. Setting **dual** on an interface sets this flag i addition to TYPEFLAG_FDUAL. Not allowed on dispinterfaces.

TYPEFLAG_FAPPOBJECT may be used on type descriptions with TypeKind = TKIND_COCLASS, and indicates that the type description describes an Application object.

Members of the Application object are globally accessible in that the Bind method of the **ITypeComp** instance associated with the library binds to the members of an Application object just as it does for type descriptions that have TypeKind = TKIND_MODULE.

The type description implicitly defines a global variable with the same name and type as the type described by the type description. This variable is also globally accessible. Specifically, when Bind is passed the name of an Application object, a VARDESC is returned describing the implicit variable. The ID of the implicitly created variable is always ID_DEFAULTINST.

When the **CreateInstance** function of an Application object type description is called, it uses **GetActiveObject** to retrieve the Application object. If **GetActiveObject** fails because the application is not running, then **CreateInstance** calls **CoCreateInstance** (which should start the application).

When TYPEFLAG_FCANCREATE is True, **ITypeInfo::CreateInstance** can create an instance of the type. Note that this is currently true only for component object classes for which a GUID has been specified.

TYPEKIND

The TYPEKIND enumeration is defined as follows:

```
typedef enum tagTYPEKIND {
      TKIND_ENUM = 0
    , TKIND_RECORD
    , TKIND_MODULE
    , TKIND_INTERFACE
    , TKIND_DISPATCH
    , TKIND_COCLASS
    , TKIND_ALIAS
    , TKIND_UNION
    , TKIND_MAX          /* end of enum marker */
} TYPEKIND;
```

Value	Description
TKIND_ALIAS	A type that is an alias for another type.
TKIND_COCLASS	A set of implemented component object interfaces.
TKIND_DISPATCH	A set of methods and properties that are accessible through **IDispatch::Invoke**. By default, dual interfaces return TKIND_DISPATCH.
TKIND_ENUM	A set of enumerators.
TKIND_INTERFACE	A type that has virtual functions, all of which are pure.
TKIND_MODULE	A module which can only have static functions and data (for instance, a DLL).
TKIND_RECORD	A struct with no methods.
TKIND_UNION	A union, all of whose members have offset zero.

VARDESC

A VARDESC structure describes a variable, constant, or data member, and is defined as follows:

```
typedef struct FARSTRUCT tagVARDESC {
    MEMBERID memid;
    OLECHAR FAR* lpstrSchema;/* reserved for future use */
    union {
                        /* VAR_PERINSTANCE - the offset of this
                           variable within the instance */
        unsigned long oInst;
```

```
                                  /* VAR_CONST—the value of the constant */
        VARIANT FAR* lpvarValue;

        }UNION_NAME(u);
        ELEMDESC elemdescVar;
        unsigned short wVarFlags;
        VARKIND varkind;
} VARDESC
```

VARFLAGS

The VARFLAGS enumeration is defined as follows:

```
typedef enum tagVARFLAGS {
        VARFLAG_FREADONLY= 1
    ,   VARFLAG_FSOURCE= 0x2
    ,   VARFLAG_FBINDABLE= 0x4
    ,   VARFLAG_FREQUESTEDIT= 0x8
    ,   VARFLAG_FDISPLAYBIND= 0x10
    ,   VARFLAG_FDEFAULTBIND= 0x20
    ,   VARFLAG_FHIDDEN= 0x40
} VARFLAGS;
```

Value	Description
VARFLAG_READONLY	Assignment to the variable should not be allowed.
VARFLAG_FSOURCE	The variable returns an object that is a source of events.
VARFLAG_FBINDABLE	The variable supports data binding.
VARFLAG_FDISPLAYBIND	The variable is displayed to the user as bindable; that is, VARFLAG_FBINDABLE must also be set.
VARFLAG_FDEFAULTBIND	The variable is the single property that best represents the object. Only one variable in a typeinfo may have this attibute.
VARFLAG_FHIDDEN	The variable should not be displayed to the user in a browser, though it exists and is bindable.

VARKIND

The VARKIND enumeration is defined as follows:

```
typedef enum tagVARKIND {
    VAR_PERINSTANCE,
    VAR_STATIC,
    VAR_CONST,
    VAR_DISPATCH
} VARKIND;
```

Value	Description
VAR_PERINSTANCE	The variable is a field or member of the type; it exists at a fixed offset within each instance of the type.
VAR_STATIC	There is only one instance of the variable.
VAR_CONST	The VARDESC describes a symbolic constant. There is no memory associated with it.
VAR_DISPATCH	The variable can only be accessed through **IDispatch::Invoke**.

ITypeInfo::AddressOfMember

HRESULT ITypeInfo::AddressOfMember(*memid*, *invkind*, *lplpvoid*)
MEMBERID *memid*
INVOKEKIND *invkind*
VOID FAR* FAR* *lplpvoid*

Retrieves the addresses of static functions or variables, such as those defined in a DLL.

Parameters

memid
    Member ID of the static member whose address is to be retrieved.
    The member ID is defined by DISPID.

invkind
    Specifies whether the member is a property, and if so, what kind.

lplpvoid
    Upon return, points to a pointer to the static member.

Return Value

The SCODE obtained from the returned HRESULT is one of the following:

SCODE	Meaning
S_OK	Success.
E_OUTOFMEMORY	Out of memory.
E_INVALIDARG	One or more of the arguments is invalid.
TYPE_E_IOERROR	The function could not read from the file.
TYPE_E_WRONGTYPEKIND	Type mismatch.
TYPE_E_INVDATAREAD	The function could not read from the file.

SCODE	Meaning
TYPE_E_UNSUPFORMAT	The type library has an old format.
TYPE_E_INVALIDSTATE	The type library could not be opened.
TYPE_E_ELEMENTNOTFOUND	The element was not found.
TYPE_E_DLLFUNCTIONNOTFOUND	The function could not be found in the DLL.
TYPE_E_CANTLOADLIBRARY	The type library or DLL could not be loaded.

Comments   The addresses are valid until the caller releases its reference to the type description. Note that the *invkind* parameter can be ignored unless the address of a property function is being requested.

If the type description inherits from another type description, this function recurses on the base type description, if necessary, to find the item with the requested member ID.

ITypeInfo::CreateInstance

HRESULT ITypeInfo::CreateInstance(*punkOuter, riid, ppvObj*)
IUnknown FAR* *punkOuter*
REFIID *riid*
VOID FAR* FAR* *ppvObj*

Creates a new instance of a type that describes a component object class (coclass).

Parameters   *punkOuter*
A pointer to the controlling IUnknown. If NULL, then a stand-alone instance is created. If valid, then an aggregate object is created.

riid
An ID for the interface the caller will use to communicate with the resulting object.

ppvObj
On return, points to a pointer to an instance of the created object.

Return Value   The SCODE obtained from the returned HRESULT is one of the following:

SCODE	Meaning
S_OK	Success.
E_OUTOFMEMORY	Out of memory.
TYPE_E_WRONGTYPEKIND	Type mismatch.
E_INVALIDARG	One or more of the arguments is invalid.

SCODE	Meaning
E_NOINTERFACE	OLE could not find an implementation of one or more required interfaces.
TYPE_E_UNSUPFORMAT	The type library has an old format.
TYPE_E_INVALIDSTATE	The type library could not be opened.
Other returns	Additional errors may be returned from **GetActiveObject** or **CoCreateInstance**.

Comments   For types that describe a component object class (coclass), **CreateInstance** creates a new instance of the class. Normally **CreateInstance** calls **CoCreateInstance** with the type description's GUID. For an Application object, it first calls **GetActiveObject**. If the application is active, **GetActiveObject** returns the active object; otherwise, if **GetActiveObject** fails, **CreateInstance** calls **CoCreateInstance**.

ITypeInfo::GetContainingTypeLib

HRESULT ITypeInfo::GetContainingTypeLib(*lplptlib***,** *lpindex***)**
ITypeLib FAR* FAR* *lplptlib*
unsigned int FAR* *lpindex*

Retrieves the containing type library and the index of the type description within that type library.

Parameters   *lplptlib*
　　　　Upon return, points to a pointer to the containing type library.

lpindex
　　　　Upon return, points to the index of the type description within the containing type library.

Return Value   The SCODE obtained from the returned HRESULT is one of the following:

SCODE	Meaning
S_OK	Success.
E_OUTOFMEMORY	Out of memory.
E_INVALIDARG	One or more of the arguments is invalid.
E_NOINTERFACE	OLE could not find an implementation of one or more required interfaces.

SCODE	Meaning
TYPE_E_IOERROR	The function could not write to the file.
TYPE_E_INVDATAREAD	The function could not read from the file.
TYPE_E_UNSUPFORMAT	The type library has an old format.
TYPE_E_INVALIDSTATE	The type library could not be opened.

ITypeInfo::GetDllEntry

HRESULT ITypeInfo::GetDllEntry(*memid*, *invkind*, *lpbstrDllName*, *lpbstrName*, *lpwOrdinal*)
MEMBERID *memid*
INVOKEKIND *invkind*
BSTR FAR* *lpbstrDllName*
BSTR FAR* *lpbstrName*
unsigned short FAR* *lpwOrdinal*

Retrieves a description or specification of an entry point for a function in a DLL.

Parameters

memid
ID of the member function whose DLL entry description is to be returned.

invkind
Specifies the kind of member identified by *memid*. This is important for properties, because one *memid* can identify up to three separate functions.

lpbstrDllName
If not NULL, the function sets **lpbstrDllName* to a BSTR containing the DLL name.

lpbstrName
If not NULL, the function sets **lpbstrName* to a BSTR containing the name of the entry point; if the entry point is specified by an ordinal, **lpbstrName* is set to NULL.

lpwOrdinal
If not NULL, and if the function is defined by ordinal, then *lpwOrdinal* is set to point to the ordinal.

Return Value   The SCODE obtained from the returned HRESULT is one of the following:

SCODE	Meaning
S_OK	Success.
E_OUTOFMEMORY	Out of memory.
E_INVALIDARG	One or more of the arguments is invalid.
E_NOINTERFACE	OLE could not find an implementation of one or more required interfaces.
TYPE_E_ELEMENTNOTFOUND	The element was not found.
TYPE_E_IOERROR	The function could not read from the file.
TYPE_E_INVDATAREAD	The function could not read from the file.
TYPE_E_UNSUPFORMAT	The type library has an old format.
TYPE_E_INVALIDSTATE	The type library could not be opened.
TYPE_E_WRONGTYPEKIND	Type mismatch.

Comments   The caller passes in a MEMID representing the member function whose entry description is desired. If the function has a DLL entry point, the name of the DLL containing the function, and either its name or ordinal identifier are placed in the passed-in pointers allocated by the caller. If there is no DLL entry point for the function, an error is returned.

If the type description inherits from another type description, this function recurses on the base type description if necessary, to find the item with the requested member ID.

The caller should use **SysFreeString**() to free the BSTRs referenced by *lpbstrName* and *lpbstrDllName*.

ITypeInfo::GetDocumentation

HRESULT ITypeInfo::GetDocumentation(*memid, lpbstrName, lpbstrDocString, lpdwHelpContext, lpbstrHelpFile*)
MEMBERID *memid*
BSTR FAR* *lpbstrName*
BSTR FAR* *lpbstrDocString*
unsigned long FAR* *lpdwHelpContext*
BSTR FAR* *lpbstrHelpFile*

Retrieves the documentation string, name of the complete Help file path and name, and the context ID for the Help topic for a specified type description.

Parameters

memid
ID of the member whose documentation is to be returned.

lpbstrName
Pointer to a BSTR allocated by the callee into which the name of the specified item is placed. If the caller does not need the item name, *lpbstrName* can be NULL.

lpbstrDocString
Pointer to a BSTR into which the documentation string for the specified item is placed. If the caller does not need the documentation string, *lpbstrDocString* can be NULL.

lpdwHelpContext
Pointer to the Help context associated with the specified item. If the caller does not need the Help context, the *lpdwHelpContext* can be NULL.

lpbstrHelpFile
Pointer to a BSTR into which the fully qualified name of the Help file is placed. If the caller does not need the Help filename, *lpbstrHelpFile* can be NULL.

Return Value

The SCODE obtained from the returned HRESULT is one of the following:

SCODE	Meaning
S_OK	Success.
E_OUTOFMEMORY	Out of memory.
E_INVALIDARG	One or more of the arguments is invalid.
TYPE_E_IOERROR	The function could not read from the file.
TYPE_E_ELEMENTNOTFOUND	The element was not found.
TYPE_E_INVDATAREAD	The function could not read from the file.
TYPE_E_UNSUPFORMAT	The type library has an old format.
TYPE_E_INVALIDSTATE	The type library could not be opened.
TYPE_E_ELEMENTNOTFOUND	The element was not found.

Comments

Provides access to the documentation for the member specified by the *memid* parameter. If the passed-in *memid* is MEMBERID_NIL, then the documentation for the type description is returned.

If the type description inherits from another type description, this function recurses on the base type description, if necessary, to find the item with the requested member ID.

The caller should use **SysFreeString**() to free the BSTRs referenced by *lpbstrName*, *lpbstrDocString*, and *lpbstrHelpFile*.

Example

```
CHECKRESULT(ptypeinfo->GetDocumentation(idMember, &bstrName, NULL, NULL,
    NULL));
    .
    .
    .
SysFreeString (bstrName);
```

ITypeInfo::GetFuncDesc

HRESULT ITypeInfo::GetFuncDesc(*index*, *lplpfuncdesc*)
unsigned int *index*
FUNCDESC FAR* FAR* *lplpfuncdesc*

Retrieves the FUNCDESC structure containing information about a specified function.

Parameters

index
Index of the function whose description is to be returned. The index should be in the range of 0 to 1 less than the number of functions in this type.

lplpfuncdesc
Upon return, points to a pointer to a FUNCDESC that describes the specified function.

Return Value

The SCODE obtained from the returned HRESULT is one of the following:

SCODE	Meaning
S_OK	Success.
E_OUTOFMEMORY	Out of memory.
E_INVALIDARG	One or more of the arguments is invalid.
TYPE_E_IOERROR	The function could not read from the file.
TYPE_E_INVDATAREAD	The function could not read from the file.
TYPE_E_UNSUPFORMAT	The type library has an old format.
TYPE_E_INVALIDSTATE	The type library could not be opened.

Comments

Provides access to a FUNCDESC that describes the function with the specified index. The FUNCDESC should be freed with **ITypeInfo::ReleaseFuncDesc()**. The number of functions in the type is one of the attributes contained in the TYPEATTR structure.

Example

```
CHECKRESULT(ptypeinfo->GetFuncDesc(i, &pfuncdesc));
idMember = pfuncdesc->elemdescFunc.ID;
CHECKRESULT(ptypeinfo->GetDocumentation(idMember, &bstrName, NULL, NULL,
NULL));
ptypeinfo->ReleaseFuncDesc(pfuncdesc);
```

ITypeInfo::GetIDsOfNames

HRESULT ITypeInfo::GetIDsOfNames(*rgszNames, cNames, rgmemid*)
OLECHAR FAR* FAR* *rgszNames*
unsigned int *cNames*
MEMBERID FAR* *rgmemid*

Maps between member names and member IDs, and parameter names and parameter IDs.

Parameters

rgszNames
   Passed-in pointer to an array of names to be mapped.

cNames
   Count of the names to be mapped.

rgmemid
   Caller-allocated array in which name mappings are placed.

Return Value

The SCODE obtained from the returned HRESULT is one of the following:

SCODE	Meaning
S_OK	Success.
STG_E_INSUFFICIENTMEMORY	Out of memory.
E_OUTOFMEMORY	Out of memory.
E_INVALIDARG	One or more of the arguments is invalid.
DISP_E_UNKNOWNNAME	One or more of the names could not be found.
DISP_E_UNKNOWNLCID	The LCID could not be found in the OLE DLLs.
TYPE_E_IOERROR	The function could not write to the file.
TYPE_E_INVDATAREAD	The function could not read from the file.
TYPE_E_UNSUPFORMAT	The type library has an old format.
TYPE_E_INVALIDSTATE	The type library could not be opened.
TYPE_E_WRONGTYPEKIND	Type mismatch.

Comments   Maps the name of a member (*rgszNames*[0]) and its parameters
(*rgszNames*[1] ...*rgszNames*[*cNames* − 1]) to the ID of the member (*rgid*[0]) and
the IDs of the specified parameters (*rgid*[1] ... *rgid*[*cNames* − 1]). Note that the
IDs of parameters are 0 for the first parameter in the member function's argument
list, 1 for the second, and so on.

If the type description inherits from another type description, this function recurses
on the base type description, if necessary, to find the item with the requested
member ID.

ITypeInfo::GetImplTypeFlags

HRESULT ITypeInfo:: GetImplTypeFlags(*index*, *pimpltypeflags*)
unsigned int *index*
MEMBERID FAR* *pimpltypeflags*

Retrieves the IMPLTYPEFLAGS for one implemented interface or base interface
in a type description.

Parameters   *index*
        Index of the implemented interface or base interface for which to get the flags.

pimpltypeflags
On return, pointer to the IMPLTYPEFLAGS.

Return Value   The SCODE obtained from the returned HRESULT is one of the following:

SCODE	Meaning
S_OK	Success.
E_OUTOFMEMORY	Out of memory.
E_INVALIDARG	One or more of the arguments is invalid.
TYPE_E_INVDATAREAD	The function could not read from the file.
TYPE_E_UNSUPFORMAT	The type library has an old format.
TYPE_E_INVALIDSTATE	The type library could not be opened.
TYPE_E_WRONGTYPEKIND	Type mismatch.

Comments   The flags are associated with the act of inheritance, not with the inherited interface.

ITypeInfo::GetMops

HRESULT ITypeInfo::GetMops(*memid*, *lpbstrMops*)
MEMBERID *memid*
BSTR FAR* *lpbstrMops*

Retrieves marshaling information.

Parameters

memid
   Member ID indicating which marshaling information is sought.

lpbstrMops
   Upon return, points to a pointer to the opcode string used in marshaling the fields of the structure described by the referenced type description, or NULL if there is no information to return.

Return Value

The SCODE obtained from the returned HRESULT is one of the following:

SCODE	Meaning
S_OK	Success.
E_OUTOFMEMORY	Out of memory.
E_INVALIDARG	One or more of the arguments is invalid.
TYPE_E_IOERROR	The function could not read from the file.
TYPE_E_UNSUPFORMAT	The type library has an old format.
TYPE_E_INVALIDSTATE	The type library could not be opened.
TYPE_E_ELEMENTNOTFOUND	The element was not found.
TYPE_E_WRONGTYPEKIND	Type mismatch.

Comments

If the passed-in member ID is MEMBERID_NIL, the function returns the opcode string for marshaling the fields of the structure described by the type description. Otherwise, it returns the opcode string for marshaling the function specified by the index.

If the type description inherits from another type description, this function recurses on the base type description, if necessary, to find the item with the requested member ID.

ITypeInfo::GetNames

HRESULT ITypeInfo::GetNames(*memid, rgbstrNames, cNameMax, lpcName*)
MEMBERID *memid*
BSTR FAR* *rgbstrNames*
unsigned int *cNameMax*
unsigned int FAR* *lpcName*

Retrieves the variable with the specified member ID, or the name of the property or method and its parameters, corresponding to the specified function ID.

Parameters

memid
ID of member whose name (or names) is to be returned.

rgbstrNames
Pointer to caller-allocated array. On return, each of these *lpcName* elements is filled in to point to a BSTR containing the name (or names) associated with the member.

cNameMax
Length of the passed-in *rgbstrNames* array.

lpcName
On return, points to number representing the number of names in *rgbstrNames* array.

Return Value

The SCODE obtained from the returned HRESULT is one of the following:

SCODE	Meaning
S_OK	Success.
E_OUTOFMEMORY	Out of memory.
E_INVALIDARG	One or more of the arguments is invalid.
TYPE_E_IOERROR	The function could not read from the file.
TYPE_E_INVDATAREAD	The function could not read from the file.
TYPE_E_UNSUPFORMAT	The type library has an old format.
TYPE_E_INVALIDSTATE	The type library could not be opened.
TYPE_E_WRONGTYPEKIND	Type mismatch.
TYPE_E_ELEMENTNOTFOUND	The element was not found.

Comments

The caller must release the returned BSTR array.

If the member ID identifies a property that is implemented with property functions, the property name is returned.

For property get functions, the names of the function and its parameters are always returned.

For property put and put reference functions, the right side of the assignment is unnamed. If *cNameMax* is less than is required to return all the names of parameters of a function, then only the names of the first *cNameMax* − 1 parameters are returned. The names of the parameters are returned in the array in the same order they appear elsewhere in the interface, for example, in the same order they appear in the parameter array associated with the FUNCDESC.

If the type description inherits from another type description, this function recurses on the base type description, if necessary, to find the item with the requested member ID.

ITypeInfo::GetRefTypeInfo

HRESULT ITypeInfo::GetRefTypeInfo(*hreftype*, *lplptinfo*)
HREFTYPE *hreftype*
ITypeInfo FAR* FAR* *lplptinfo*

If a type description references other type descriptions, this function retrieves the referenced type descriptions.

Parameters

hreftype
　　Handle to the referenced type description to be returned.

lplptinfo
　　Points to a pointer to the referenced type description.

Return Value

The SCODE obtained from the returned HRESULT is one of the following:

SCODE	Meaning
S_OK	Success.
E_OUTOFMEMORY	Out of memory.
E_INVALIDARG	One or more of the arguments is invalid.
TYPE_E_IOERROR	The function could not read from the file.
TYPE_E_INVDATAREAD	The function could not read from the file.

SCODE	Meaning
TYPE_E_UNSUPFORMAT	The type library has an old format.
TYPE_E_INVALIDSTATE	The type library could not be opened.
TYPE_E_WRONGTYPEKIND	Type mismatch.
TYPE_E_ELEMENTNOTFOUND	The element was not found.
TYPE_E_REGISTRYACCESS	There was an error accessing the system registration database.
TYPE_E_LIBNOTREGISTERED	The type library was not found in the system registration database.

Comments

On return, the second parameter contains a pointer to a pointer to a type description that is referenced by this type description. A type description must have a reference to each type description that occurs as the type of any of its variables, function parameters, or function return types. For example, if the type of a data member is a record type, the typeinfo for that data member contains the *hreftype* of a referenced type description. To get a pointer to the type description, the reference is passed to **GetRefTypeInfo**.

ITypeInfo::GetRefTypeOfImplType

HRESULT ITypeInfo::GetRefTypeOfImplType(*index*, *lphreftype*)
unsigned int *index*
HREFTYPE FAR* *lphreftype*

If this type description describes a component object class, the function retrieves the type description of the specified implemented interface types. For an interface, **GetRefTypeOfImplType** returns the type information for inherited interfaces, if any exist.

Parameters

index
Index of the implemented type whose handle is returned. The valid range is 0 to the *cImplTypes* field in the TYPEATTR structure.

lphreftype
Upon return, points to a handle for the implemented interface (if any). This handle can be passed to **ITypeInfo::GetRefTypeInfo** to get the type description.

Return Value   The SCODE obtained from the returned HRESULT is one of the following:

SCODE	Meaning
S_OK	Success.
TYPE_E_ELEMENTNOTFOUND	Passed index is outside the range 0 to 1 less than the number of function descriptions.
E_INVALIDARG	One or more of the arguments is invalid.
TYPE_E_IOERROR	The function could not read from the file.
TYPE_E_INVDATAREAD	The function could not read from the file.
TYPE_E_UNSUPFORMAT	The type library has an old format.
TYPE_E_INVALIDSTATE	The type library could not be opened.
TYPE_E_IOERROR	The function could not write to the file.
TYPE_E_INVDATAREAD	The function could not read from the file.
TYPE_E_UNSUPFORMAT	The type library has an old format.
TYPE_E_INVALIDSTATE	The type library could not be opened.

Comments   If you have the TKIND_DISPATCH typeinfo for a dual interface, you can get the TKIND_INTERFACE typeinfo by calling **GetRefTypeOfImplType** with an *Index* of –1, and passing the returned *lpHRefType* handle to **GetRefTypeInfo** to retrieve the typeinfo.

ITypeInfo::GetTypeAttr

HRESULT ITypeInfo::GetTypeAttr(*lplptypeattr***)**
TYPEATTR FAR* FAR* *lplptypeattr*

Retrieves a TYPEATTR structure containing the attributes of the type description.

Parameter   *lplptypeattr*
    Upon return, points to a pointer to a structure that contains the attributes of this type description.

Return Value   The SCODE obtained from the returned HRESULT is one of the following:

SCODE	Meaning
S_OK	Success.
E_OUTOFMEMORY	Out of memory.
E_INVALIDARG	One or more of the arguments is invalid.

SCODE	Meaning
TYPE_E_IOERROR	The function could not write to the file.
TYPE_E_INVDATAREAD	The function could not read from the file.
TYPE_E_UNSUPFORMAT	The type library has an old format.
TYPE_E_INVALIDSTATE	The type library could not be opened.

Comments   To free the TYPEATTR structure, use **ITypeInfo::ReleaseTypeAttr.**

Example
```
CHECKRESULT(ptypeinfoCur->GetTypeAttr(&ptypeattrCur));
    .
    .
    .
ptypeinfoCur->ReleaseTypeAttr(ptypeattrCur);
```

ITypeInfo::GetTypeComp

HRESULT ITypeInfo::GetTypeComp(*lplpcomp*)
ITypeComp FAR* FAR* *lplpcomp*

Retrieves the **ITypeComp** interface for the type description, which enables a client compiler to bind to the type description's members.

Parameter   *lplpcomp*
Upon return, points to a pointer to the **ITypeComp** of the containing type library.

Return Value   The SCODE obtained from the returned HRESULT is one of the following:

SCODE	Meaning
S_OK	Success.
E_OUTOFMEMORY	Out of memory.
E_INVALIDARG	One or more of the arguments is invalid.
TYPE_E_IOERROR	The function could not read from the file.
TYPE_E_INVDATAREAD	The function could not read from the file.
TYPE_E_UNSUPFORMAT	The type library has an old format.
TYPE_E_INVALIDSTATE	The type library could not be opened.
TYPE_E_WRONGTYPEKIND	Type mismatch.

Comments   A client compiler can use the **ITypeComp** interface to bind to members of the type.

ITypeInfo::GetVarDesc

HRESULT ITypeInfo::GetVarDesc(*index*, *lplpvardesc*)
unsigned int *index*
VARDESC FAR* FAR* *lplpvardesc*

Retrieves a VARDESC structure describing the specified variable.

Parameters

index
Index of the variable whose description is to be returned. The index should be in the range of 0 to 1 less than the number of variables in this type.

lplpvardesc
Upon return, points to a pointer to a VARDESC that describes the specified variable.

Return Value

The SCODE obtained from the returned HRESULT is one of the following:

SCODE	Meaning
S_OK	Success.
E_OUTOFMEMORY	Out of memory.
E_INVALIDARG	One or more of the arguments is invalid.
TYPE_E_IOERROR	The function could not read from the file.
TYPE_E_INVDATAREAD	The function could not read from the file.
TYPE_E_UNSUPFORMAT	The type library has an old format.
TYPE_E_INVALIDSTATE	The type library could not be opened.

Comments

To free the VARDESC structure, use **ReleaseVarDesc**.

Example

```
CHECKRESULT(ptypeinfo->GetVarDesc(i, &pvardesc));
idMember = pvardesc->memid;
CHECKRESULT(ptypeinfo->GetDocumentation(idMember, &bstrName, NULL, NULL,
        NULL));
ptypeinfo->ReleaseVarDesc(pvardesc);
```

ITypeInfo::Invoke

HRESULT ITypeInfo::Invoke(*lpvInstance*, *memid*, *wFlags*, *pdispparams*, *pvargResult*, *pexcepinfo*, *puArgErr*)
VOID FAR* *lpvInstance*
MEMBERID *memid*
unsigned short *wFlags*
DISPPARAMS FAR* *pdispparams*
VARIANT FAR* *pvargResult*
EXCEPINFO FAR* *pexcepinfo*
unsigned int FAR* *puArgErr*

Invokes a method or accesses a property of an object that implements the interface described by the type description.

Parameters

lpvInstance
Pointer to an instance of the interface described by this type description.

memid
Identifies the interface member.

wFlags
Flags describing the context of the invoke call, as follows:

Value	Description
DISPATCH_METHOD	The member was accessed as a method. If there is ambiguity, both this and the DISPATCH_PROPERTYGET flag may be set.
DISPATCH_PROPERTYGET	The member is being retrieved as a property or data member.
DISPATCH_PROPERTYPUT	The member is being changed as a property or data member.
DISPATCH_PROPERTYPUTREF	The member is being changed by using a reference assignment, rather than a value assignment. This value is only valid when the property accepts a reference to an object.

pdispparams

Points to a structure containing an array of arguments, an array of DISPIDs for named arguments, and counts of the number of elements in each array.

pvargResult

Should be NULL if the caller expects no result; otherwise, it should be a pointer to the location at which the result is to be stored. If *wFlags* specifies DISPATCH_PROPERTYPUT or DISPATCH_PROPERTYPUTREF, *pvargResult* is ignored.

pexcepinfo

Points to an exception information structure, which is filled in only if DISP_E_EXCEPTION is returned. If *pexcepinfo* is NULL on input, only an HRESULT error will be returned.

puArgErr

If **Invoke** returns DISP_E_TYPEMISMATCH, *puArgErr* indicates the index (within *rgvarg*) of the argument with incorrect type. If more than one argument has an error, *puArgErr* indicates only the first argument with an error. Note that arguments in *pdispparams->rgvarg* appear in reverse order, so the first argument is the one having the highest index in the array. Can't be NULL.

Return Value

The SCODE obtained from the returned HRESULT is one of the following:

SCODE	Meaning
S_OK	Success.
E_INVALIDARG	One or more of the arguments is invalid.
DISP_E_EXCEPTION	The member being invoked has returned an error HRESULT. If the member implements **IErrorInfo**, details are available in the error object. Otherwise, the *pexcepinfo* parameter contains details.
TYPE_E_IOERROR	The function could not read from the file.
TYPE_E_INVDATAREAD	The function could not read from the file.
TYPE_E_UNSUPFORMAT	The type library has an old format.
TYPE_E_REGISTRYACCESS	There was an error accessing the system registration database.
TYPE_E_LIBNOTREGISTERED	The type library was not found in the system registration database.
TYPE_E_INVALIDSTATE	The type library could not be opened.
TYPE_E_WRONGTYPEKIND	Type mismatch.
TYPE_E_ELEMENTNOTFOUND	The element was not found.
TYPE_E_BADMODULEKIND	The module does not support **Invoke**.
Other returns	Any of the **IDispatch::Invoke** errors may also be returned.

Comments   Use **ITypeInfo::Invoke** to access a member of an object or invoke a method that implements the interface described by this type description. For objects that support the **IDispatch** interface, **Invoke** can be used to implement **IDispatch::Invoke**.

ITypeInfo::Invoke takes a pointer to an instance of the class. Otherwise, its parameters are the same as **IDispatch::Invoke**, except that **ITypeInfo::Invoke** omits the REFIID and LCID parameters. When called, **ITypeInfo::Invoke** performs the actions described by the **IDispatch::Invoke** parameters on the specified instance.

For VTBL interface members, **ITypeInfo::Invoke** passes the LCID of the typeinfo into parameters tagged with the **lcid** attribute, and the returned value into the **retval** parameter.

If the type description inherits from another type description, this function recurses on the base type description if necessary, to find the item with the requested member ID.

ITypeInfo::ReleaseFuncDesc

VOID ITypeInfo::ReleaseFuncDesc(*lpfuncdesc*)
FUNCDESC FAR* *lpfuncdesc*

Releases a FUNCDESC previously returned by **GetFuncDesc**.

Parameter   *lpfuncdes*
Pointer to the FUNCDESC to be freed.

Comments   **ReleaseFuncDesc** releases a FUNCDESC that was returned through **ITypeInfo::GetFuncDesc**.

Example   `ptypeinfoCur->ReleaseFuncDesc(pfuncdesc);`

ITypeInfo::ReleaseTypeAttr

VOID ITypeInfo::ReleaseTypeAttr(*lptypeattr*)
TYPEATTR FAR* *lptypeattr*

Releases a TYPEATTR previously returned by **GetTypeAttr**.

Parameter   *lptypeattr*
Pointer to the TYPEATTR to be freed.

Comments   **ReleaseTypeAttr** releases a TYPEATTR that was returned through
         ITypeInfo::GetTypeAttr.

ITypeInfo::ReleaseVarDesc

    VOID ITypeInfo::ReleaseVarDesc(*lpvardesc*)
    VARDESC FAR* *lpvardesc*

    Releases a VARDESC previously returned by **GetVarDesc**.

Parameter   *lpvardesc*
      Pointer to the VARDESC to be freed.

Comments   **ReleaseVarDesc** releases a VARDESC that was returned through
         ITypeInfo::GetVarDesc.

Example
```
VARDESC    FAR *pvardesc;
CHECKRESULT(ptypeinfo->GetVarDesc(i, &pvardesc));
idMember = pvardesc->memid;
CHECKRESULT(ptypeinfo->GetDocumentation(idMember, &bstrName, NULL, NULL,
    NULL));
ptypeinfo->ReleaseVarDesc(pvardesc);
```

ITypeComp Interface

Implemented by	Used by	Header filename
OLEAUT32.DLL (32-bit systems)	Tools that compile references to objects contained in type libraries.	**OLEAUTO.H**
TYPELIB.DLL (16-bit systems)		**DISPATCH.H**

Binding is the process of mapping names to types and type members. The
ITypeComp interface provides a fast way to access information that compilers
need when binding to and instantiating structures and interfaces.

Structures and Enumerations

The **ITypeComp** interface uses the following structures and enumerations:

BINDPTR

A union containing a pointer to a FUNCDESC, VARDESC, or an **ITypeComp** interface.

```
typedef union tagBINDPTR {
    FUNCDESC FAR* lpfuncdesc;
    VARDESC FAR* lpvardesc;
    ITypeComp FAR* lptcomp;
} BINDPTR;
```

DESCKIND

Identifies the type of the type description being bound to.

```
typedef enum tagDESCKIND {
    DESCKIND_NONE,
    DESCKIND_FUNCDESC,
    DESCKIND_VARDESC,
    DESCKIND_TYPECOMP,
    DESCKIND_IMPLICITAPPOBJ
} DESCKIND;
```

Comments

Value	Description
DESCKIND_NONE	No match was found.
DESCKIND_FUNCDESC	A FUNCDESC was returned.
DESCKIND_VARDESC	A VARDESC was returned.
DESCKIND_TYPECOMP	A TYPECOMP was returned.
DESCKIND_IMPLICITAPPOBJ	An IMPLICITAPPOBJ was returned.

ITypeComp::Bind

HRESULT ITypeComp::Bind(*szName, lHashVal, wFlags, lplptinfo, lpdesckind, lpbindptr*)
OLECHAR FAR* *szName*
unsigned long *lHashVal*
unsigned short *wFlags*
ITypeInfo FAR* FAR* *lplptinfo*
DESCKIND FAR* *lpdesckind*
BINDPTR FAR* *lpbindptr*

Maps a name to a member of a type, or binds global variables and functions contained in a type library.

Parameters

szName
> Name to be bound.

lHashVal
> Hash value for the name computed by **LHashValOfNameSys**.

wFlags
> Flags word containing one or more of the INVOKE flags defined in the INVOKEKIND enumeration. Specifies whether the name was referenced as a method or as a property. When binding to a variable, specify the INVOKE_PROPERTYGET flag. Specify 0 to bind to any type of member.

lplptinfo
> If a FUNCDESC or VARDESC was returned, then *lplptinfo* points to a pointer to the type description that contains the item to which it is bound.

lpdesckind
> Pointer to a DESCKIND enumerator that indicates whether the name bound to a VARDESC, FUNCDESC, or TYPECOMP. Points to DESCKIND_NONE if there was no match.

lpbindptr
> Upon return, contains a pointer to the bound-to VARDESC, FUNCDESC, or **ITypeComp**.

Return Value

The SCODE obtained from the returned HRESULT is one of the following:

SCODE	Meaning
S_OK	Success.
E_OUTOFMEMORY	Out of memory.
E_INVALIDARG	One or more of the arguments is invalid.
TYPE_E_IOERROR	The function could not read from the file.

SCODE	Meaning
TYPE_E_INVDATAREAD	The function could not read from the file.
TYPE_E_UNSUPFORMAT	The type library has an old format.
TYPE_E_INVALIDSTATE	The type library could not be opened.
TYPE_E_AMBIGUOUSNAME	More than one instance of this name occurs in the type library.

Comments

Used for binding to the variables and methods of a type, or for binding to the global variables and methods in a type library. The returned DESCKIND pointer *lpdesckind* indicates whether the name was bound to a VARDESC, a FUNCDESC, or an **ITypeComp** instance. The returned *lpbindptr* points to the VARDESC, FUNCDESC, or **ITypeComp**.

If a data member or method is bound to, then *lplptinfo* points to the type description that contains the method or data member.

If **Bind** binds the name to a nested binding context, it returns a pointer to an **ITypeComp** instance in lpbindptr and a NULL type description pointer in lplptinfo. For example, if you pass the name of a type description for a module (TKIND_MODULE), enumeration (TKIND_ENUM), or coclass (TKIND_COCLASS) **Bind** returns the **ITypeComp** instance of the type description for the module, enumeration, or coclass. This feature supports languages like Visual Basic that allow references to the members of a type description to be qualified by the name of the type description. For example, a function in a module can be referenced by modulename.functionname.

The members of TKIND_ENUM, TKIND_MODULE, and TKIND_COCLASS types marked as Application objects can be directly bound to from **ITypeComp**, without specifying the name of the module. The **ITypeComp** of a coclass defers to the **ITypeComp** of its default interface.

As with other methods of **ITypeComp**, **ITypeInfo**, and **ITypeLib**, the calling code is responsible for releasing the returned object instances or structures. If a VARDESC or FUNCDESC is returned, the caller is responsible for deleting it via the returned type description and releasing the type description instance itself; otherwise, if an **ITypeComp** instance is returned, the caller must release it.

Special rules apply if you call a type library's **Bind** method, passing it the name of a member of an Application object class (that is, a class that has the TYPEFLAG_FAPPOBJECT flag set). In this case, **Bind** returns DESCKIND_IMPLICITAPPOBJ in *lpdesckind,* a VARDESC that describes the Application object in *lpbindptr*, and the **ITypeInfo** of the Application object class in *lplptinfo*. To bind to the object, you must call **ITypeInfo::GetTypeComp** to get the **ITypeComp** of the Application object class, and then reinvoke its **Bind** method with the name initially passed to the type library's **ITypeComp**.

The caller should use the returned **ITypeInfo** pointer (*lplptinfo*) to get the address of the member.

Note that the *wflags* parameter is the same as the *wflags* parameter in **IDispatch::Invoke**.

ITypeComp::BindType

HRESULT **ITypeComp::BindType**(*szName, lHashVal, lplpitinfo, lplpitcomp*
OLECHAR FAR* *szName*
unsigned long *lHashVal*
ITypeInfo FAR* FAR* *lplptinfo*
ITypeComp FAR* FAR* *lplptcomp*

Binds to the type descriptions contained within a type library.

Parameters

szName
    Name to be bound.

lHashVal
    Hash value for the name computed by **LHashValOfName**.

lplptinfo
    Upon return, contains a pointer to a pointer to an **ITypeInfo** of the type to which the name was bound.

lplptcomp
    Reserved for future use. Pass NULL.

Return Value

The SCODE obtained from the returned HRESULT is one of the following:

SCODE	Meaning
S_OK	Success.
E_OUTOFMEMORY	Out of memory.
E_INVALIDARG	One or more of the arguments is invalid.
TYPE_E_IOERROR	The function could not read from the file.
TYPE_E_INVDATAREAD	The function could not read from the file.
TYPE_E_UNSUPFORMAT	The type library has an old format.
TYPE_E_INVALIDSTATE	The type library could not be opened.
TYPE_E_AMBIGUOUSNAME	More than one instance of this name occurs in the type library.

Comments   Used for binding a type name to the **ITypeInfo** that describes the type. This
function is invoked on the **ITypeComp** returned by **ITypeLib::GetTypeComp** to
bind to types defined within that library. It could also be used in the future for
binding to nested types.

Type Compilation Functions

LHashValOfName

unsigned long LHashValOfName(*lcid*, *szName*)
LCID *lcid*
OLECHAR FAR* *szName*

Computes a hash value for a name that can then be passed to **ITypeComp::Bind**,
ITypeComp::BindType, **ITypeLib::FindName**, or **ITypeLib::IsName**.

Parameters   *lcid*
        The locale ID for the string.

szName
        String whose hash value is to be computed.

Return Value   A 32-bit hash value representing the name passed in.

Comments   This function is equivalent to **LHashValOfNameSys**. The OLEAUTO.H header
file contains macros that define **LHashValOfName** as **LHashValOfNameSys**
with the target operating system (*syskind*), based on your build preprocessor flags.

LHashValOfName computes a 32-bit hash value for a name which can then be
passed to **ITypeComp::Bind**, **ITypeComp::BindType**, **ITypeLib::FindName**,
or **ITypeLib::IsName**. The returned hash value is independent of the case of the
characters in *szName* as long as the language of the name is one of the languages
supported by the OLE National Language Specification API. Specifically, for any
two strings, if those strings match when a case-insensitive comparison is done using
any language, then they will produce the same hash value.

LHashValOfNameSys

unsigned long LHashValOfName(*syskind*, *lcid*, *szName*)
SYSKIND *syskind*
LCID *lcid*
OLECHAR FAR* *szName*

Computes a hash value for a name that can then be passed to **ITypeComp::Bind**, **ITypeComp::BindType**, **ITypeLib::FindName**, or **ITypeLib::IsName**.

Parameters   *syskind*
    The SYSKIND of the target operating system.

lcid
    The locale ID for the string.

szName
    String whose hash value is to be computed.

Return Value   A 32-bit hash value representing the name passed in.

Type Library Loading and Registration Functions

LoadTypeLib

HRESULT LoadTypeLib(*szFileName*, *lplptlib*)
OLECHAR FAR* *szFileName*
ITypeLib FAR* FAR* *lplptlib*

Loads and registers a type library.

Parameters   *szFileName*
    Contains the name of the file from which **LoadTypeLib** should attempt to load a type library.

lplptlib
    On return, contains a pointer to a pointer to the loaded type library.

Return Value   The SCODE obtained from the returned HRESULT is one of the following:

SCODE	Meaning
S_OK	Success.
E_OUTOFMEMORY	Out of memory.
E_INVALIDARG	One or more of the arguments is invalid.
TYPE_E_IOERROR	The function could not write to the file.
TYPE_E_INVALIDSTATE	The type library could not be opened.
TYPE_E_INVDATAREAD	The function could not read from the file.
TYPE_E_UNSUPFORMAT	The type library has an old format.
TYPE_E_INVALIDSTATE	The type library could not be opened.
TYPE_E_UNKNOWNLCID	The LCID could not be found in the OLE support DLLs.
TYPE_E_CANTLOADLIBRARY	The type library or DLL could not be loaded.
Other returns	All FACILITY_STORAGE errors may be returned.

Comments   **LoadTypeLib** loads and registers a type library (usually created with MkTypLib) that is stored in the specified file. If *szFileName* specifies only a filename, with no path, **LoadTypeLib** searches for the file and proceeds as follows:

- If the file is a stand-alone type library implemented by TYPELIB.DLL, the library is loaded directly.

- If the file is a DLL or .EXE, the file is loaded. By default, the type library is extracted from the first resource of type ITypeLib. To load a different type library resource, append an integer index to *szFileName*. For example:

```
LoadTypeLib("C:\MONTANA\EXE\MFA.EXE\3", lplptlib)
```

  This statement loads the type library resource 3 from the file MFA.EXE.

- If the file is none of the above, the filename is parsed into a moniker (an object that represents a file-based link source), then bound to the moniker. This approach allows **LoadTypeLib** to be used on foreign type libraries, including in-memory type libraries. Foreign type libraries can't reside in a DLL or .EXE file. See the *OLE Programmer's Guide and Reference* for more information on monikers.

If the type library is already loaded, **LoadTypeLib** increments the type library's reference count and returns a pointer to the type library.

LoadRegTypeLib

HRESULT LoadRegTypeLib(*guid*, *wVerMajor*, *wVerMinor*, *lcid*, *lplptlib*)
REFGUID *guid*
unsigned short *wVerMajor*
unsigned short *wVerMinor*
LCID *lcid*
ITypeLib FAR* FAR* *lplptlib*

Uses registry information to load a type library.

Parameters

guid
    ID of the library being loaded.

wVerMajor
    Major version number of library being loaded.

wVerMinor
    Minor version number of library being loaded.

lcid
    National language code of library being loaded.

lplptlib
    On return, points to a pointer to the loaded type library.

Return Value

The SCODE obtained from the returned HRESULT is one of the following:

SCODE	Meaning
S_OK	Success.
E_OUTOFMEMORY	Out of memory.
E_INVALIDARG	One or more of the arguments is invalid.
TYPE_E_IOERROR	The function could not read from the file.
TYPE_E_INVALIDSTATE	The type library could not be opened.
TYPE_E_INVDATAREAD	The function could not read from the file.
TYPE_E_UNSUPFORMAT	The type library has an old format.
TYPE_E_INVALIDSTATE	The type library could not be opened.
TYPE_E_UNKNOWNLCID	The passed in LCID could not be found in the OLE support DLLs.
TYPE_E_CANTLOADLIBRARY	The type library or DLL could not be loaded.
Other returns	All FACILITY_STORAGE and system registry errors may also be returned.

Comments   **LoadRegTypeLib** defers to **LoadTypeLib** to load the file.

LoadRegTypeLib compares the requested version numbers against those found in the system registry and takes one of the following actions:

- If one of the registered libraries exactly matches both the requested major and minor version numbers, then that type library is loaded.

- If one or more registered type libraries exactly match the requested major version number and have a greater minor version number than that requested, the one with the greatest minor version number is loaded.

- If none of the registered type libraries exactly match the requested major version number or if none of those which do exactly match the major version number also have a minor version number greater than or equal to the requested minor version number, then **LoadRegTypeLib** returns an error.

RegisterTypeLib

HRESULT **RegisterTypeLib**(*ptlib*, *szFullPath*, *szHelpDir*)
ITypeLib FAR* *ptlib*
OLECHAR FAR* *szFullPath*
OLECHAR FAR* *szHelpDir*

Adds information about a type library to the system registry.

Parameters   *ptlib*
Pointer to the type library being registered.

szFullPath
Fully qualified path specification for the type library being registered.

szHelpDir
Directory in which the Help file for the library being registered can be found. May be NULL.

Return Value   The SCODE obtained from the returned HRESULT is one of the following:

SCODE	Meaning
S_OK	Success.
E_OUTOFMEMORY	Out of memory.
E_INVALIDARG	One or more of the arguments is invalid.
TYPE_E_IOERROR	The function could not write to the file.
TYPE_E_REGISTRYACCESS	The system registration database could not be opened.
TYPE_E_INVALIDSTATE	The type library could not be opened.

Comments   **RegisterTypeLib** can be used during application initialization to correctly register the application's type library.

In addition to filling in a complete registry entry under the **TypeLib** key, **RegisterTypeLib** adds entries for each of the dispinterfaces and OLE Automation-compatible interfaces, including dual interfaces. This information is required in order to create instances of these interfaces.

QueryPathOfRegTypeLib

HRESULT QueryPathOfRegTypeLib(*guid*, *wVerMajor*, *wVerMinor*, *lcid*, *lpBstrPathName*)
REFGUID *guid*
unsigned short *wVerMajor*
unsigned short *wVerMinor*
LCID *lcid*
LPBSTR *lpBstrPathName*

Retrieves the path of a registered type library.

Parameters   *guid*
    ID of the library whose path is to be queried.

wVerMajor
    Major version number of the library whose path is to be queried.

wVerMinor
    Minor version number of the library whose path is to be queried.

lcid
    National language code for the library whose path is to be queried.

lpBstrPathName
    Caller-allocated BSTR in which the type library name is returned.

Return Value   The SCODE obtained from the returned HRESULT is one of the following:

SCODE	Meaning
S_OK	Success

Comments   Returns the fully qualified filename specified for the type library in the registry. The caller allocates the BSTR that is passed in, and must free it after use.

CHAPTER 9

Type Building Interfaces

The type building interfaces, **ICreateTypeInfo** and **ICreateTypeLib**, are used to build tools that automate the process of generating type descriptions and creating type libraries. The MkTypLib tool, for example, uses these interfaces to create type libraries. See Chapter 7, "MkTypLib and Object Description Language" for more information on MkTypLib.

Generally, you do not need to write custom implementations of these interfaces; MkTypLib itself uses the default implementations, which are returned by the **CreateTypeLib** function. If you want to create tools similar to MkTypLib, calling the default implementations should suffice.

Implemented by	Used by	Header filename	Import library name
OLEAUT32.DLL (32-bit systems) TYPELIB.DLL (16-bit systems)	Applications that expose programmable objects.	OLEAUTO.H DISPATCH.H	OLEAUT32.LIB TYPELIB.LIB

ICreateTypeInfo Interface

The type building interfaces include the following member functions:

Interface	Member name	Purpose
ICreateTypeInfo	AddFuncDesc	Adds a function description as a type description.
	AddImplType	Specifies an inherited interface.
	AddRefTypeInfo	Adds a type description to those referenced by the type description being created.
	AddVarDesc	Adds a data member description as a type description.

Interface	Member name	Purpose
ICreateTypeInfo (*continued*)	**DefineFuncAsDllEntry**	Associates a DLL entry point with a function that has a specified index.
	LayOut	Assigns VTBL offsets for virtual functions and instance offsets for per-instance data members.
	SetAlignment	Specifies data alignment for types of TKIND_RECORD.
	SetDocString	Sets the documentation string displayed by type browsers.
	SetFuncAndParamNames	Sets the function name and names of its parameters.
	SetFuncDocString	Sets the documentation string for a function.
	SetFuncHelpContext	Sets the Help context for a function.
	SetGuid	Sets the globally unique ID for the type library.
	SetHelpContext	Sets the Help context of the type description.
	SetImplTypeFlags	Sets the attributes for an implemented or inherited interface of a type.
	SetMops	Sets the opcode string for a type description.
	SetSchema	Reserved for future use.
	SetTypeDescAlias	Sets the type description for which this type description is an alias, if TYPEKIND=TKIND_ALIAS.
	SetTypeFlags	Sets type flags of the type description being created.
	SetTypeIdlDesc	Reserved for future use.
	SetVarDocString	Sets the documentation string for a variable.
	SetVarHelpContext	Sets the Help context for a variable.
	SetVarName	Sets the name of a variable.
	SetVersion	Sets version numbers for the type description.

Interface	Member name	Purpose
ICreateTypeLib	**CreateTypeInfo**	Creates a new type description instance within the type library.
	SaveAllChanges	Saves the **ICreateTypeLib** instance.
	SetDocString	Sets the documentation string for the type library.
	SetHelpContext	Sets the Help context for general information about the type library in the Help file.
	SetHelpFileName	Sets the Help filename.
	SetLcid	Sets the locale code indicating the national language associated with the library.
	SetLibFlags	Sets library flags, such as LIBFLAG_FRESTRICTED.
	SetName	Sets the name of the type library.
	SetGuid	Sets the globally unique ID for the type library.
	SetVersion	Sets major and minor version numbers for the type library.
Library creation functions	**CreateTypeLib**	Gives access to a new object instance that supports the **ICreateTypeLib** interface.

Structures and Enumerations

The type building interfaces use the following structures and enumerations.

LIBFLAGS

The LIBFLAGS enumeration defines flags that apply to type libraries. LIBFLAGS is defined as follows:

```
typedef enum tagLIBFLAGS {
    LIBFLAG_FRESTRICTED = 0x01
    , LIBFLAG_FCONTROL = 0x02
    , LIBFLAG_FHIDDEN = 0x04
} LIBFLAGS;
```

Value	Description
LIBFLAG_FCONTROL	The type library describes controls and should not be displayed in type browsers intended for nonvisual objects.
LIBFLAG_FRESTRICTED	The type library is restricted and should not be displayed to users.
LIBFLAG_FHIDDEN	The type library should not be displayed to users, although its use is not restricted. To be used by controls; hosts should create a new type library that wraps the control with extended properties.

SYSKIND

The SYSKIND identifies the target operating system platform.

```
typedef enum tagSYSKIND[
    SYS_WIN16,
    SYS_WIN32,
    SYS_MAC
] SYSKIND;
```

Value	Description
SYS_WIN16	The target operating system for the type library is 16-bit Windows systems. By default, data members are packed.
SYS_WIN32	The target operating system for the type library is 32-bit Windows systems. By default, data members are naturally aligned (for example, 2-byte integers are aligned on even-byte boundaries; 4-byte integers are aligned on quad-word boundaries, and so forth).
SYS_MAC	The target operating system for the type library is Macintosh. By default, all data members are aligned on even-byte boundaries.

ICreateTypeInfo::AddFuncDesc

HRESULT ICreateTypeInfo::AddFuncDesc(*index*, *lpFuncDesc*)
unsigned int *index*
FUNCDESC FAR* *lpFuncDesc*

Parameters

index
Index of the new FUNCDESC in the type information.

lpFuncDesc
Pointer to a FUNCDESC structure that describes the function. The *bstrIDLInfo* field in the FUNCDESC should be set to NULL for future compatibility.

Return Value

The SCODE value of the returned HRESULT is one of the following:

SCODE	Meaning
S_OK	Success.
STG_E_INSUFFICIENTMEMORY	Out of memory.
E_OUTOFMEMORY	Out of memory.
E_INVALIDARG	One or more of the arguments is invalid.
E_ACCESSDENIED	Can't write to destination.
TYPE_E_WRONGTYPEKIND	Type mismatch.

Comments

AddFuncDesc is used to add a function description to the type description. The index specifies the order of the functions within the type information. The first function has an index of zero. If an index is specified that exceeds one less than the number of functions in the type information, then an error is returned. Calling this function does not pass ownership of the FUNCDESC structure to **ICreateTypeInfo**. Therefore, the caller must still deallocate the FUNCDESC structure.

The passed-in VTBL field (*oVft*) of the FUNCDESC is ignored. This attribute is set when **ICreateTypeInfo::LayOut** is called.

AddFuncDesc uses the passed-in member ID fields within each FUNCDESC for classes with TYPEKIND = TKIND_DISPATCH or TKIND_INTERFACE. If the member IDs are set to MEMID_NIL, **AddFuncDesc** assigns member IDs to the functions. Otherwise, the member ID fields within each FUNCDESC are ignored.

Note that any HREFTYPE fields in the FUNCDESC structure must have been produced by the same instance of **ITypeInfo** for which **AddFuncDesc** is called.

The get and put accessor functions for the same property must have the same DISPID.

ICreateTypeInfo::AddImplType

HRESULT ICreateTypeInfo::AddImplType(*index, hreftype*)
unsigned int *index*
HREFTYPE *hreftype*

Parameters

index
　　Index of the implementation class to be added; specifies the order of the type
　　relative to the other type.

hreftype
　　Handle to the referenced type description obtained from **AddRefType**
　　description.

Return Value

The SCODE value of the returned HRESULT is one of the following:

SCODE	Meaning
S_OK	Success.
STG_E_INSUFFICIENTMEMORY	Out of memory.
E_OUTOFMEMORY	Out of memory.
E_ACCESSDENIED	Can't write to destination.
TYPE_E_WRONGTYPEKIND	Type mismatch.

Comments

AddImplType is used only for specifying an inherited interface or an interface
implemented by a component object class.

ICreateTypeInfo::AddRefTypeInfo

HRESULT ICreateTypeInfo::AddRefTypeInfo(*lptinfo, lphreftype*)
ITypeInfo FAR* *lptinfo*
HREFTYPE FAR* *lphreftype*

Parameters

lptinfo
　　Pointer to the type description to be referenced.

lphreftype
　　On return, pointer to the handle that this type description associates with the
　　referenced type information.

Return Value	The SCODE value of the returned HRESULT is one of the following:

SCODE	Meaning
S_OK	Success.
STG_E_INSUFFICIENTMEMORY	Out of memory.
E_OUTOFMEMORY	Out of memory.
E_INVALIDARG	One or more of the arguments is invalid.
E_ACCESSDENIED	Can't write to destination.
TYPE_E_WRONGTYPEKIND	Type mismatch.

Comments   Adds a type description to those referenced by the type description being created. The second parameter returns a pointer to the handle of the added type information. If **AddRefTypeInfo** has previously been called for the same type information, the index that was returned by the previous call is returned in *lphreftype*.

ICreateTypeInfo::AddVarDesc

HRESULT ICreateTypeInfo::AddVarDesc(*index*, *lpVarDesc*)
unsigned int *index*
VARDESC FAR* *lpVarDesc*

Parameters   *index*
  Index of the variable or data member to be added to the type description.

  lpVarDesc
  Pointer to the variable or data member description to be added.

Return Value   The SCODE value of the returned HRESULT is one of the following:

SCODE	Meaning
S_OK	Success.
STG_E_INSUFFICIENTMEMORY	Out of memory.
E_OUTOFMEMORY	Out of memory.
E_INVALIDARG	One or more of the arguments is invalid.
E_ACCESSDENIED	Can't write to destination.
TYPE_E_WRONGTYPEKIND	Type mismatch.

Comments   Adds a variable or data member description to the type description. The index specifies the order of the variables. The first variable has an index of zero. **ICreateTypeInfo::AddVarDesc** returns an error if the specified index is greater than the number of variables currently in the type information. Calling this function does not pass ownership of the VARDESC structure to **ICreateTypeInfo**. Note that the Instance field (*oInst*) of the VARDESC structure is ignored; this attribute is set when **ICreateTypeInfo::LayOut** is called. Also, the member ID fields within the VARDESCs are ignored unless the TYPEKIND of the class is TKIND_DISPATCH.

Any HREFTYPE fields in the VARDESC structure must have been produced by the same instance of **ITypeInfo** for which **AddVarDesc** is called.

AddVarDesc ignores the contents of the *idldesc* field of the ELEMDESC.

ICreateTypeInfo::DefineFuncAsDllEntry

HRESULT **ICreateTypeInfo::DefineFuncAsDllEntry**(*index*, *szDllName*, *szProcName*)
unsigned int *index*
OLECHAR FAR* *szDllName*
OLECHAR FAR* *szProcName*

Parameters   *index*
    Index of the function.

szDllName
    Name of the DLL containing the entry point.

szProcName
    Name of the entry point or an ordinal (if the high word is zero).

Return Value   The SCODE value of the returned HRESULT is one of the following:

SCODE	Meaning
S_OK	Success.
STG_E_INSUFFICIENTMEMORY	Out of memory.
E_OUTOFMEMORY	Out of memory.
E_INVALIDARG	One or more of the arguments is invalid.
TYPE_E_ELEMENTNOTFOUND	The element can't be found.
TYPE_E_WRONGTYPEKIND	Type mismatch.

Comments   Associates a DLL entry point with the function that has the specified index. If the high word of *szProcName* is zero, then the low word must contain the ordinal of the entry point; otherwise, *szProcName* points to the zero-terminated name of the entry point.

ICreateTypeInfo::LayOut

HRESULT ICreateTypeInfo::LayOut()

Return Value   The SCODE value of the returned HRESULT is one of the following:

SCODE	Meaning
S_OK	Success.
STG_E_INSUFFICIENTMEMORY	Out of memory.
E_OUTOFMEMORY	Out of memory.
SCODE	**Meaning**
E_ACCESSDENIED	Can't write to destination.
TYPE_E_UNDEFINEDTYPE	Bound to unrecognized type.
TYPE_E_INVALIDSTATE	The type library's state is not valid for this operation.
TYPE_E_WRONGTYPEKIND	Type mismatch.
TYPE_E_ELEMENTNOTFOUND	The element can't be found.
TYPE_E_AMBIGUOUSNAME	More than one item exists with this name.
TYPE_E_SIZETOOBIG	The type information is too large to lay out.
TYPE_E_TYPEMISMATCH	Type mismatch.

Comments   **LayOut** assigns VTBL offsets for virtual functions and instance offsets for per-instance data members, and creates the two typeinfos for dual interfaces. **LayOut** also assigns member ID numbers to the functions and variables unless the TYPEKIND of the class is TKIND_DISPATCH. **LayOut** should be called after all members of the type information are defined and before the type library is saved.

Use **SaveAllChanges** to save the type information after calling **LayOut**. Don't call other members of the **ICreateTypeInfo** interface after calling **LayOut**.

Note that different implementations of **ICreateTypeInfo** or other interfaces that create type information are free to assign any member ID numbers, provided that all members, including inherited members, have unique IDs.

ICreateTypeInfo::SetAlignment

HRESULT ICreateTypeInfo::SetAlignment(*cbAlignment*)
unsigned short *cbAlignment*

Parameters

cbAlignment
Alignment method for the type. A value of 0 indicates alignment on the 64K boundary; 1 indicates no special alignment. For other values, *n* indicates alignment on byte *n*.

Return Value

The SCODE value of the returned HRESULT is one of the following:

SCODE	Meaning
S_OK	Success.
STG_E_INSUFFICIENTMEMORY	Out of memory.
E_OUTOFMEMORY	Out of memory.
E_ACCESSDENIED	Can't write to destination.
TYPE_E_INVALIDSTATE	The type library's state is not valid for this operation.

Comments

Specifies the data alignment for an item of TYPEKIND=TKIND_RECORD. The alignment is the minimum of the natural alignment (for example, byte data on byte boundaries, word data on word boundaries, and so on) and the alignment denoted by *cbAlignment*.

ICreateTypeInfo::SetDocString

HRESULT ICreateTypeInfo::SetDocString(*szDoc*)
OLECHAR FAR* *szDoc*

Parameters

szDoc
Pointer to the documentation string.

Return Value   The SCODE value of the returned HRESULT is one of the following:

SCODE	Meaning
S_OK	Success.
STG_E_INSUFFICIENTMEMORY	Out of memory.
E_OUTOFMEMORY	Out of memory.
E_ACCESSDENIED	Can't write to destination.
TYPE_E_INVALIDSTATE	The type library's state is not valid for this operation.

Comments   Sets the documentation string displayed by type browsers. The documentation string is a brief description of the type description being created.

ICreateTypeInfo::SetFuncAndParamNames

HRESULT ICreateTypeInfo::SetFuncAndParamNames(*index, rgszNames, cNames*)
unsigned int *index*
OLECHAR FAR* FAR* *rgszNames*
unsigned int *cNames*

Parameters   *index*
Index of the function whose function name and parameter names are to be set.

rgszNames
Array of pointers to names. The first element is the function name; subsequent elements are names of parameters.

cNames
Number of elements in the *rgszNames* array.

Return Value   The SCODE value of the returned HRESULT is one of the following:

SCODE	Meaning
S_OK	Success.
STG_E_INSUFFICIENTMEMORY	Out of memory.
E_OUTOFMEMORY	Out of memory.
E_INVALIDARG	One or more of the arguments is invalid.
E_ACCESSDENIED	Can't write to destination.
TYPE_E_ELEMENTNOTFOUND	The element can't be found.

Comments   Sets the name of a function and the names of its parameters to the names in the array of pointers *rgszNames*. You only need to use **SetFuncAndParamNames** once for each property, because all property accessor functions are identified by one name. For property functions, provide names for the named parameters only; the last parameter for put and putref accessor functions is unnamed.

ICreateTypeInfo::SetFuncDocString

HRESULT ICreateTypeInfo::SetFuncDocString(*index*, *szDocString***)**
unsigned int *index*
OLECHAR FAR* *szDocString*

Parameters   *index*
　　　　Index of the function.

　　　　szDocString
　　　　Pointer to the documentation string.

Return Value   The SCODE value of the returned HRESULT is one of the following:

SCODE	Meaning
S_OK	Success.
STG_E_INSUFFICIENTMEMORY	Out of memory.
E_OUTOFMEMORY	Out of memory.
E_INVALIDARG	One or more of the arguments is invalid.
E_ACCESSDENIED	Can't write to destination.
TYPE_E_ELEMENTNOTFOUND	The element can't be found.

Comments Sets the documentation string for the function with the specified *index*. The documentation string is a brief description of the function intended for use by tools like type browsers. You only need to use **SetFuncDocString** once for each property, because all property accessor functions are identified by one name.

ICreateTypeInfo::SetFuncHelpContext

HRESULT ICreateTypeInfo::SetFuncHelpContext(*index, dwHelpContext*)
unsigned int *index*
unsigned long *dwHelpContext*

Parameters *index*
  Index of the function.

dwHelpContext
  A Help context ID for the Help topic.

Return Value The SCODE value of the returned HRESULT is one of the following:

SCODE	Meaning
S_OK	Success.
STG_E_INSUFFICIENTMEMORY	Out of memory.
E_OUTOFMEMORY	Out of memory.
E_ACCESSDENIED	Can't write to destination.
TYPE_E_ELEMENTNOTFOUND	The element can't be found.
E_INVALIDARG	One or more of the arguments is invalid.

Comments Sets the Help context for the function with the specified index. You only need to use **SetFuncHelpContext** once for each property, because all property accessor functions are identified by one name.

ICreateTypeInfo::SetGuid

HRESULT ICreateTypeInfo::SetGuid(*guid*)
REFGUID *guid*

Parameters *guid*
  Globally unique ID to be associated with the type description.

Return Value   The SCODE value of the returned HRESULT is one of the following:

SCODE	Meaning
S_OK	Success.
STG_E_INSUFFICIENTMEMORY	Out of memory.
E_OUTOFMEMORY	Out of memory.
E_ACCESSDENIED	Can't write to destination.

Comments   Sets the globally unique ID (GUID) associated with the type description. For an interface, this is an interface ID; for a coclass, it is a class ID. See Chapter 7, "MkTypLib and Object Description Language" for information on GUIDs.

ICreateTypeInfo::SetHelpContext

HRESULT ICreateTypeInfo::SetHelpContext(*dwHelpContext*)
unsigned long *dwHelpContext*

Parameters   *dwHelpContext*
    Handle to the Help context.

Return Value   The SCODE value of the returned HRESULT is one of the following:

SCODE	Meaning
S_OK	Success.
STG_E_INSUFFICIENTMEMORY	Out of memory.
E_OUTOFMEMORY	Out of memory.
E_INVALIDARG	One or more of the arguments is invalid.
E_ACCESSDENIED	Can't write to destination.

Comments   Sets the Help context of the type information.

ICreateTypeInfo::SetImplTypeFlags

HRESULT ICreateTypeInfo::SetImplTypeFlags(*index, impltypeflags*)
unsigned int *index*
int *impltypeflags*

Parameters

index
Index of the interface for which to set type flags.

impltypeflags
IMPLTYPE flags to set.

Return Value

The SCODE value of the returned HRESULT is one of the following:

SCODE	Meaning
S_OK	Success.
STG_E_INSUFFICIENTMEMORY	Out of memory.
E_OUTOFMEMORY	Out of memory.
E_INVALIDARG	One or more of the arguments is invalid.
E_ACCESSDENIED	Can't write to destination.

Comments

Sets the IMPLTYPE flags for the indexed interface. See the "IMPLTYPEFLAGS" section in Chapter 8, "Type Description Interfaces."

ICreateTypeInfo::SetMops

HRESULT ICreateTypeInfo::SetMops(*index, bstrMops*)
unsigned int *index*
BSTR *bstrMops*

Parameters

index
Index of the member for which to set the opcode string. If index is –1, sets the opcode string for the type description.

bstrMops
The marshaling opcode string.

Return Value   The SCODE value of the returned HRESULT is one of the following:

SCODE	Meaning
S_OK	Success.
STG_E_INSUFFICIENTMEMORY	Out of memory.
E_OUTOFMEMORY	Out of memory.
E_INVALIDARG	One or more of the arguments is invalid.
E_ACCESSDENIED	Can't write to destination.

Comments   Sets the marshaling opcode string associated with the type description or the function.

ICreateTypeInfo::SetTypeDescAlias

HRESULT ICreateTypeInfo::SetTypeDescAlias(*lptDescAlias***)**
TYPEDESC FAR* *lptDescAlias*

Parameters   *lptDescAlias*
     Pointer to a type description that describes the type for which this is an alias.

Return Value   The SCODE value of the returned HRESULT is one of the following:

SCODE	Meaning
S_OK	Success.
STG_E_INSUFFICIENTMEMORY	Out of memory.
E_OUTOFMEMORY	Out of memory.
E_INVALIDARG	One or more of the arguments is invalid.
E_ACCESSDENIED	Can't write to destination.
TYPE_E_WRONGTYPEKIND	Type mismatch.

Comments   Call **SetTypeDescAlias** for a type description whose TYPEKIND is TKIND_ALIAS to set the type for which it is an alias.

ICreateTypeInfo::SetTypeFlags

HRESULT ICreateTypeInfo::SetTypeFlags(*uTypeFlags*)
unsigned int *uTypeFlags*

Parameter

uTypeFlags
Settings for the type flags.

Return Value

The SCODE value of the returned HRESULT is one of the following:

SCODE	Meaning
S_OK	Success.
STG_E_INSUFFICIENTMEMORY	Out of memory.
E_OUTOFMEMORY	Out of memory.
E_INVALIDARG	One or more of the arguments is invalid.
E_ACCESSDENIED	Can't write to destination.
TYPE_E_WRONGTYPEKIND	Type mismatch.

Comments

Use **SetTypeFlags** to set the flags for the type description. See the "TYPEFLAGS" section in Chapter 8, "Type Description Interfaces" for details.

ICreateTypeInfo::SetVarDocString

HRESULT ICreateTypeInfo::SetVarDocString(*index, szDocString*)
unsigned int *index*
OLECHAR FAR* *szDocString*

Parameters

index
Index of the variable being documented.

szDocString
The documentation string to be set.

Return Value　　The SCODE value of the returned HRESULT is one of the following:

SCODE	Meaning
S_OK	Success.
STG_E_INSUFFICIENTMEMORY	Out of memory.
E_OUTOFMEMORY	Out of memory.
E_ACCESSDENIED	Can't write to destination.
TYPE_E_ELEMENTNOTFOUND	The element was not found.

Comments　　Sets the documentation string for the variable with the specified *index*.

ICreateTypeInfo::SetVarHelpContext

HRESULT ICreateTypeInfo::SetVarHelpContext(*index***, ***dwHelpContext***)**
unsigned int *index*
unsigned long *dwHelpContext*

Parameters　　*index*
　　　　Index of the variable described by the type description.

　　dwHelpContext
　　　　Handle to the Help context for the Help topic on the variable.

Return Value　　The SCODE value of the returned HRESULT is one of the following:

SCODE	Meaning
S_OK	Success.
STG_E_INSUFFICIENTMEMORY	Out of memory.
E_OUTOFMEMORY	Out of memory.
E_ACCESSDENIED	Can't write to destination.
TYPE_E_ELEMENTNOTFOUND	The element can't be found.

Comments　　Sets the Help context for the variable with the specified *index*.

ICreateTypeInfo::SetVarName

HRESULT ICreateTypeInfo::SetVarName(*index, szName*)
unsigned int *index*
OLECHAR FAR* *szName*

Parameters
index
    Index of the variable whose name is being set.

szName
    Name for the variable.

Return Value
The SCODE value of the returned HRESULT is one of the following:

SCODE	Meaning
S_OK	Success.
STG_E_INSUFFICIENTMEMORY	Out of memory.
E_OUTOFMEMORY	Out of memory.
E_ACCESSDENIED	Can't write to destination.
TYPE_E_ELEMENTNOTFOUND	The element can't be found.

Comments
Sets the name of a variable.

ICreateTypeInfo::SetVersion

HRESULT ICreateTypeInfo::SetVersion(*wMajorVerNum, wMinorVerNum*)
unsigned short *wMajorVerNum*
unsigned short *wMinorVerNum*

Parameters
wMajorVerNum
    Major version number for the type.

wMinorVerNum
    Minor version number for the type.

Return Value   The SCODE value of the returned HRESULT is one of the following:

SCODE	Meaning
S_OK	Success.
E_ACCESSDENIED	Can't write to destination.
TYPE_E_INVALIDSTATE	The type library's state is not valid for this operation.

Comments   Sets the major and minor version number of the type information.

ICreateTypeLib Interface

ICreateTypeLib::CreateTypeInfo

HRESULT ICreateTypeLib::CreateTypeInfo(*szName*, *tkind*, *lplpctinfo*)
OLECHAR FAR* *szName*
TYPEKIND *tkind*
ICreateTypeInfo FAR* FAR* *lplpctinfo*

Parameters   *szName*
      Name of the new type.

tkind
      TYPEKIND of the type description to be created.

lplpctinfo
      On return, contains a pointer to the type description.

Return Value   The SCODE value of the returned HRESULT is one of the following:

SCODE	Meaning
S_OK	Success.
STG_E_INSUFFICIENTMEMORY	Out of memory.
E_OUTOFMEMORY	Out of memory.
E_INVALIDARG	One or more of the arguments is invalid.
TYPE_E_INVALIDSTATE	The type library's state is not valid for this operation.
TYPE_E_NAMECONFLICT	The provided name is not unique.
TYPE_E_WRONGTYPEKIND	Type mismatch.

Comments   Use **CreateTypeInfo** to create a new type description instance within the library. An error is returned if the specified name already appears in the library. Valid *tkind* values are described in the "TYPEKIND" section in Chapter 8, "Type Description Interfaces."

ICreateTypeLib::SaveAllChanges

HRESULT ICreateTypeLib::SaveAllChanges()

Return Value   The SCODE value of the returned HRESULT is one of the following:

SCODE	Meaning
S_OK	Success.
STG_E_INSUFFICIENTMEMORY	Out of memory.
E_OUTOFMEMORY	Out of memory.
E_INVALIDARG	One or more of the arguments is invalid.
TYPE_E_IOERROR	The function can't write to the file.
TYPE_E_INVALIDSTATE	The type library's state is not valid for this operation.
Other returns	All FACILITY_STORAGE errors.

Comments   Saves the **ICreateTypeLib** instance following the layout of the type information. Do not call any other **ICreateTypeLib** methods after calling **SaveAllChanges**.

ICreateTypeLib::SetDocString

HRESULT ICreateTypeLib::SetDocString(*szDoc***)**
OLECHAR FAR* *szDoc*

Parameters   *szDoc*
     A documentation string that briefly describes the type library.

Return Value

The SCODE value of the returned HRESULT is one of the following:

SCODE	Meaning
S_OK	Success.
STG_E_INSUFFICIENTMEMORY	Out of memory.
E_OUTOFMEMORY	Out of memory.
E_INVALIDARG	One or more of the arguments is invalid.

Comments

Sets the documentation string associated with the library. The documentation string is a brief description of the library intended for use by type information browsing tools.

ICreateTypeLib::SetGuid

HRESULT ICreateTypeLib::SetGuid(*guid*)
REFGUID *guid*

Parameters

guid
> The universal unique ID to be assigned to the library.

Return Value

The SCODE value of the returned HRESULT is one of the following:

SCODE	Meaning
S_OK	Success.
STG_E_INSUFFICIENTMEMORY	Out of memory.
E_OUTOFMEMORY	Out of memory.
E_INVALIDARG	One or more of the arguments is invalid.
TYPE_E_INVALIDSTATE	The type library's state is not valid for this operation.

Comments

Sets the universal unique ID (UUID) associated with the type library. UUIDs are described in Chapter 7, "MkTypLib and Object Description Language."

ICreateTypeLib::SetHelpContext

HRESULT ICreateTypeLib::SetHelpContext(*dwHelpContext*)
unsigned long *dwHelpContext*

Parameters   *dwHelpContext*
              Help context to be assigned to the library.

Return Value   The SCODE value of the returned HRESULT is one of the following:

SCODE	Meaning
S_OK	Success.
STG_E_INSUFFICIENTMEMORY	Out of memory.
E_OUTOFMEMORY	Out of memory.
E_INVALIDARG	One or more of the arguments is invalid.
TYPE_E_INVALIDSTATE	The type library's state is not valid for this operation.

Comments   Sets the Help context for retrieving general Help information for the type library.
              Note that calling **SetHelpContext** with a Help context of zero is equivalent to not
              calling it at all, because zero indicates a NULL Help context.

ICreateTypeLib::SetHelpFileName

HRESULT ICreateTypeLib::SetHelpFileName(*szFileName*)
OLECHAR FAR* *szFileName*

Parameters   *szFileName*
              The name of the Help file for the library.

Return Value   The SCODE value of the returned HRESULT is one of the following:

SCODE	Meaning
S_OK	Success.
STG_E_INSUFFICIENTMEMORY	Out of memory.
E_OUTOFMEMORY	Out of memory.
E_INVALIDARG	One or more of the arguments is invalid.
TYPE_E_INVALIDSTATE	The type library's state is not valid for this operation.

Comments   Sets the name of the Help file. Each type library can reference a single Help file.

The **GetDocumentation** method of the created **ITypeLib** returns a fully qualified path for the Help file, which is formed by appending the name passed into *szFileName* to the registered Help directory for the type library. The Help directory is registered under:

\TYPELIB**<*guid of library*>**<*Major.Minor version* >**\HELPDIR**

ICreateTypeLib::SetLibFlags

HRESULT ICreateTypeLib::SetLibFlags(*uLibFlags***)**
unsigned int *uLibFlags*

Parameters   *uLibFlags*
                         The flags to set for the library.

Return Value   The SCODE value of the returned HRESULT is one of the following:

SCODE	Meaning
S_OK	Success.
STG_E_INSUFFICIENTMEMORY	Out of memory.
E_OUTOFMEMORY	Out of memory.
E_INVALIDARG	One or more of the arguments is invalid.
TYPE_E_INVALIDSTATE	The type library's state is not valid for this operation.

Comments   Valid *uLibFlags* values are listed in "LIBFLAGS," earlier in this chapter.

ICreateTypeLib::SetLcid

HRESULT ICreateTypeLib::SetLcid(*lcid***)**
LCID *lcid*

Parameters   *lcid*
                         An LCID representing the locale ID for the type library.

Return Value The SCODE value of the returned HRESULT is one of the following:

SCODE	Meaning
S_OK	Success.
STG_E_INSUFFICIENTMEMORY	Out of memory.
E_OUTOFMEMORY	Out of memory.
E_INVALIDARG	One or more of the arguments is invalid.
TYPE_E_INVALIDSTATE	The type library's state is not valid for this operation.

Comments Sets the binary Microsoft national language ID associated with the library. For more information on national language IDs, see "Supporting Multiple National Languages," in Chapter 2, "Exposing OLE Automation Objects." For additional information for 16-bit systems, refer to Appendix A, "National Language Support Functions." For 32-bit systems, refer to the Windows NT documentation on the NLS API.

ICreateTypeLib::SetName

HRESULT ICreateTypeLib::SetName(*szName*)
OLECHAR FAR* *szName*

Parameters *szName*
  Name to be assigned to the library.

Return Value The SCODE value of the returned HRESULT is one of the following:

SCODE	Meaning
S_OK	Success.
STG_E_INSUFFICIENTMEMORY	Out of memory.
E_OUTOFMEMORY	Out of memory.
E_INVALIDARG	One or more of the arguments is invalid.
TYPE_E_INVALIDSTATE	The type library's state is not valid for this operation.

Comments Sets the name of the type library.

ICreateTypeLib::SetVersion

HRESULT ICreateTypeLib::SetVersion(*wMajorVerNum*, *wMinorVerNum*)
unsigned short *wMajorVerNum*
unsigned short *wMinorVerNum*

Parameters

wMajorVerNum
Major version number for the library.

wMinorVerNum
Minor version number for the library.

Return Value

The SCODE value of the returned HRESULT is one of the following:

SCODE	Meaning
S_OK	Success.
TYPE_E_INVALIDSTATE	The type library's state is not valid for this operation.

Comments

Sets the major and minor version numbers of the type library.

CreateTypeLib

HRESULT CreateTypeLib(*syskind*, *szFile*, *lplpctlib*)
SYSKIND *syskind*
OLECHAR FAR* *szFile*
ICreateTypeLib FAR* FAR* *lplpctlib*

Parameters

syskind
The target operating system for which to create a type library.

szFile
The name of the file to create.

lplpctlib
Pointer to an instance supporting the **ICreateTypeLib** interface.

Return Value The SCODE value of the returned HRESULT is one of the following:

SCODE	Meaning
S_OK	Success.
STG_E_INSUFFICIENTMEMORY	Out of memory.
E_OUTOFMEMORY	Out of memory.
E_INVALIDARG	One or more of the arguments is invalid.
TYPE_E_IOERROR	The function could not create the file.
Other returns	All FACILITY_STORAGE errors.

Comments **CreateTypeLib** sets its output parameter (*lplpctlib*) to point to a newly created object that supports the **ICreateTypeLib** interface.

C H A P T E R   1 0

Error Handling Interfaces

Objects that are invoked through VTBL binding need to use the OLE Automation error handling interfaces to define and return error information. The interfaces include the following:

- **ICreateErrorInfo** interface—Sets error information.

- **IErrorInfo** interface—Returns information from an error object.

- **ISupportErrorInfo** interface—Identifies this object as supporting the **ErrorInfo** interface.

- Error handling functions.

This chapter covers the error handling interfaces in detail. The member functions of each interface are listed in the following table.

Category	Member name	Purpose
IErrorInfo	**GetDescription**	Returns a textual description of the error.
	GetGUID	Returns the GUID for the interface that defined the error.
	GetHelpContext	Returns the Help context ID for the error.
	GetHelpFile	Returns the path of the Help file that describes the error.
	GetSource	Returns the ProgID for the class or application that returned the error.

Category	Member name	Purpose
ICreateErrorInfo	SetDescription	Sets a textual description of the error.
	SetGUID	Sets the GUID for the interface that defined the error.
	SetHelpContext	Sets the Help context ID for the error.
	SetHelpFile	Sets the path of the Help file that describes the error.
	SetSource	Sets the ProgID for the class or application that returned the error.
ISupportErrorInfo	InterfaceSupportsErrorInfo	Indicates whether an interface supports the IErrorInfo interface.
Error handling functions	CreateErrorInfo	Creates a generic error object.
	GetErrorInfo	Retrieves and clears the current error object.
	SetErrorInfo	Sets the current error object.

Returning Error Information

▶   **To return error information**

1. Implement the **ISupportErrorInfo** interface.
2. Call the CreateErrorInfo function to create an instance of the generic error object.
3. Use the **ICreateErrorInfo** methods to set its contents.
4. Call the **SetErrorInfo** function to associate the error object with the current logical thread.

The following figure illustrates this procedure.

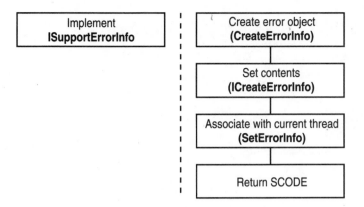

The error handling interfaces create and manage an error object, which provides information about the error. The error object is not the same as the object that encountered the error; it is a separate object that is associated with the current thread of execution.

Retrieving Error Information

► **To retrieve error information, an object**

1. Checks whether the returned SCODE represents an error that the object is prepared to handle.

2. Calls **QueryInterface** to get a pointer to the **ISupportErrorInfo** interface, then calls **InterfaceSupportsErrorInfo** to verify that the error was raised by the object that returned it, and that the error object pertains to the current error and not to a previous call.

3. Calls the **GetErrorInfo** function to get a pointer to the error object.

4. Uses the **IErrorInfo** methods to retrieve information from the error object.

The following figure illustrates this procedure.

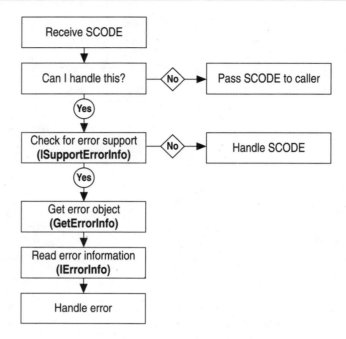

If the object is not prepared to handle the error, but needs to propagate the error information further down the call chain, it should simply pass the SCODE to its caller. Because the **GetErrorInfo** function clears the error information and passes ownership of the error object to the caller, the function should be called only by the object that handles the error.

ICreateErrorInfo Interface

Implemented by	Used by	Header filename	Import library name
OLEAUT32.DLL (32-bit systems)	Applications that return rich error information.	OLEAUTO.H	OLEAUT32.LIB
OLE2DISP.DLL (16-bit systems)		DISPATCH.H	OLE2DISP.LIB

ICreateErrorInfo::SetDescription

HRESULT ICreateErrorInfo::SetDescription(*szDescription*)
LPSTR * *szDescription*

Sets the textual description of the error.

Parameters

szDescription
   A brief, zero-terminated string that describes the error.

Return Value

The SCODE obtained from the returned HRESULT is:

SCODE	Meaning
S_OK	Success
E_OUTOFMEMORY	Insufficient memory to complete the operation.

Comments

The text should be supplied in the language specified by the LCID that was passed to the method that raised the error. See "The LCID Attribute," in Chapter 7, for more information.

Example

```
hr = CreateErrorInfo(&pcerrinfo);
if (m_excepinfo.bstrDescription)
    pcerrinfo->SetDescription(m_excepinfo.bstrDescription);
```

ICreateErrorInfo::SetGUID

HRESULT ICreateErrorInfo::SetGUID(*rguid*)
REFGUID *rguid*

Sets the GUID of interface that defined the error.

Parameters

rguid
   The GUID of the interface that defined the error, or GUID_NULL, if the error was defined by the operating system.

Return Value   The SCODE obtained from the returned HRESULT is:

SCODE	Meaning
S_OK	Success
E_OUTOFMEMORY	Insufficient memory to complete the operation.

Comments   **ICreateErrorInfo::SetGUID** sets the GUID of the interface that defined the error. If the error was defined by the system, **ICreateError::SetGUID** should set GUID_NULL.

Note that this GUID does not necessarily represent the source of the error, however; the source is the class or application that raised the error. Using the GUID, applications can handle errors in an interface independent of the class that implements the interface.

Example
```
hr = CreateErrorInfo(&pcerrinfo);
pcerrinfo->SetGUID(IID_IHello);
```

ICreateErrorInfo::SetHelpContext

HRESULT ICreateErrorInfo::SetHelpContext(*dwHelpContext*)
DWORD *dwHelpContext*

Sets the Help context ID for the error.

Parameters   *dwHelpContext*
    The Help context ID for the error.

Return Value   The SCODE obtained from the returned HRESULT is:

SCODE	Meaning
S_OK	Success
E_OUTOFMEMORY	Insufficient memory to complete the operation.

Comments   **ICreateErrorInfo::SetHelpContext** sets the Help context ID for the error. To establish the Help file to which it applies, use **ICreateErrorInfo::SetHelpFile**.

Example
```
hr = CreateErrorInfo(&pcerrinfo);
pcerrinfo->SetHelpContext(dwhelpcontext);
```

ICreateErrorInfo::SetHelpFile

HRESULT ICreateErrorInfo::SetHelpFile(*szHelpFile*)
LPSTR *szHelpFile*

Sets the path of the Help file that describes the error.

Parameters   *szHelpFile*
The fully qualified path of the Help file that describes the error.

Return Value   The SCODE obtained from the returned HRESULT is:

SCODE	Meaning
S_OK	Success
E_OUTOFMEMORY	Insufficient memory to complete the operation.

Comments   **ICreateErrorInfo::SetHelpFile** sets the fully qualified path of the Help file that describes the current error. Use **ICreateError::SetHelpContext** to set the Help context ID for the error within the Help file.

Example
```
hr = CreateErrorInfo(&pcerrinfo);
pcerrinfo->SetHelpFile("C:\myapp\myapp.hlp");
```

ICreateErrorInfo::SetSource

HRESULT ICreateErrorInfo::SetSource(*szSource*)
LPSTR *szSource*

Sets the language-dependent ProgID for the class or application that raised the error.

Parameters   *szSource*
A programmatic ID, in the form *progname.objectname*.

Return Value   The SCODE obtained from the returned HRESULT is:

SCODE	Meaning
S_OK	Success
E_OUTOFMEMORY	Insufficient memory to complete the operation.

Comments Use **ICreateErrorInfo::SetSource** to identify the class or application that is the source of the error. The language for the returned ProgID depends on the LCID that was passed into the method at invocation.

Example
```
hr = CreateErrorInfo(&pcerrinfo);
if (m_excepinfo.bstrSource)
    pcerrinfo->SetSource(m_excepinfo.bstrSource);
```

IErrorInfo Interface

Implemented by	Used by	Header filename	Import library name
OLEAUT32.DLL (32-bit systems)	Applications that receive rich information.	OLEAUTO.H	OLEAUT32.LIB
OLE2DISP.DLL (16-bit systems)		DISPATCH.H	OLE2DISP.LIB

IErrorInfo::GetDescription

HRESULT IErrorInfo::GetDescription(*pbstrDescription*)
BSTR * *pbstrDescription*

Returns a textual description of the error.

Parameters *pbstrDescription*
Pointer to a brief string that describes the error.

Return Value The SCODE obtained from the returned HRESULT is:

SCODE	Meaning
S_OK	Success

Comments The text is returned in the language specified by the LCID that was passed to **IDispatch::Invoke** for the method that encountered the error.

IErrorInfo::GetGUID

HRESULT IErrorInfo::GetGUID(*pguid*)
GUID * *pguid*

Returns the GUID of interface that defined the error.

Parameters

pguid
    Pointer to a GUID, or GUID_NULL, if the error was defined by the operating
    system.

Return Value

The SCODE obtained from the returned HRESULT is:

SCODE	Meaning
S_OK	Success

Comments

IErrorInfo::GetGUID returns the GUID of the interface that defined the error. If
the error was defined by the system, **IError::GetGUID** returns GUID_NULL.

Note that this GUID does not necessarily represent the source of the error; the
source is the class or application that raised the error. Using the GUID, an
application can handle errors in an interface independent of the class that
implements the interface.

IErrorInfo::GetHelpContext

HRESULT IErrorInfo::GetHelpContext(*pdwHelpContext*)
DWORD * *pdwHelpContext*

Returns the Help context ID for the error.

Parameters

pdwHelpContext
    Pointer to the Help context ID for the error.

Return Value

The SCODE obtained from the returned HRESULT is:

SCODE	Meaning
S_OK	Success

Comments

IErrorInfo::GetHelpContext returns the Help context ID for the error. To find
the Help file to which it applies, use **IErrorInfo::GetHelpFile**.

IErrorInfo::GetHelpFile

HRESULT IErrorInfo::GetHelpFile(*pbstrHelpFile*)
BSTR * *pbstrHelpFile*

Returns the path of the Help file that describes the error.

Parameters

pbstrHelpFile
Pointer to a string containing the fully qualified path of the Help file.

Return Value

The SCODE obtained from the returned HRESULT is:

SCODE	Meaning
S_OK	Success

Comments

IErrorInfo::GetHelpFile returns the fully qualified path of the Help file that describes the current error. Use **IError::GetHelpContext** to find the Help context ID for the error within the Help file.

IErrorInfo::GetSource

HRESULT IErrorInfo::GetSource(*pbstrSource*)
BSTR * *pbstrSource*

Returns the language-dependent ProgID for the class or application that raised the error.

Parameters

pbstrSource
Pointer to a string containing a ProgID, in the form *progname.objectname*.

Return Value

The SCODE obtained from the returned HRESULT is:

SCODE	Meaning
S_OK	Success

Comments

Use **IErrorInfo::GetSource** to determine the class or application that is the source of the error. The language for the returned ProgID depends on the LCID that was passed into the method at invocation.

ISupportErrorInfo Interface

Implemented by	Used by	Header filename	Import library name
Applications that return error information.	Applications that retrieve error information.	OLEAUTO.H (32-bit systems) DISPATCH.H (16-bit systems)	None

ISupportErrorInfo::InterfaceSupportsErrorInfo

HRESULT ISupportErrorInfo::InterfaceSupportsErrorInfo(*riid*)
REFIID *riid*

Indicates whether an interface supports the **IErrorInfo** interface.

Parameters

riid
    Pointer to an interface ID.

Return Value

The SCODE obtained from the returned HRESULT is:

SCODE	Meaning
S_OK	Interface supports **IErrorInfo.**
S_FALSE	Interface doesn't support **IErrorInfo**.

Comments

Objects that support the **IErrorInfo** mechanism must implement this interface.

Programs that receive an error SCODE should call **QueryInterface** to get a pointer to the **ISupportErrorInfo** interface, then call **InterfaceSupportsErrorInfo** with the *riid* of the interface that returned the SCODE. If **InterfaceSupportsErrorInfo** returns S_FALSE, then the error object doesn't represent an error returned from the caller, but from somewhere else. In this case, the error object can be considered incorrect and should be discarded.

If **InterfaceSupportsErrorInfo** returns S_OK, use **GetErrorInfo** to get a pointer to the error object.

Example   The following example implements the **ISupportErrorInfo** for the Lines sample.
Note that the **IErrorInfo** implementation also supports the **AddRef**, **Release**, and
QueryInterface members inherited from **IUnknown**.

```
CSupportErrorInfo::CSupportErrorInfo(IUnknown FAR* punkObject, REFIID
riid)
{
    m_punkObject = punkObject;
    m_iid = riid;
}


STDMETHODIMP
CSupportErrorInfo::QueryInterface(REFIID iid, void FAR* FAR* ppv)
{
    return m_punkObject->QueryInterface(iid, ppv);
}


STDMETHODIMP_(ULONG)
CSupportErrorInfo::AddRef(void)
{
    return m_punkObject->AddRef();
}

STDMETHODIMP_(ULONG)
CSupportErrorInfo::Release(void)
{
    return m_punkObject->Release();
}

STDMETHODIMP
CSupportErrorInfo::InterfaceSupportsErrorInfo(REFIID riid)
{
    return (riid == m_iid) ? NOERROR : ResultFromScode(S_FALSE);
}
```

Error Handling Functions

For 32-bit systems, the error handling functions are provided in OLEAUT32.DLL; the header file is OLEAUTO.H, and the import library is OLEAUT32.LIB. For 16-bit systems, the error handling functions are provided in OLE2DISP.DLL; the header file is DISPATCH.H, and the import library is OLE2DISP.LIB.

CreateErrorInfo

HRESULT CreateErrorInfo(*ppcerrinfo*)
ICreateErrorInfo * * *ppcerrinfo*

Creates an instance of a generic error object.

Parameters

ppcerrinfo
> Pointer to a system-implemented generic error object.

Return Value

The SCODE obtained from the returned HRESULT is one of the following:

SCODE	Meaning
S_OK	Success.
E_OUTOFMEMORY	Could not create the error object.

Comments

This function returns a pointer to a generic error object, which can be used with **QueryInterface** on **ICreateErrorInfo** to set its contents. The resulting object can then be passed to **SetErrorInfo**(). The generic error object implements both **ICreateErrorInfo** and **IErrorInfo**.

Example

```
ICreateErrorInfo *pcerrinfo;
HRESULT hr;

hr = CreateErrorInfo(&pcerrinfo);
```

GetErrorInfo

HRESULT GetErrorInfo(*pperrinfo*)
IErrorInfo * * *pperrinfo*

Gets the error information pointer set by the previous call to **SetErrorInfo** in the current logical thread.

Parameters   *pperrinfo*
    Pointer to a pointer to an error object.

Return Value   The SCODE obtained from the returned HRESULT is one of the following:

SCODE	Meaning
S_OK	Success
S_FALSE	There was no error object to return.

Comments   This function returns a pointer to the most recently set **IErrorInfo** pointer in the current logical thread. It transfers ownership of the error object to the caller and clears the error state for the thread.

SetErrorInfo

HRESULT SetErrorInfo(*perrinfo*)
IErrorInfo * *perrinfo*

Sets the error information object for the current thread of execution.

Parameters   *perrinfo*
    Pointer to an error object.

Return Value   The SCODE obtained from the returned HRESULT is:

SCODE	Meaning
S_OK	Success

Comments

This function releases the existing error information object (if one exists) and sets the pointer to *perrinfo*. Use this function after creating an error object to associate the object with the current thread of execution.

Example

```
ICreateErrorInfo *pcerrinfo;
    IErrorInfo *perrinfo;
    HRESULT hr;

hr = CreateErrorInfo(&pcerrinfo);
hr = pcerrinfo->QueryInterface(IID_IErrorInfo, (LPVOID FAR*) &perrinfo);
if (SUCCEEDED(hr))
    {
        SetErrorInfo(0, perrinfo);
        perrinfo->Release();
    }
    pcerrinfo->Release();
```

P A R T 3

Appendixes

A P P E N D I X   A

National Language Support Functions

The National Language Support (NLS) functions provide support for applications that deal with multiple locales at once, especially for applications supporting OLE Automation. Locale information is passed to allow the application to interpret both the member names and the argument data in the proper locale context. On 32-bit Windows systems, an NLS API is part the system software; the information in this appendix applies only to 16-bit Windows systems.

Implemented by	Used by	Header filename	Import library name
OLE2NLS.DLL	Applications that support multiple national languages.	OLENLS.H	OLE2NLS.LIB

For OLE Automation, applications need to get locale information and to compare and transform strings into the proper format for each locale.

A *locale* is simply user preference information that denotes the user's language and sublanguage, represented as a list of values. National language support incorporates several disparate definitions of a locale into one coherent model. It is designed to be general enough at a low level to support multiple distinct high-level functions, such as the ANSI C locale functions.

A *code page* is the mapping between character glyphs (shapes) and the 1- or 2-byte numeric values that are used to represent them. Microsoft Windows version 3.1 uses one of several code pages, depending on the localized version of Windows installed. For example, the Russian version uses code page 1251 (Cyrillic), while the English/US and Western European versions use code page 1252 (Multilingual). For historical reasons, the Windows code page in effect is referred to as the ANSI code page.

Because only one code page is in effect at a time, it is impossible for a computer running English/US Windows version 3.1 to correctly display or print data from the Cyrillic code page; the fonts do not contain the Cyrillic characters. However, it can still manipulate the characters internally, and they will display correctly again if moved back to a machine running Russian Windows.

All NLS functions use the locale ID to identify which code page a piece of text is assumed to lie in; for example, when returning locale information (like month names) for Russian, the returned string can be meaningfully displayed in the Cyrillic code page only, because other code pages don't contain the appropriate characters. Similarly, when attempting to change the case of a string with the Russian locale, the case-mapping rules assume the characters are in the Cyrillic code page.

These functions can be divided into two categories:

- String transformation—NLS functions support uppercasing, lowercasing, generating sort keys (all locale-dependent), and getting string type information.
- Locale manipulation—NLS functions return information about installed locales for use in string transformations.

Overview of Functions

The following table lists the NLS functions.

Function	Purpose
CompareStringA	Compares two strings of the same locale.
LCMapStringA	Transforms the case or sort order of a string.
GetLocaleInfoA	Retrieves locale information from the user's system.
GetStringTypeA	Retrieves locale type information about each character in a string.
GetSystemDefaultLangID	Retrieves the default LANGID from a user's system.[1]
GetSystemDefaultLCID	Retrieves the default LCID from a user's system.
GetUserDefaultLangID	Retrieves the default LANGID from a user's system.
GetUserDefaultLCID	Retrieves the default LCID from a user's system.[1]

[1] Because Microsoft Windows is a single-user system, **GetUserDefaultLangID** and **GetUserDefaultLCID** return the same information as **GetSystemDefaultLangID** and **GetSystemDefaultLCID**.

Localized Member Names

An application may expose a set of objects whose members have names that differ across localized versions of the product. This poses a problem for programming languages that want to access such objects because it means that late binding will be sensitive to the locale of the application. The **IDispatch** and VTBL interfaces allow software developers a range of solutions which vary in cost of implementation and quality of national language support. All methods of the **IDispatch** interface that are potentially sensitive to language are passed a locale ID (LCID).

Following are some of the possible approaches a class implementation may take:

- Accept any LCID and use the same member names in all locales. This is acceptable if the interface will typically be accessed only by advanced users. For example, the member names for OLE interfaces will never be localized.

- Simply return an error (DISP_E_UNKNOWNLCID) if the caller's LCID doesn't match the localized version of the class. This would prevent users from being able to write late-bound code which runs on machines with different localized implementations of the class.

- Recognize the particular version's localized names, as well as one language which is recognized in all versions. For example, a French version might accept French and English names, where English is the language supported in all versions. This would constrain users, who want to write code which runs in all countries, to use English.

- Accept all LCIDs supported by all versions of the product. This means that the implementation of **GetIDsOfNames** would need to interpret the passed array of names based on the given LCID. This is the preferred solution because users would be able to write code in their national language and run the code on any localized version of the application.

At the very least, the application must check the LCID before interpreting member names. Also note that the meaning of parameters passed to a member function may depend on the caller's national language. For example, a spreadsheet application might interpret the arguments to a **SetFormula** method differently, depending on the LCID.

Locale ID (LCID)

The **IDispatch** interface uses the 32-bit Windows definition of a locale ID (LCID) to identify locales. An LCID is a DWORD value which contains the language ID (LANGID) in the lower word and a reserved value in the upper word. The bits are as follows:

Reserved		LANGID	
31	16	15	0	Bits

This LCID has the components necessary to uniquely identify one of the installed system-defined locales.

```
/*
 * LCID creation/extraction macros:
 *
 *       MAKELCID - construct locale ID from language ID and
 *                  country code.
 */
#define MAKELCID(1) ((DWORD)(((WORD)(1)) | (((DWORD)((WORD)(0))) <<
16)))
```

There are two predefined LCID values: LOCALE_SYSTEM_DEFAULT is the system default locale, and LOCALE_USER_DEFAULT is the current user's locale. However, when querying the NLS APIs for several pieces of information, it is more efficient to query once for the current locale with **GetSystemDefaultLCID** or **GetUserDefaultLCID**, rather than using these constants.

Language ID (LANGID)

A LANGID is a 16-bit value which is the combination of a primary and sublanguage ID. The bits are as follows:

Sublanguage ID						Primary Language ID										
15	14	13	12	11	10	9	8	7	6	5	4	3	2	1	0	Bits

Macros are provided for constructing a LANGID and extracting the fields:

```
/*
 * Language ID creation/extraction macros:
 *
 *    MAKELANGID - construct language ID from primary language ID and
 *                 sublanguage ID.
 *    PRIMARYLANGID - extract primary language ID from a language ID.
 *    SUBLANGID - extract sublanguage ID from a language ID.
 *    LANGIDFROMLCID - get the language ID from a locale ID.
 */
#define MAKELANGID(p, s)        (((((USHORT)(s)) << 10) | (USHORT)(p))
#define PRIMARYLANGID(lgid)     ((USHORT)(lgid) & 0x3ff)
#define SUBLANGID(lgid)         ((USHORT)(lgid) >> 10)
#define LANGIDFROMLCID(lcid)    ((WORD)(lcid))
```

The following three combinations of primary and sublanguage IDs have special meanings:

PRIMARYLANGID	SUBLANGID	Meaning
LANG_NEUTRAL	SUBLANG_NEUTRAL	Language neutral
LANG_NEUTRAL	SUBLANG_SYS_DEFAULT	System default language
LANG_NEUTRAL	SUBLANG_DEFAULT	User default language

For primary language IDs, the range 0x200 to 0x3ff is user definable. The range 0x000 to 0x1ff is reserved for system use. The following table lists the primary language IDs supported by OLE Automation:

Language	PRIMARYLANGID
Neutral	0x00
Chinese	0x04
Czech	0x05
Danish	0x06
Dutch	0x13
English	0x09
Finnish	0x0b
French	0x0c

Language	PRIMARYLANGID
German	0x07
Greek	0x08
Hungarian	0x0e
Icelandic	0x0F
Italian	0x10
Japanese	0x11
Korean	0x12
Norwegian	0x14
Polish	0x15
Portuguese	0x16
Russian	0x19
Serbo Croatian	0x1a
Slovak	0x1b
Spanish	0x0a
Swedish	0x1d
Turkish	0x1F

For sublanguage IDs, the range 0x20 to 0x3f is user definable. The range 0x00 to 0x1f is reserved for system use. The following table lists the sublanguage IDs supported by OLE Automation:

Sublanguage	SUBLANGID
Neutral	0x00
Default	0x01
System Default	0x02
Chinese (Simplified)	0x02
Chinese (Traditional)	0x01
Dutch	0x01
Dutch (Belgian)	0x02
English (US)	0x01
English (UK)	0x02
English (Australian)	0x03
English (Canadian)	0x04
English (Irish)	0x06
English (New Zealand)	0x05

Sublanguage	SUBLANGID
French	0x01
French (Belgian)	0x02
French (Canadian)	0x03
French (Swiss)	0x04
German	0x01
German (Swiss)	0x02
German (Austrian)	0x03
Greek	0x01
Icelandic	0x01
Italian	0x01
Italian (Swiss)	0x02
Japanese	0x01
Korean	0x01
Norwegian (Bokmal)	0x01
Norwegian (Nynorsk)	0x02
Portuguese	0x02
Portuguese (Brazilian)	0x01
Serbo Croatian (Latin)	0x01
Spanish (Castilian)1	0x01
Spanish (Mexican)	0x02
Spanish (Modern)1	0x03
Turkish	0x01

1 The only difference between Spanish (Castilian) and Spanish (Modern) is the sort ordering. All of
the LCType values are the same.

Locale Constants (LCTYPE)

An LCTYPE is a constant which specifies a particular piece of locale information.

```
typedef  DWORD  LCTYPE;
```

The list of supported LCTYPES follows. All values are null-terminated, variable
length strings. Numeric values are expressed as strings of decimal digits unless
otherwise noted. The values in the brackets indicate the maximum number of
characters allowed for the string (including the null-termination). If no maximum is
indicated, the string may be of variable length.

Constant name	Description
LOCALE_ILANGUAGE	A language ID represented in hexadecimal digits; see previous sections. [5]
LOCALE_SLANGUAGE	The full localized name of the language.
LOCALE_SENGLANGUAGE	The full English name of the language from the ISO Standard 639. This will always be restricted to characters that can be mapped into the ASCII 127-character subset.
LOCALE_SABBREVLANGNAME	The abbreviated name of the language, created by taking the two-letter language abbreviation, as found in ISO Standard 639, and adding a third letter as appropriate to indicate the sublanguage.
LOCALE_SNATIVELANGNAME	The native name of the language.
LOCALE_ICOUNTRY	The country code, based on international phone codes, also referred to as IBM country codes. [6]
LOCALE_SCOUNTRY	The full localized name of the country.
LOCALE_SENGCOUNTRY	The full English name of the country. This will always be restricted to characters that can be mapped into the ASCII 127-character subset.
LOCALE_SABBREVCTRYNAME	The abbreviated name of the country as found in ISO Standard 3166.
LOCALE_SNATIVECTRYNAME	The native name of the country.
LOCALE_IDEFAULTLANGUAGE	Language ID for the principal language spoken in this locale. This is provided so that partially specified locales can be completed with default values. [5]
LOCALE_IDEFAULTCOUNTRY	Country code for the principal country in this locale. This is provided so that partially specified locales can be completed with default values. [6]

Constant name	Description
LOCALE_IDEFAULTANSICODEPAGE	The ANSI code page associated with this locale. Format: 4 Unicode decimal digits plus a Unicode null-terminator. [10] [6]
LOCALE_IDEFAULTCODEPAGE	The OEM code page associated with the country. [6]
LOCALE_SLIST	Characters used to separate list items; for example, comma is used in many locales.
LOCALE_IMEASURE	This value is "0" for the metric system (S.I.) and "1" for the U.S. system of measurements. [2]
LOCALE_SDECIMAL	Characters used for the decimal separator.
LOCALE_STHOUSAND	Characters used as the separator between groups of digits left of the decimal.
LOCALE_SGROUPING	Sizes for each group of digits to the left of the decimal. An explicit size is required for each group; sizes are separated by semicolons. If the last value is 0, the preceding value is repeated. To group thousands, specify "3;0."
LOCALE_IDIGITS	The number of fractional digits. [3]
LOCALE_ILZERO	Whether to use leading zeros in decimal fields. [2] A setting of 0 means use no leading zeros; 1 means use leading zeros.
LOCALE_SNATIVEDIGITS	The ten characters that are the native equivalent of the ASCII '0-9'.
LOCALE_INEGNUMBER	Negative number mode. [2] "0" (1.1) "1" -1.1 "2" -1.1 "3" 1.1 "4" 1.1
LOCALE_SCURRENCY	The string used as the local monetary symbol.

Constant name	Description
LOCALE_SINTLSYMBOL	Three characters of the International monetary symbol specified in ISO 4217 *Codes for the Representation of Currencies and Funds,* followed by the character separating this string from the amount.
LOCALE_SMONDECIMALSEP	Characters used for the monetary decimal separators.
LOCALE_SMONTHOUSANDSEP	Characters used as monetary separator between groups of digits left of the decimal.
LOCALE_SMONGROUPING	Sizes for each group of monetary digits to the left of the decimal. An explicit size is needed for each group; sizes are separated by semicolons. If the last value is 0, the preceding value is repeated. To group thousands, specify "3;0".
LOCALE_ICURRDIGITS	Number of fractional digits for the local monetary format. [3]
LOCALE_IINTLCURRDIGITS	Number of fractional digits for the international monetary format. [3]
LOCALE_ICURRENCY	Positive currency mode. [2]
	"0" Prefix, no separation "1" Suffix, no separation "2" Prefix, 1-character separation "3" Suffix, 1-character separation
LOCALE_INEGCURR	Negative currency mode. [2]
	"0" ($1.1) "1" -$1.1 "2" $-1.1 "3" $1.1- "4" $(1.1$) "5" -1.1$ "6" 1.1-$ "7" 1.1$- "8" -1.1 $ (space before $) "9" -$ 1.1 (space after $) "10" 1.1 $- (space before $)

Constant name	Description
LOCALE_ICALENDARTYPE	The type of calendar currently in use. [2]
	"1" Gregorian (as in U.S.)
	"2" Gregorian (always English strings)
	"3" Era: Year of the Emperor (Japan)
	"4" Era: Year of the Republic of China
	"5" Tangun Era (Korea)
LOCALE_IOPTIONALCALENDAR	The additional calendar types available for this LCID; can be a null-separated list of all valid optional calendars. [2]
	"0" None available
	"1" Gregorian (as in U.S.)
	"2" Gregorian (always English strings)
	"3" Era: Year of the Emperor (Japan)
	"4" Era: Year of the Republic of China
	"5" Tangun Era (Korea)
LOCALE_SDATE	Characters used for the date separator.
LOCALE_STIME	Characters used for the time separator.
LOCALE_STIMEFORMAT	Time formatting string. [80]
LOCALE_SSHORTDATE	Short Date_Time formatting strings for this locale.
LOCALE_SLONGDATE	Long Date_Time formatting strings for this locale.
LOCALE_IDATE	Short Date format ordering specifier. [2]
	"0" Month–Day–Year
	"1" Day–Month–Year
	"2" Year–Month–Day
LOCALE_ILDATE	Long Date format ordering specifier. [2]
	"0" Month–Day–Year
	"1" Day–Month–Year
	"2" Year–Month–Day

Constant name	Description
LOCALE_ITIME	Time format specifier. [2]
	"0" AM/PM 12-hour format "1" 24-hour format
LOCALE_ITIMEMARKPOSN	Whether the time marker string (AM|PM) precedes or follows the time string. (The registry value is named ITimePrefix for previous Far East version compatibility.)
	"0" Suffix (9:15 AM)
	"1" Prefix (AM 9:15)
LOCALE_ICENTURY	Whether to use full 4-digit century. [2]
	"0" Two digit "1" Full century
LOCALE_ITLZERO	Whether to use leading zeros in time fields. [2]
	"0" No leading zeros "1" Leading zeros for hours
LOCALE_IDAYLZERO	Whether to use leading zeros in day fields. [2]
	"0" No leading zeros "1" Leading zeros
LOCALE_IMONLZERO	Whether to use leading zeros in month fields. [2]
	"0" No leading zeros "1" Leading zeros
LOCALE_S1159	String for the AM designator.
LOCALE_S2359	String for the PM designator.

Constant name	Description
LOCALE_IFIRSTWEEKOFYEAR	Specifies which week of the year is considered first. [2]
	"0" Week containing 1/1 is the first week of the year.
	"1" First full week following 1/1 is the first week of the year.
	"2" First week with at least 4 days is the first week of the year.
LOCALE_IFIRSTDAYOFWEEK	Specifies the day considered first in the week. [2]
	"0" SDAYNAME1
	"1" SDAYNAME2
	"2" SDAYNAME3
	"3" SDAYNAME4
	"4" SDAYNAME5
	"5" SDAYNAME6
	"6" DAYNAME7
LOCALE_SDAYNAME1	Long name for Monday.
LOCALE_SDAYNAME2	Long name for Tuesday.
LOCALE_SDAYNAME2	Long name for Tuesday.
LOCALE_SDAYNAME3	Long name for Wednesday.
LOCALE_SDAYNAME4	Long name for Thursday.
LOCALE_SDAYNAME5	Long name for Friday.
LOCALE_SDAYNAME6	Long name for Saturday.
LOCALE_SDAYNAME7	Long name for Sunday.
LOCALE_SABBREVDAYNAME1	Abbreviated name for Monday.
LOCALE_SABBREVDAYNAME2	Abbreviated name for Tuesday.
LOCALE_SABBREVDAYNAME3	Abbreviated name for Wednesday.
LOCALE_SABBREVDAYNAME4	Abbreviated name for Thursday.

Constant name	Description
LOCALE_SABBREVDAYNAME5	Abbreviated name for Friday.
LOCALE_SABBREVDAYNAME6	Abbreviated name for Saturday.
LOCALE_SABBREVDAYNAME7	Abbreviated name for Sunday.
LOCALE_SMONTHNAME1	Long name for January.
LOCALE_SMONTHNAME2	Long name for February.
LOCALE_SMONTHNAME3	Long name for March.
LOCALE_SMONTHNAME4	Long name for April.
LOCALE_SMONTHNAME5	Long name for May.
LOCALE_SMONTHNAME6	Long name for June.
LOCALE_SMONTHNAME7	Long name for July.
LOCALE_SMONTHNAME8	Long name for August.
LOCALE_SMONTHNAME9	Long name for September.
LOCALE_SMONTHNAME10	Long name for October.
LOCALE_SMONTHNAME11	Long name for November.
LOCALE_SMONTHNAME12	Long name for December.
LOCALE_SMONTHNAME13	Native name for 13th month, if it exists.
LOCALE_SABBREVMONTHNAME1	Abbreviated name for January.
LOCALE_SABBREVMONTHNAME2	Abbreviated name for February.
LOCALE_SABBREVMONTHNAME3	Abbreviated name for March.
LOCALE_SABBREVMONTHNAME4	Abbreviated name for April.
LOCALE_SABBREVMONTHNAME5	Abbreviated name for May.
LOCALE_SABBREVMONTHNAME6	Abbreviated name for June.
LOCALE_SABBREVMONTHNAME7	Abbreviated name for July.
LOCALE_SABBREVMONTHNAME8	Abbreviated name for August.
LOCALE_SABBREVMONTHNAME9	Abbreviated name for September.
LOCALE_SABBREVMONTHNAME10	Abbreviated name for October.
LOCALE_SABBREVMONTHNAME11	Abbreviated name for November.
LOCALE_SABBREVMONTHNAME12	Abbreviated name for December.

Constant name	Description
LOCALE_SABBREVMONTHNAME13	Native abbreviated name for 13th month, if it exists.
LOCALE_SPOSITIVESIGN	String value for the positive sign.
LOCALE_SNEGATIVESIGN	String value for the negative sign.
LOCALE_IPOSSIGNPOSN	Formatting index for positive values. [2]

    "0"   Parentheses surround the amount and the monetary symbol.

    "1"   The sign string precedes the amount and the monetary symbol.

    "2"   The sign string precedes the amount and the monetary symbol.

    "3"   The sign string precedes the amount and the monetary symbol.

    "4"   The sign string precedes the amount and the monetary symbol.

Constant name	Description
LOCALE_INEGSIGNPOSN	Formatting index for negative values. [2]

    "0"   Parentheses surround the amount and the monetary symbol.

    "1"   The sign string precedes the amount and the monetary symbol.

    "2"   The sign string precedes the amount and the monetary symbol.

    "3"   The sign string precedes the amount and the monetary symbol.

    "4"   The sign string precedes the amount and the monetary symbol.

Constant name	Description
LOCALE_IPOSSYMPRECEDES	"1" if the monetary symbol precedes; "0" if it succeeds a positive amount. [2]
LOCALE_IPOSSEPBYSPACE	"1" if the monetary symbol is separated by a space from a positive amount; "0" otherwise. [2]
LOCALE_INEGSYMPRECEDES	"1" if the monetary symbol precedes; "0" if it succeeds a negative amount. [2]
LOCALE_INEGSEPBYSPACE	"1" if the monetary symbol is separated by a space from a negative amount; "0" otherwise. [2]

The following table shows the equivalence between LCTYPE values and the information stored in the [intl] section of WIN.INI. These values will be retrieved from WIN.INI if information for the current system locale is queried. Values for LCTYPEs not in the following table do not depend on information stored in WIN.INI.

WIN.INI settings	LCTYPE
sLanguage[1]	LOCALE_SABBREVLANGNAME
iCountry	LOCALE_ICOUNTRY
sCountry	LOCALE_SCOUNTRY
sList	LOCALE_SLIST
iMeasure	LOCALE_IMEASURE
sDecimal	LOCALE_SDECIMAL
sThousand	LOCALE_STHOUSAND
iDigits	LOCALE_IDIGITS
iLZero	LOCALE_ILZERO
sCurrency	LOCALE_SCURRENCY
iCurrDigits	LOCALE_ICURRDIGITS
iCurrency	LOCALE_ICURRENCY
iNegCurr	LOCALE_INEGCURR
sDate	LOCALE_SDATE
sTime	LOCALE_STIME
sShortDate	LOCALE_SSHORTDATE
sLongDate	LOCALE_SLONGDATE
iDate	LOCALE_IDATE
iTime	LOCALE_ITIME
iTLZero	LOCALE_ITLZERO
s1159	LOCALE_S1159
s2359	LOCALE_S2359

[1] Unlike in WIN.INI, values returned by LOCALE_SABBREVLANGNAME are always in uppercase.

CompareStringA

> **int CompareStringA**(*LCID*, *dwCmpFlags*, *lpString1*, *cchCount1*, *lpString2*,
> *cchCount2*)
> **LCID** *LCID*
> **DWORD** *dwCmpFlags*
> **LPCSTR** *lpString1*
> **int** *cchCount1*
> **LPCSTR** *lpString2*
> **int** *cchCount2*

Compares two character strings of the same locale according to the supplied LCID.

Parameters

LCID

Locale context for the comparison. The strings are assumed to be represented in the default ANSI code page for this locale.

dwCmpFlags

Flags that indicate the character traits to use or ignore when comparing the two strings. Several flags can be combined (in the case of this function, there are no illegal combinations of flags), or none can be used at all. Compare flags include the following.

Value	Meaning
NORM_IGNORECASE	Ignore case; default is OFF.
NORM_IGNOREKANATYPE	Ignore Japanese hiragana/katakana character differences; default is OFF.
NORM_IGNORENONSPACE	Ignore nonspacing marks (accents, diacritics and vowel marks); default is OFF.
NORM_IGNORESYMBOLS	Ignore symbols; default is OFF.
NORM_IGNOREWIDTH	Ignore character width, default is OFF.

lpString1 and *lpString2*

The two strings to be compared.

cchCount1 and *cchCount2*

The character counts of the two strings. The count does *not* include the null-terminator (if any). If either *cchCount1* or *cchCount2* is −1, the corresponding string is assumed to be null-terminated and the length will be calculated automatically.

Return Value

Value	Meaning
0	Failure.
1	lpString1 is less than lpString2.
2	lpString1 is equal to lpString2.
3	lpString1 is greater than lpString2.

Comments

When used without any flags, this function uses the same sorting algorithm as **lstrcmp** in the given locale. When used with NORM_IGNORECASE, the same algorithm as **lstrcmpi** is used.

For DBCS locales, the flag NORM_IGNORECASE has an effect on all the wide (two-byte) characters as well as the narrow (one-byte) characters. This includes the wide Greek and Cyrillic characters.

In Chinese Simplified, the sorting order used to compare the strings is based on the following sequence: symbols, digit numbers, English letters and Chinese Simplified characters. The characters within each group sort in character code order.

In Chinese Traditional, the sorting order used to compare the strings is based on the "number of strokes" in the characters. Symbols, digit numbers, and English characters are considered to have zero strokes. The sort sequence is symbols, digit numbers, English letters and Chinese Traditional characters. The characters within each stroke-number group sort in character code order.

In Japanese, the sorting order used to compare the strings is based on the Japanese 50-on sorting sequence. The Kanji ideographic characters sort in character code order.

In Japanese, the flag NORM_IGNORENONSPACE has an effect on the daku-on, handaku-on, chou-on, you-on, and soku-on modifiers, and on the repeat kana/kanji characters.

In Korean, the sort order is based on the sequence: symbols, digit numbers, Jaso and Hangeul, Hanja, and English. Within the Jaso-Hangeul group, each Jaso character is followed by the Hangeuls that start with that Jaso. Hanja characters are sorted in Hangeul pronunciation order. Where multiple Hanja have the same Hangeul pronounciation they are sorted in character code order.

The NORM_IGNORENONSPACE flag only has an effect for the locales in which accented characters are sorted in a second pass from main characters (that is, all characters in the string are first compared without regard to accents and, if the strings are equal, a second pass over the strings to compare accents is performed). In this case, this flag causes the second pass to not be performed. Some locales sort accented characters in the first pass, in which case this flag will have no effect.

Note that if the return value is 2, the two strings are "equal" in the collation sense, though not necessarily identical (case might be ignored, and so on).

If the two strings are of different lengths, they are compared up to the length of the shortest one. If they are equal to that point, the return value will indicate that the longer string is greater.

To maintain the C run-time convention of comparing strings, the value 2 can be subtracted from a nonzero return value. The meaning of < 0, $== 0$, and > 0 is then consistent with the C run-time conventions.

LCMapStringA

int LCMapStringA(*LCID*, *dwMapFlags*, *lpSrcStr*, *cchSrc*, *lpDestStr*, *cchDest*)
LCID *LCID*
DWORD *dwMapFlags*
LPCSTR *lpSrcStr*
int *cchSrc*
LPSTR *lpDestStr*
int *cchDest*

Parameters   *LCID*

Locale context for the mapping. The strings are assumed to be represented in the default ANSI code page for this locale.

dwMapFlags

Flags that indicate what type of transformation is to occur during mapping. Several flags can be combined on a single transformation (though some combinations are illegal). Mapping options include the following.

Name	Meaning
LCMAP_LOWERCASE	Lowercase.
LCMAP_UPPERCASE	Uppercase.
LCMAP_SORTKEY	Character sort key.
LCMAP_HALFWIDTH	Narrow characters (where applicable).
LCMAP_FULLWIDTH	Wide characters (where applicable).
LCMAP_HIRAGANA	Hiragana.
LCMAP_KATAKANA	Katakana.
NORM_IGNORECASE	Ignore case; default is OFF.

Name	Meaning
NORM_IGNORENONSPACE	Ignore nonspacing; default is OFF.
NORM_IGNOREWIDTH	Ignore character width; default is OFF.
NORM_IGNOREKANATYPE	Ignore Japanese hiragana/katakana character differences; default is OFF.
NORM_IGNORESYMBOLS	Ignore symbols; default is OFF.

The latter five options (NORM_IGNORECASE, NORM_IGNORENONSPACE, NORM_IGNOREWIDTH, NORM_IGNOREKANATYPE,and NORM_IGNORESYMBOLS) are normalization options that can only be used in combination with the LCMAP_SORTKEY conversion option.

Conversion options can be combined only when they are taken from the following three groups, and then only when there is no more than one option from each group:

- Casing options (LCMAP_LOWERCASE, LCMAP_UPPERCASE)
- Width options (LCMAP_HALFWIDTH, LCMAP_FULLWIDTH)
- Kana options (LCMAP_HIRAGANA, LCMAP_KATAKANA)

lpSrcStr
Pointer to the supplied string to be mapped.

cchSrc
Character count of the input string buffer. If–1, *lpSrcStr* is assumed to be null-terminated and the length will be calculated automatically.

lpDestStr
Pointer to the memory buffer to store the resulting mapped string.

cchDest
Character count of the memory buffer pointed to by *lpDestStr*. If *cchDest* is 0, then the return value of this function is the number of characters required to hold the mapped string. The *lpDestStr* pointer is not referenced in this case.

Return Value

Value	Meaning
0	Failure
The number of characters written to *lpDestSt*	Success

Comments

LCMapStringA maps one character string to another, performing the specified locale-dependent translation.

The flag LCMAP_UPPER produces the same result as **AnsiUpper** in the given locale; the flag LCMAP_LOWER produces the same result as **AnsiLower**. In particular, like these functions, this function always maps a single character to a single character.

The mapped string will be null-terminated if the source string is null-terminated.

When used with LCMAP_UPPER and LCMAP_LOWER, the *lpSrcStr* and *lpDestStr* may be the same to produce an in-place mapping. When LCMAP_SORTKEY is used, the *lpSrcStr* and *lpDestStr* pointers may *not* be the same; an error will result in this case.

The LCMAP_SORTKEY transformation transforms two strings such that when compared with the standard C library function **strcmp** (by strict numerical valuation of their characters), the same order would result as if the original strings were compared with **CompareStringA**. When LCMAP_SORTKEY is specified, the output string will be a string (without NULLs, except for the terminator), but the "character" values will not be meaningful display values. This is similar behavior to the ANSI C function **strxfrm**.

GetLocaleInfoA

int **GetLocaleInfoA**(*LCID*, *LCType*, *lpLCData*, *cchData*)
LCID *LCID*
LCTYPE *LCType*
LPSTR *lpLCData*
int *cchData*

Parameters
LCID
ID for a locale. The returned string will be represented in the default ANSI code page for this locale.

LCType
Flag that indicates the type of information to be returned by the call. See the listing of constant values in this chapter. LOCALE_NOUSEROVERRIDE | LCTYPE indicates that the desired information will always be retrieved from the locale database, even if the LCID is the current one, and the user has changed some of the values with the control panel. If this flag is not specified, values in WIN.INI take precedence over the database settings when getting values for the current system default locale.

lpLCData
Pointer to the memory where **GetLocaleInfoA** will return the requested data. This pointer is not referenced if *cchData* is 0.

cchData
Character count of the supplied *lpLCData* memory buffer. If *cchData* is 0, the return value is the number of characters required to hold the string, including the terminating NULL character. *lpLCData* is not referenced in this case.

Return Value	**Value**	**Meaning**
	0	Failure
	The number of characters copied, including the terminating NULL character	Success

Comments   **GetLocaleInfoA** returns one of the various pieces of information about a locale by querying the stored locale database or WIN.INI. The call also indicates how much memory is necessary to contain the desired information.

The information returned is always a null-terminated string. No integers are returned by this function; numeric values are returned as text (see format descriptions under LCTYPE).

GetStringTypeA

BOOL GetStringTypeA(*LCID*, *dwInfoType*, *lpSrcStr*, *cchSrc, lpCharType*)
LCID *LCID*
DWORD *dwInfoType*
LPCSTR *lpSrcStr*
int *cchSrc*
LPWORD *lpCharType*

Parameters   *LCID*
> Locale context for the mapping. The string is assumed to be represented in the default ANSI code page for this locale.

dwInfoType
> Type of character information to retrieve. The various types are divided into different levels (see Comments for a list of the information included in each type). The options are mutually exclusive. The following types are supported:
> - CT_CTYPE1
> - CT_CTYPE2
> - CT_CTYPE3

lpSrcStr
> String for which character types are requested. If *cchSrc* is −1, *lpSrcStr* is assumed to be null-terminated.

cchSrc

    Character count of *lpSrcStr*. If *cchSrc* is −1, *lpSrcStr* is assumed to be null-terminated. Note that this must also be the character count of *lpCharType*.

lpCharType

    Array of the same length as *lpSrcStr* (*cchSrc*). On output, the array contains one word corresponding to each character in *lpSrcStr*.

Return Value

Value	Meaning
0	Failure
1	Success

Comments

The *lpSrcStr* and *lpCharType* pointers may *not* be the same; in this case the error ERROR_INVALID_PARAMETER results.

The character type bits are divided up into several levels. One level's information can be retrieved by a single call.

This function supports three character types:

- Ctype 1
- Ctype 2
- Ctype 3

Ctype 1 types support ANSI C and POSIX character typing functions. A bitwise OR of these values is returned when *dwInfoType* is set to CT_CTYPE1. For DBCS locales, the Ctype 1 attributes apply to both the narrow characters and the wide characters. The Japanese hiragana and katakana characters, and the kanji ideograph characters all have the C1_ALPHA attribute.

The following table lists the Ctype 1 character types.

Name	Value	Meaning
C1_UPPER	0x0001	Uppercase1
C1_LOWER	0x0002	Lowercase1
C1_DIGIT	0x0004	Decimal digits
C1_SPACE	0x0008	Space characters
C1_PUNCT	0x0010	Punctuation

Name	Value	Meaning
C1_CNTRL	0x0020	Control characters
C1_BLANK	0x0040	Blank characters
C1_XDIGIT	0x0080	Hexadecimal digits
C1_ALPHA	0x0100	Any letter

1 The Windows version 3.1 functions **IsCharUpper** and **IsCharLower** do not always produce correct results for characters in the range 0x80-0x9f, so they may produce different results than this function for characters in that range. (For example, the German Windows version 3.1 language driver incorrectly reports 0x9a, lowercase s hacek, as uppercase).

Ctype 2 types support the proper layout of text. For DBCS locales, Ctype 2 applies to both narrow and wide characters. The directional attributes are assigned so that the BiDi layout algorithm standardized by Unicode produces the correct results. See *The Unicode Standard: Worldwide Character Encoding* from Addison-Wesley for more information on the use of these attributes.

	Name	Value	Meaning
Strong	C2_LEFTTORIGHT	0x1	Left to right
	C2_RIGHTTOLEFT	0x2	Right to left
Weak	C2_EUROPENUMBER	0x3	European number, European digit
	C2_EUROPESEPARATOR	0x4	European numeric separator
	C2_EUROPETERMINATOR	0x5	European numeric terminator
	C2_ARABICNUMBER	0x6	Arabic number
	C2_COMMONSEPARATOR	0x7	Common numeric separator
Neutral	C2_BLOCKSEPARATOR	0x8	Block separator
	C2_SEGMENTSEPARATOR	0x9	Segment separator
	C2_WHITESPACE	0xA	White space
	C2_OTHERNEUTRAL	0xB	Other neutrals
Not applicable	C2_NOTAPPLICABLE	0x0	No implicit direction (for example, control codes)

Ctype 3 types are general text-processing information. A bitwise OR of these values is returned when *dwInfoType* is set to CT_CTYPE3. For DBCS locales, the Ctype 3 attributes apply to both the narrow characters and the wide characters. The Japanese hiragana and katakana characters and the kanji ideograph characters all have the C3_ALPHA attribute.

Name	Value	Meaning
C3_NONSPACING	0x1	Nonspacing mark
C3_DIACRITIC	0x2	Diacritic nonspacing mark
C3_VOWELMARK	0x4	Vowel nonspacing mark
C3_SYMBOL	0x8	Symbol
C3_KATAKANA	0x10	Katakana character
C3_HIRAGANA	0x20	Hiragana character
C3_HALFWIDTH	0x40	Narrow character
C3_FULLWIDTH	0x80	Wide character
C3_IDEOGRAPH	0x100	Ideograph
C3_ALPHA	0x8000	Any letter
C3_NOTAPPLICABLE	0x0	Not applicable

GetSystemDefaultLangID

Returns the system default language ID.

LANGID GetSystemDefaultLangID(void);

Return Value

Value	Meaning
0	Failure
The system default LANGID	Success

Comments   See **GetSystemDefaultLCID** for information on how this value is determined.

GetSystemDefaultLCID

Returns the system default LCID.

LCID GetSystemDefaultLCID(void)

Return Value

Value	Meaning
0	Failure
System default locale ID	Success

Comments   The return value is determined by examining the values of *sLanguage* and *iCountry* in WIN.INI, and comparing the values to those in the stored locale database. If no matching values are found, or the required values cannot be read from WIN.INI, or if the stored locale database cannot be loaded, the value 0 is returned.

GetUserDefaultLangID

Returns the user default LANGID.

LANGID GetUserDefaultLangID(void)

Return Value

Value	Meaning
0	Failure
The user default LANGID	Success

Comments   Because Windows version 3.1 is a single-user system, the value returned from this function is always the same as that returned from **GetSystemDefaultLangID**.

GetUserDefaultLCID

Returns the user default LCID.

LCID GetUserDefaultLCID(void)

Return Value

Value	Meaning
0	Failure
The user default locale ID	Success

Comments   Because Windows version 3.1 is a single-user system, the value returned by this function is always the same as that returned from **GetSystemDefaultLCID**.

APPENDIX B

Files You Need

To use OLE Automation, you need the following files. The filenames shown in **bold** are required by your application at run time. Note that you should not ship the files with your 32-bit Windows application; these files are provided as part of the 32-bit Windows operating system.

32-bit filenames	16-bit filenames	Purpose
None	OLE2.REG	Registers OLE and OLE Automation. OLE is a system component on 32-bit systems, and therefore no .REG file is required.
None	**OLE2NLS.DLL** OLE2NLS.LIB OLENLS.H	Provides functions for applications that support multiple national languages. Note that on 32-bit systems, NLS features are provided by the Win32 NLS API.
OLEPRX32.DLL	**OLE2PROX.DLL**	Coordinates object access across processes.
MKTYPLIB.EXE	MKTYPLIB.EXE	Builds type libraries from interface descriptions.
OLEAUT32.DLL OLEAUT32.LIB OLEAUTO.H	**TYPELIB.DLL** DISPATCH.H	Accesses type libraries.

32-bit filenames	16-bit filenames	Purpose
	OLE2DISP.DLL	Provides functions for creating OLE Automation objects and retrieving active objects at run time. Accesses OLE Automation objects by invoking methods and properties.
	OLE2DISP.LIB	
	DISPATCH.H	
OLE32.DLL	**OLE2.DLL**	Provides OLE functions that may be used by OLE objects or containers.
OLE32.LIB	OLE2.LIB	
OLE2.H	OLE2.H	
	COMPOBJ.DLL	Supports component object creation and access.
	COMPOBJ.LIB	
	OLE2.H	
	COMPOBJ.H	
	STORAGE.DLL	Supports access to subfiles, such as type libraries, within compound documents.
	STORAGE.LIB	
	OLE2.H	
	STORAGE.H	

APPENDIX C

Information for Visual Basic Programmers

Visual Basic provides full support for OLE Automation. The following table lists how Visual Basic statements translate into OLE APIs.

Visual Basic Statement	OLE APIs
CreateObject (*"ProgID"*)	**CLSIDFromProgID**()
	CoCreateInstance()
	QueryInterface() to get **IDispatch** interface
GetObject (*"filename"*, *"ProgID"*)	**CLSIDFromProgID**()
	CoCreateInstance()
	QueryInterface() for **IPersistFile** interface
	Load() on **IPersistFile** interface
	QueryInterface() to get **IDispatch** interface
GetObject (*"filename"*)	**CreateBindCtx**() creates the bind context for the subsequent functions.
	MkParseDisplayName() returns a moniker handle for **BindMoniker**.
	BindMoniker() returns a pointer to the IDispatch interface.
	Release() on moniker handle.
	Release() on context.
GetObject (, *"ProgID"*)	**CLSIDFromProgID**()
	GetActiveObject() on class ID.
	QueryInterface() to get **IDispatch** interface.
Dim *x* **As New** *interface*	Find CLSID for *interface*.
	CoCreateInstance()
	QueryInterface()

APPENDIX D

How OLE Automation Compares Strings

This appendix describes how the OLE Automation implementations compare strings. Understanding these comparisons is useful when creating applications that support national languages that use accents and digraphs. The information in this appendix applies to the following:

- **CreateStdDispatch** (OLEAUT32.DLL on 32-bit Windows systems, OLE2DISP.DLL on 16-bit Windows systems)

- **DispGetIDsOfNames** (OLEAUT32.DLL on 32-bit Windows systems, OLE2DISP.DLL on 16-bit Windows systems)

- **ITypeLib::FindName** (OLEAUT32.DLL on 32-bit Windows systems, TYPELIB.DLL on 16-bit Windows systems)

- **ITypeLib::GetIDsOfNames** (OLEAUT32.DLL on 32-bit Windows systems, TYPELIB.DLL on 16-bit Windows systems)

- MkTypLib (MKTYPLIB.EXE)

When comparing strings, the listed OLE Automation components use the following rules:

- Comparisons are sensitive to locale based on the string's LCID. A string must have an LCID that is supported by the application or type library. Locales and LCIDs are described in the section "Supporting Multiple National Languages," in Chapter 2.

- Accent characters are ignored. For example, the string "à" compares the same as "a."

- Case is ignored. For example, the string "A" compares the same as "a."

- Comparisons are sensitive to digraphs. For example, the string "Æ" is not the same as "AE."

- For Japanese, Korean, and Chinese locales, **ITypeLib::FindName** and **ITypeLib::GetIDsOfNames** ignore width and kanatype.

A P P E N D I X   E

Handling GUIDs

Globally unique identifiers (GUIDs) appear in many places in a typical OLE Automation application. GUID errors can cause persistent bugs. To help you avoid GUID problems, this appendix lists all the places GUIDs appear in a typical OLE Automation application, describes common characteristics of GUID bugs, and offers some GUID management techniques.

GUIDs are the same as UUIDs (Universally Unique Identifiers). A class identifier (CLSID) is a UUID/GUID that refers to a class.

The System Registry

The system registry is a central repository containing information about objects. GUIDs are used to index that information. You can view the registration information on your system by running REGEDIT with the /V option:

```
regedit /v
```

Typically, a name is connected with a GUID (for example, "Hello.Application" maps to a GUID) and then the GUID is connected to all the other relevant aspects (for example, the GUID maps to "HELLO.EXE").

You create GUIDs with the tool GUIDGEN.EXE. Running GUIDGEN.EXE produces a huge hex number which uniquely identifies your object, whether it be a class, an interface, a library, or some other kind of object.

Where GUIDs Live

GUIDs appear in the following places:

- .REG files—When you create an application, you usually create one or more .REG files. The .REG files contain the GUIDs for the classes that your application exposes. These GUIDs are added to the registry when you run REGEDIT.EXE to register your classes, or when you register type information with **LoadTypeLib**.

- The system registry—Contains the GUIDs for your classes in multiple places. This is where OLE and applications get information about your classes.

- .ODL files—When you describe objects in an Object Description Language (.ODL) file, you provide a GUID for each object. Compiling the .ODL file with MKTYPLIB.EXE places the GUIDs in a type library, which usually exists as a .TLB file. If you change a GUID in an .ODL file, make sure that you run MkTypLib again.

- .TLB files—Type libraries describe your classes, and this information includes the GUIDs for the classes. You can browse .TLB files using the TIBROWSE sample application supplied with OLE.

- .H files—Most application developers will declare CLSIDs for their classes in a header file using the DEFINE_GUID macro.

Troubleshooting

The following are common problems with GUIDs.

Problem   "**GetObject** can't seem to create an instance of my application."

Solution   Visual Basic uses the OLE calls listed in Appendix C to find the .EXE file that creates your application instance.

▶ **Visual Basic proceeds as follows:**

1. Looks up the GUID for your object. For the Hello application, Visual Basic maps the ProgID Hello.Application into a GUID.
2. Finds the object's server. This is HELLO.EXE for the Hello application.
3. Launches the application.

If an error occurs, check the following:

- Did you remember to run the .REG file?
- Are the entries in the registry correct? Check to see if all the GUIDs match.
- Can the application be launched? The executable (.EXE) file for the application, listed in the LocalServer entry, should either be on the path or it should be fully specified, for example, `c:\ole2\sample\hello\hello.bin`.

Problem
"When I use **GetObject**, the application launches and then the **GetObject** call fails."

Solution
Normally, a class factory is registered using **CoRegisterClassObject** when your application is started. Some applications register their class factories only when launched with the **/Automation** switch. If you inherited code or copied a sample, you should find out whether it checks for this switch. The **/Automation** option could appear in the .REG file, the registry, or in your development environment.

Problem

"**GetTypeInfoOfGuid**() is failing to get the type information from my type library."

Solution

When you call **GetTypeInfoOfGuid**, you provide a GUID. If this GUID doesn't match the GUID in your .TLB file, no type information will be returned. The GUID in your code is likely to be declared in a header file. You can check the GUID in your .TLB file by using BROWSE, which is provided with OLE, or with the Visual Basic Object Browser.

GUID Management

The problem with managing GUIDs is that they are pervasive, and their length prohibits simple comparisons.

The single most important technique in managing GUIDs is to keep a central list of all the GUIDs you use. Use the MAKE_GUID macro or the GUIDGEN tool with the **-n** option to generate the required number of GUIDs, and place the resulting strings in the first column of a spreadsheet. Each time you use a new GUID, enter a description of its purpose in the second column of the spreadsheet.

Keeping a central list has several advantages:

- Listing all the GUIDs in one location may prevent you from accidentally reusing a GUID. This often happens when you clone an application in order to create another one.

- You can use the spreadsheet to compare GUIDs. You can check that a GUID is correct by copying it from the place where it is being used (for example, a .REG file), pasting it into the spreadsheet, and then comparing the two cells with the "="operator.

- You'll have a record of your GUID use in case of future problems, and you'll have a single source of information to find the GUID for your object.

Glossary

A

accessor function A function that sets or retrieves the value of a property. Most properties have a pair of accessor functions; properties that are read-only may have only one accessor function.

Application object The top-level object in an application's object hierarchy. The Application object identifies the application to the system and typically becomes active when the application starts. Specified by the **appobj** attribute in the type library.

C

class factory
An object that implements the **IClassFactory** interface, which allows it to create other objects of a specific class.

class identifier (CLSID)
A unique identifier (UUID) that identifies an OLE object. An object registers its CLSID in the system registration database so that it can be loaded and programmed by other applications.

coclass Component object model class; a top-level object in the object hierarchy.

collection object A grouping of exposed objects. A collection object enables you to address multiple occurrences of an object as a unit, for example, to draw a set of points.

component object A Windows object identified by a unique class identifier (CLSID), which associates the object with a DLL or an .EXE file.

compound document A document that suppports linked or embedded objects, such as sound clips, spreadsheets, text, and bitmaps, created by different applications as well as its own data. Compound documents are stored by container applications.

container application An application that provides storage, a display site, and access to a compound document object.

D

Dispatch identifier (DISPID) The number by which a member function, parameter, or data member of an object is known internally to **IDispatch**.

dispinterface An **IDispatch** interface that responds only to a certain fixed set of names. The properties and methods of the dispinterface are not in the virtual function table (VTBL) for the object.

dual interface An interface that supports both **IDispatch** and VTBL binding.

E

event An action recognized by an object, such as clicking the mouse or pressing a key, and for which you can write code to respond. In OLE Automation, an event is a method that is called, rather than implemented, by an OLE Automation object.

event sink A function that handles events. The code associated with a Visual Basic form, which contains event handlers for one or more controls, is an event sink.

event source A control that experiences events and calls an event handler to dispose of them.

exposed object *See OLE Automation object.*

H

HRESULT A value returned from a function call to an interface, consisting of a severity code, context information, a facility code, and a status code that describes the result. For 16-bit Windows systems, the HRESULT is an opaque result handle defined to be zero for a successful return from a function, and nonzero if error or status information is to be returned. To convert an HRESULT into the more detailed SCODE, applications call **GetSCode()**. *See SCODE.*

I

ID binding The ability to bind member names to DISPIDs at compile time, for example, by obtaining the IDs from a type library. This approach eliminates the need for calls to **IDispatch::GetIDsOfNames** and results in improved performance over late-bound calls. *See also late binding.*

in-place activation The ability to activate an object from within an OLE control and to associate a verb with that activation (for example, edit, play, change). Sometimes referred to as in-place editing or visual editing.

in-process server An OLE component that runs in the same process space as the OLE Automation controller.

interface One or more well-defined base classes providing member functions that, when implemented in an application, provide a specific service. Interfaces may include compiled support functions to simplify their implementation.

L

late binding The ability to bind names to IDs at run time, rather than compile time.

local server *See out-of-process server.*

locale identifier (LCID) A 32-bit value that identifies the human language preferred by a user, region, or application.

M

marshaling The process of packaging and sending interface parameters across process boundaries.

member function One of a group of related functions that make up an interface. *See also method and property.*

method Member functions of an exposed object that perform some action on the object, such as saving it to disk.

multiple-document interface (MDI) application An application that can support multiple documents from one application instance. MDI object applications can simultaneously service a user and one or more embedding containers. *See also single-document interface (SDI) application.*

O

object A unit of information that resides in a compound document and whose behavior is constant no matter where it is located or used.

Object Description Language (ODL) A scripting language used to describe exposed libraries, objects, types, and interfaces. ODL scripts are compiled into type libraries by the MkTypLib tool.

OLE An object-based technology for sharing information and services across process and machine boundaries.

OLE Automation A technology that provides a way to manipulate objects defined by an application or library from outside the application. OLE Automation enables programmability.

OLE Automation controller An application, programming tool, or scripting language that accesses OLE Automation objects. Microsoft Visual Basic is an OLE Automation controller.

OLE Automation object An object that is exposed to other applications or programming tools through OLE Automation interfaces.

OLE Automation server An application, type library, or other source that makes OLE Automation objects available for programming by other applications, programming tools, or scripting languages.

out-of-process server
An OLE server implemented as an .EXE file that runs outside the process of the OLE Automation controller.

P

programmable object *See OLE Automation object.*

property A data member of an exposed object. Properties are set or returned by means of get and put accessor functions.

proxy An interface-specific object that packages parameters for that interface in preparation for a remote method call. A proxy runs in the address space of the sender and communicates with a corresponding stub in the receiver's address space. *See also stub, marshaling, and unmarshaling.*

S

safe array An array that contains information about the number of dimensions and the bounds of its dimensions. Safe arrays are passed by **IDispatch::Invoke** within VARIANTARGs. Their base type is VT_tag | VT_ARRAY.

SCODE A DWORD value that is used to pass detailed information to the caller of an interface member or API function. The status codes for OLE interfaces and APIs are defined in FACILITY_ITF. *See HRESULT.*

single-document interface (SDI) application
An application that can support only one document at a time. Multiple instances of an SDI application must be started to service both an embedded object and a user. *See also multiple-document interface (MDI) application.*

stub An interface-specific object that unpackages the parameters for that interface after they are marshaled across the process boundary, and makes the requested method call. The stub runs in the address space of the receiver and communicates with a corresponding proxy in the sender's address space. *See proxy, marshaling, and unmarshaling.*

T

type description
The information used to build the type information for one or more aspects of an application's interface. Type descriptions are written in Object Description Language (ODL) and include both programmable and nonprogrammable interfaces.

type information Information that describes the interfaces of an application. Type information is created from type descriptions using OLE Automation tools, such as MkTypLib or the **CreateDispTypeInfo** function. Type information may be accessed through the **ITypeInfo** interface.

type information element
A unit of information identified by one of these
statements in a type description: typedef, enum,
struct, module, interface, dispinterface, or coclass.

type library A file or component within another
file that contains OLE Automation standard
descriptions of exposed objects, properties, and
methods. Object library (.OLB) files contain type
libraries. Type libraries are created from type
descriptions using MkTypLib, and may be
accessed through the **ITypeLib** interface.

U

unmarshaling The process of unpackaging
parameter that have been sent across process
boundaries.

V

Value property The property that defines the
default behavior of an object when no other
methods or properties are specified. You indicate
the Value property by specifying the **default**
attribute in ODL.

virtual function table (VTBL) A table of function
pointers, such as an implementation of a class in
C++. The pointers in the VTBL point to the
members of the interfaces that an object supports.

Index

Register Today!
Return this
OLE Automation Programmer's Reference
registration card for a
Microsoft Press® catalog

U.S. and Canada addresses only. Fill in information below and mail postage-free. Please mail only the bottom half of this page.

1-55615-851-3A   *OLE Automation Programmer's Reference*   *Owner Registration Card*

NAME

INSTITUTION OR COMPANY NAME

ADDRESS

CITY   STATE   ZIP

Microsoft®Press
Quality Computer Books

For a free catalog of
Microsoft Press® products, call
1-800-MSPRESS

BUSINESS REPLY MAIL
FIRST-CLASS MAIL   PERMIT NO. 53   BOTHELL, WA

POSTAGE WILL BE PAID BY ADDRESSEE

MICROSOFT PRESS REGISTRATION
OLE AUTOMATION PROGRAMMER'S
REFERENCE
PO BOX 3019
BOTHELL   WA   98041-9946